ACCOUNTABILITY
IN HUMAN
RESOURCE
MANAGEMENT

ACCOUNTABILITY IN HUMAN RESOURCE MANAGEMENT

...

JACK J. PHILLIPS

Gulf Publishing Company
Houston, London, Paris, Tokyo, Zurich

Accountability in Human Resource Management

Gulf Publishing Company
Book Division
P.O. Box 2608 □ Houston, Texas 77252-2608

10 9 8 7 6 5 4 3 2 1

Library of Congress Cataloging-in-Pulication Data

Phillips, Jack J., 1945–
    Accountability in human resource management / Jack J. Phillips.
      p. cm.
    Includes bibliographical references and index.
    ISBN 0-88415-396-7
    1. Personnel management—Evaluation. I. Title.
HF5549.P4588 1996
658.3—dc20

95-42091
CIP

Dedicated to my daughter, Jackie,
who grew up during the development of this book.

Contents

PART ONE
General Framework for Evaluation

CHAPTER ONE
The Need for a Results-Based Approach _____ 1
Important Trends Related to HR Contribution 5, The Importance of These
Trends 21, Challenges 21, Paradigm Shifts 22, Conclusion: Payoff of
Measuring the HR Contribution 24, A Self-Assessment Tool 25,
References 29

CHAPTER TWO
Measuring the HR Contribution: A Survey of Appoaches _____ 33
Surveys 34, HR Reputation 35, Human Resources Accounting 36, HR
Auditing 37, HR Case Studies 38, HR Cost Monitoring 39, Competitive
Benchmarking 40, Key Indicators 41, HR Effectiveness Index 42, HR
Management by Objectives 45, HR Profit Centers 45, Return on
Investment 46, Summary 46, References 48

Acknowledgment

No book represents the work of the author alone. Many people contribute to the final product, and this book is no exception. Many colleagues have shared their ideas, which have been refined and developed and ultimately presented here. Over the years, many colleagues who are human resource managers and executives have shared their thoughts on this important topic. To all of them, I owe much appreciation for their contribution. I would like to thank Ken Lowery for reviewing the manuscript and offering suggestions. Ken is a very professional human resources manager who understands the need for a results-based approach.

Several individuals made direct contribution to this work. Through the years, I have worked closely with Jac Fitz-enz of the Saratoga Institute. Throughout his career, Jac has made a tremendous contribution to the measurement and evaluation process. The Saratoga Institute conducted one of the studies designed especially for this book. For their efforts and assistance, I owe them many thanks. To Dr. Anson Seers, at the University of Alabama, I owe much gratitude. He encouraged me to pursue a major research project on the development of a human resources effectiveness index. He was helpful, supportive, and encouraging throughout the entire project. He is truly an excellent researcher, scholar, and professor who understands the HR function and knows how to bring closure to projects.

Many thanks to my assistant Tammy Bush, who has been very helpful, creative, and resourceful as this book developed over the course of several years. Without her persistence, this book would still be under development. To the professional team at Gulf Publishing Company: thanks for the support. BJ Lowe and Joyce Alff were very patient with me as I took too much time to develop this book.

Finally, I owe much appreciation to my wife Johnnie, who provides encouragement, support, and assistance on all of my efforts, including this book. She always makes many sacrifices for me to pursue my work.

Preface

FOCUS OF THE BOOK

The initial research and development for this book began in the '80s. I examined hundreds of studies, surveys, and interviews to identify the most effective practices and processes to show the human resources (HR) contribution. The lengthy development process allowed me to apply new techniques and models within operations and analyze them for effectiveness before including them in the book. Two major studies were initiated specifically for this book and their results are reported in several chapters. After a decade of development, this significant work should be a valuable contribution to the field.

I have been fortunate to tackle HR measurement and evaluation from several perspectives. First and most importantly, as a human resource executive for many years, I struggled directly with the issue of accountability and attempted to bring a bottom-line focus to the human resources function. Second, as a top executive in a major financial institution, I viewed human resources from a completely different perspective, as a user of the services. Third, as an experienced author and researcher, I explored, examined, and reported on this topic for several years. Using available research, I attempted to show human resources practitioners the best practices. Finally, as a consultant, I have been fortunate to work with a variety of organizations to help them improve the contribution of the human resources function.

From these perspectives, several impressions begin to emerge about the HR profession, all underscoring the need for increased accountability of the HR function. Collectively, these perspectives provided a unique vantage point from which to write this book. The final product should be a valuable contribution to help human resources managers tackle this important issue.

IMPORTANCE OF MEASURING THE CONTRIBUTION

The evidence is very clear: the human resources function in organizations is continuing to grow in importance and influence. Among the reasons for the increasing influence are:

- Growing budgets that make human resources the greatest single expenditure in most organizations.
- The consequences of improper and ineffective human resource practices.
- The vast potential for using human resources to enhance productivity, improve quality, spur innovation, contain costs, and satisfy customers.
- The integration of human resources into the mainstream functions in the organization.

With this high-profile posturing, all HR executives are faced with an important challenge: A need exists to ensure that the function is managed appropriately and that programs are subjected to a system of accountability. In short, there must be some way to measure the contribution of human resources so that viable existing programs are managed appropriately, new programs are only approved where there is potential return, and marginal or ineffective programs are revised or eliminated altogether.

Among the hottest issues in the human resources field are the subjects of ensuring accountability, calculating the return on investment, developing a value-added approach, and making a bottom-line contribution. When any of these topics are discussed, they attract attention. Why? Because there is now more pressure to show this contribution than ever before. The pressure comes from top executives who demand accountability for the tremendous investment in human resources. Key operating managers also ask the HR function to help them get results by building a more productive and effective organization. Finally, today's progressive human resources managers are business managers first and professional HR managers second. They recognize that they must contribute to the organization in real terms and in ways that executives fully understand—bottom-line impact.

While this trend toward HR accountability is highly visible and significant, many HR professionals are still reluctant to accept this responsibility and meet the demands of accountability. They often contend that measurement and evaluation systems are too difficult and costly, and in some cases, impossible. In reality, a measurement and evaluation system can be simplified and implemented with little cost. It requires upfront planning, some additional tasks, and more importantly, a change in philosophy and attitude of not only the human resources staff, but of those it serves.

TARGET AUDIENCE

The primary target audience for this book is practicing human resource professionals. The book equips HR professionals with the tools necessary to show the contribution of programs. Presented in a systematic format, from a practical viewpoint with many examples and illustrations, it is based on actual experiences, accepted practices, and a strong research base. Each technique and idea has been tested and proven in actual practice.

A second target audience is students of human resources management who are preparing for assignments in this important field. This book will help them develop a results-based approach to the study of human resources practices in organizations. It also provides the tools necessary for job success in the HR field.

A third target audience is middle and top level managers who want to know more about how human resources can contribute to the bottom line of the organization. It shows managers how to help the HR staff become results-based contributors to the organization.

STRUCTURE OF THE BOOK

The book is divided into four parts. Part One (Chapters 1–2) presents a general framework for evaluating the human resources function. Chapter One explains the need for a results-based approach, and it is included to convince those individuals who do not yet fully embrace the concept. It shows important trends and challenges and opportunities that exist when measuring the return on investment. Chapter Two focuses on the approaches, outlining 13 different ways organizations now use to measure the HR contribution. Each is presented with a brief assessment of its usefulness. It is from this list that specific approaches are identified for expanded coverage in other chapters.

Part Two (Chapters 3–4) presents the issues involved in developing a results-based approach to human resources. Chapter Three describes a nine-step result-based model to implement a new HR program. It discusses a variety of fundamental concepts and issues, including the purposes of evaluation, the myths of evaluation, the levels of evaluation, the various obstacles to evaluation, and the responsibilities of evaluation. The attitude of the staff is also explored because it is so critical to the success of the effort. The chapter ends with an application of the model. Chapter Four highlights the important role of management in the success of the human resource contribution. It addresses specific strategies to strengthen relationships with key managers. Techniques for improving management commitment, support, and reinforcement for programs are fully explored, along with specific ways to get managers more involved in human resources function.

Part Three (Chapters 5–9) is the heart of the book and focuses on specific ways to measure the contribution of human resources. Chapter Five presents data collection techniques using surveys, questionnaires, interviews, focus groups, observations, and performance data, which can be used in various combinations to collect the data necessary to measure the contribution. Chapter Six explores evaluation design and implementation issues. Common designs are presented along with techniques to obtain feedback on human resources programs and activities. Useful techniques for measuring improvement are outlined, including action planning and performance contracting. Chapter Seven presents ways in which the total human resources effort can be measured and highlights five important measures that collectively should determine much of the success of human resources. This chapter presents an important study, with a useful model that details how these measures can be combined to form an HR effectiveness index. Chapter Eight presents measures from each specific human resources functional unit. More than 100 measures are presented in this chapter. Finally, Chapter Nine discusses benchmarking as a way to measure HR effectiveness and compare it with other organizations. The various phases of benchmarking are presented, showing step-by-step how an organization can develop its own benchmarking survey.

Part Four (Chapters 10-12) explores data analysis and presentation of results. Chapter Ten reports on human resources costs and shows the various ways in which costs can be monitored and used to measure the contribution. The impact costs of human resources are explored as important variables closely related to human resources practices. Chapter Eleven explains data analysis and data interpretation and shows how the influence of the HR program is isolated from other factors. It discusses various ways to convert data to monetary units to include the actual calculation of the return on investment. Chapter 12 discusses communication of HR program results to demonstrate how the successes of HR contribute to the organization.

Appendices provide additional information and examples of tools and techniques used in the chapters. Overall, each chapter is self-contained, although some chapters build on information presented earlier. It is not necessary to read the book in sequence. The reader may absorb only the chapters of particular interest.

WHAT THIS BOOK WILL DO FOR YOU

This book explores the key issues of human resources measurement and evaluation. After completing the book, the reader should know how to:

- Assess the current status of measuring the HR contribution in the organization
- Explain the importance of and necessity for measuring the contribution
- Identify the various approaches that can be used to measure the contribution
- Develop programs with an emphasis on accountability
- Establish a results-based approach when implementing HR programs
- Design data collection instruments and techniques for measurement and evaluation
- Improve management commitment and support for the HR function
- Build partnership relationships with key managers
- Select the optimum evaluation strategy for the organization
- Determine the costs of HR programs
- Isolate the effects of HR programs from other variables
- Convert HR program data to monetary values
- Calculate the return on investment in HR programs
- Communicate the results of HR programs

In summary, this is the first book to communicate concise, practical methods to evaluate any type of HR program. With its systematic process, ranging from developing the framework for evaluation to communicating the results, this book is designed to be a standard reference on measurement and evaluation for every HR professional.

CHAPTER ONE

The Need for a Results-Based Approach

During the last decade, the Human Resources (HR) function experienced drastic change in its role, status, and influence. Some HR executives recognized the change and stepped up to the challenge. A panel of top-level Human Resources executives recently assembled by *Personnel Journal* agreed that "HR is moving away from the transactional, paper-pushing, hiring/firing support function it has been and is becoming a bottom-line business decision maker."[1] Indeed HR is becoming a strategic business partner. But how does HR become more involved in business decisions? How does this affect the day-to-day role of HR?

A sample of the comments from panel members revealed details of this trend. "Being a strategic partner means understanding the business direction of the company, including what the product is, what it's capable of doing, who the typical customers are and how the company is positioned competitively in the marketplace," explains Tim Harris, senior vice president of HR for Novell Inc. in San Jose, California.

Tim Epps, vice president of People Systems for Saturn Corp., in Troy, Michigan, adds, "HR must become bottom-line valid. It must demonstrate its validity to the business, its ability to accomplish business objectives and its ability to speak of accomplishments in business language. The HR function must perform in a measurable and accountable way for the business to reach its objectives."

The ways in which HR becomes "bottom-line" vary depending on a company's strategic objectives. Generally speaking, traditional HR responsibilities, such as training, compensation and performance management, are linked to tangible business goals and measuring the contribution to those goals. John McMahon, corporate vice president of HR for Stride Rite Corp. in Cambridge, Massachusetts, explains that his company has developed an HR strategic plan that details the HR implications of each of the company's overall business goals.

What makes this strategic HR role possible in many companies is the HR department's shift from being a doer to an enabler, from being a staff function that delivers prepackaged HR services to the rest of the company to being a service that helps line managers create and manage their own customized HR policies.

That's what has taken place at Dallas-based Texas Instruments Inc. "My job early on was to make people happy . . . to worry about training, pay and benefits, communication and employee satisfaction," says Chuck Nielson, vice president of HR, who has been with TI since 1965. "But when we viewed our role in HR as keeping people happy, we found ourselves on a separate track from operating managers who were concerned with such things as yield, billing, scrap and other hard business issues. Operating people weren't supposed to spend any time on personnel—it detracted from their "real" jobs. Today, one of the most dramatic changes in our company is that HR folks are in partnership with the operating managers.

There is no doubt that the HR field is in the midst of this change, yet few HR managers are equipped to deal with it. Perhaps the situation is best described in a recent article on accountability:

> Sooner or later it all boils down to money. Human resource executives can grapple with such issues as rising health care costs, a widening skills gap, an increasingly diverse work force, the conflicting demands of work and family, and government regulation, and can develop responses to each. Ultimately, however, every idea—however innovative, farsighted and workable it may seem—must undergo the scrutiny of some tough questions: "Where will we get the money to pay for it? Will we see a return on investment? And perhaps the two most fundamental questions, Can we afford to do it? And its corollary, Can we afford not to do it?[2]

Because human resources represents a significant cost to the organization, the effectiveness of the function can influence the overall success or failure of the organization. Indeed, some organizations have failed because of ineffective HR policies. For example, many experts agree that much of the Eastern Airlines failure can be pinned on ineffective employee relations practices. The decline of the U.S. steel industry is blamed, in part, to costly employee and labor relations policies. A contributing factor to the recent problems of IBM, General Motors, and

Sears are their HR policies that left these three organizations saddled with tremendous human resources costs.

In perhaps its largest gesture of big spending, GM capitulated repeatedly to the United Auto Workers, thereby burdening itself with enormous wage and benefit costs. One kind of cost, health benefits for retirees that were to be paid in the future, was for many years invisible because accounting rules did not require it to be recorded as current expense.[3] In 1992, the new accounting rules brought the retiree health benefit problem into perspective, and GM took a monumental charge of $33 billion in pre-tax costs. This charge left GM with a loss for 1992 of $23.5 billion, far and away the largest loss of a Fortune 500 company in U.S business history.

For years, IBM has been trying to come up with innovative ways to get the employees to leave. Through a variety of incentive packages and finally shelving of its no-layoff policy, IBM is taking huge hits for employee costs. The layoff policy, which seemed to be one of the cornerstones of IBM's success, became one of the problems in trying to remain profitable.[4] Other examples are abundant throughout business in which human resources costs make organizations unprofitable and very uncompetitive in today's global economy.

Because they expect an adequate return on their investment in human, as well as other resources, some executives question whether the HR department should continue to expand if there is not a clear connection between its activities and the overall results of the organization. One chief financial officer of a Fortune 100 company was quoted as saying to his company's director of human resources: "I invest in human resource planning programs the way I invest in a machine tool. If you can't show me an ROI equal to this firm's cost of capital, I'm not buying and your budget is going to be cut."[5] This blunt demand is becoming typical of the new bottom-line orientation to human resource management that now dominates most major corporations.

On the positive side, the success of many outstanding companies today, such as 3M, Procter & Gamble, Motorola, Federal Express, Merck, and Coca-Cola. can be traced to effective HR policies. Chief executives, striving to improve productivity and achieve performance goals, are demanding—and getting—cost effective and productive approaches from their HR function. At America's top organizations, chief executives are recognizing the link between the people and the bottom line. Faced with issues as diverse as re-engineering, executive succession, and government regulation, they see how important employee relations can be to competitiveness.[6] The literature is laced with hundreds of examples of organizations making a tremendous contribution with the human resource function. HR departments are taking significant strides in reducing costs, enhancing customer service, improving profits, and boosting productivity. They accomplish this through a rigorous program of accountability for the function, and at the heart of accountability is measurement and evaluation. An important tenet of continuous process improvement (CPI) is *nothing improves until it is measured.* The CPI corollary is that when something is measured, it automatically begins to improve. This phenomenon is put into practice and is paying off in handsome dividends.[7]

The Human Resources department is, in effect, a function charged with advising and directing management on the investment of its human assets. Though it has traditionally been viewed as an expense center, its efforts can have significant impact on productivity and profits. The magnitude of employee costs alone should command the attention of top executives. For example, Texas Instruments, a high tech electronics firm with 65,000 employees worldwide, calculates its employee costs at 55 percent of operating costs. Even in capital intensive organizations where employee costs are relatively low, the long-term investment in employees is significant. For example, consider the investment in an employee for the total length of employment based on reasonable assumptions about expected duration of employment, anticipated salary increases, and expected increases in benefit costs. When the initial salary is adjusted upward to reflect predicted salary and benefit increases, the investment in an employee quickly becomes staggering. A major study conducted in the Upjohn Company revealed that the average cost of an employee over the full length of employment was 160 times the initial starting salary. For example, a $25,000 starting salary would result in a $4-million investment for a 30-year duration of employment.[8] When discounted to today's values, the figure is over a million dollars. Thus, a decision to hire an employee could be viewed as a million-dollar decision if the employee remains with the organization for 30 years. Although this may be exaggeration, the point is crystal clear: HR decisions are expensive. With this perspective, it seems logical that an organization should maximize the effectiveness of human resources and ensure that employees are properly selected, trained, and supported, and are always producing at optimum performance levels.

Another view of this issue is to consider the consequences of incorrect decisions on human resources issues. Improper decisions, based on subjective data, can result in serious consequences for the organization, possibly reducing its profitability or, in some cases, even leading to serious losses or bankruptcy. For example, a disastrous communications breakdown in New York City caused by AT&T was traced to a shortage of one or two technicians in a critical area. The technicians had been dispatched to attend a training program. Sears Roebuck and Company faced a significant decline in its auto repair business after allegations of widespread fraudulent behavior in several shops became public. Sears blamed an improperly designed incentive compensation plan.[9] HR decisions must be based on all the objective data that can be assimilated on an economical basis.

Unfortunately, a results-based approach is far from common practice in HR departments. One estimate is that 60 to 70 percent of HR departments are not using any method to measure their effectiveness.[10] While there are several obstacles to introducing measurement and evaluation of HR functions, in many cases HR professionals do not know how to measure the results of their efforts. Measurement and evaluation is not usually a part of their professional preparation. In other cases, managers do not want to be measured, living in the echoes of the past when it was generally accepted that the function was subjective and difficult to measure. Also, top management has not always demanded measurable results from HR. Without top management encouragement, many departments have not vigorously pursued quantitative evaluation.

The pressure to remain competitive in a dynamic, international economy has forced some organizations to develop a results-based approach. For these organizations to remain competitive in today's economy, they must have innovative products and services, excellent quality control and customer service, and efficient operations and delivery systems. This can only be accomplished through proper investment in HR programs designed to recruit quality employees, train them adequately, and keep them involved, challenged, and motivated.

This book focuses on the process of, and the techniques for, measuring the contribution of the HR function. It demonstrates methods to determine whether the investment in human resources produces a return. This initial chapter provides the foundation by reviewing the basic principles of the HR contribution.

Important Trends Related to HR Contribution

Emerging trends, issues, and priorities of the HR function are getting their share of attention. Peter Drucker predicted these changes in *The Wall Street Journal* over ten years ago when he asserted that the personnel department, in addition to changing its name to human resources, must behave quite differently and follow the line mode of behavior rather than the staff mode. Line managers are involved in producing, distributing, or selling the organization's products or services and are concerned about output, quantity, and cost. Staff employees provide support and assistance and are often less concerned about these issues. According to Drucker, "Above all, the personnel department would have to redirect itself away from concern with the cost of employees to concern with their yield."[11] This important concept has had and will continue to have a major influence on organizations. HR executives can help shape the future direction of their organizations by focusing on specific strategies to implement the changes suggested by Drucker.

From recent articles, reports, books, and interviews on the subject, seven trends can be identified that have a significant impact on an organization's bottom-line results and the HR function's role in the process. These trends include the increased importance of the HR function, increased accountability, organization-al change and quality programs, improvement in productivity, adoption of human resources strategies, growing use of human resources' information systems, and reliance on partnership relationships. Collectively these trends enhance or com-plement the efforts of the HR department to monitor and improve its contribution to organizational performance.

Increased Importance of the HR Function

The importance of the HR function and its connection to the bottom line is sometimes subtle, occasionally mysterious, and at times very convincing. Above all, it seems to be well publicized. Probably the most publicized reports come from the popular press's treatment of the importance of HR practices in organi-zations. List after list appears for the most profitable, fastest growing, most admired, and best managed companies in America. Among the lists are *Fortune* magazine's annual list of most admired companies, *Business Week's* annual list of America's most competitive companies, *Inc.* magazine's list of the best small companies to work for in America, and other publications such as *The 100 Best Companies to Work for in America.*[12] The basis for many of these lists is often the HR practices of these organizations. Even a magazine not known for its admira-tion of business, *Mother Jones,* has developed its own list. Among the issues examined were such variables as the workplace, treatment of employees, and the degree of company ownership.

Top executives' attitudes about the importance of the HR function have a signif-icant impact on an organization's bottom line. In a major study involving top U.S. businesses, executives were asked about the critical competitive issues facing U.S. companies and their suggestions for strengthening U.S. business competitiveness. The study clearly showed that top executives believe that internal management and human resources improvements are the best ways to improve the quality of U.S. goods and services and to make them more competitive in the world market.[13] This viewpoint was particularly underscored by larger organizations.

The importance of HR is recognized in many ways. Probably no recognition has been more meaningful than the awards given by *Personnel Journal,* a practi-tioner publication serving the human resources field. The Optimas awards, with ten categories, were created in 1991 to recognize the importance of HR and its value to the organization. Table 1-1 presents the winners for the 1995 awards and shows the range of the awards and types of programs. The 1995 award winners share two things in common: They are all important participants in the corporate decision-making process, and they all contribute to the organization's bottom line. Overall, the awards show the importance of the function and its contribution to organizations.[14] It is interesting to note that the general excellence award was won by the City of Hampton, Virginia. Previous award winners in this category include First Chicago Corporation, Levis-Strauss & Co., Hewlett Packard Co., and AT&T Corporation. Hampton has been working diligently implementing a variety of value-added and high-impact programs similar to those used in the cor-

TABLE 1-1
PERSONNEL JOURNAL OPTIMAS AWARD

AWARD CATEGORY	1995 WINNER	BASIS FOR AWARD
General Excellence	City of Hampton, Virginia	A public deployment of corporate tactics
Competitive Advantage	Mirage Resorts, Inc.	Selective staffing and commitment to training gives Mirage Resorts a competitive edge
Financial Impact	Springfield Remanufac- turing Corp.	Springfield Remanufactur- ing turns financial training into a game and workers into entrepreneurs
Global Outlook	Colgate-Palmolive Co.	Out of a year-long strate- gy-development process came a global HR system linked to business goals
Innovation	Hotel del Coronado San Diego, CA	To cover Mexican work- ers' dependents, Hotel del Coronado established the first Mexican HMO
Managing Change	The Seattle Times Co.	Diversity training and content audits help keep *The Seattle Times* current with its community
Partnership	Intel Corp.	Intel teaches an Arizona school quality manage- ment principles in exchange for educational involvement
Quality of Life	Calvert Group	Benefits programs at this investment firm address social responsibility as well as individual needs

(continued on next page)

TABLE 1-1 (CONTINUED)
PERSONNEL JOURNAL OPTIMAS AWARD

AWARD CATEGORY	1995 WINNER	BASIS FOR AWARD
Service	PepsiCo, Inc.	A stock-option program for all full-time employees supports this firm's entrepreneurial culture
Vision	Minnesota Mining and Manufacturing Co. (3M)	A decade-old strategy has helped 3M prevent downsizing while continuing to recruit new talent

Source: Halcrow, A. "Optimas Awards Recognize Triumphs in HR," Personnel Journal, January 1995, pp. 66–80.

porate sector. Many of their programs are producing results and adding to the bottom line.

The competencies required for the HR function underscore the changing role and importance of the function. A comprehensive study of HR competencies in the 90s revealed some important trends for success in the function. The study identified a three-part framework for conceptualizing HR competencies including a knowledge of business, delivery of HR practices, and managing the change process. As shown in Figure 1-1, business capabilities are an important part of this framework. According to the study, HR professionals fail to add their full value to an organization if they do not understand how the business operates. Knowledge of an organization's financial, strategic, and technological capabilities is essential to any strategic discussion. HR professionals who are knowledgeable exclusively in industrial, employee, or human relations may be competent in their discipline, but fail to understand the essentials of the business world in which their firms are involved.[15]

Probably one of the most visible indicators of the developing importance of the HR function is the status, influence, and position of the HR manager in major organizations. More and more, human resource executives are making their way to CEO positions and into corporate boardrooms. It is not unusual to find an employee who worked in HR for most of his or her career promoted to CEO, as is the case of Mike R. Bowlin, an HR veteran who leads ARCO, one of the world's largest oil companies.[16] While many HR executives attend board meetings as observers of the process (as non-voting participants), in some cases, they serve as directors.[17]

One of the most dramatic developments has been the shift in reporting relationship of HR executives. Often the title of the person to whom the function

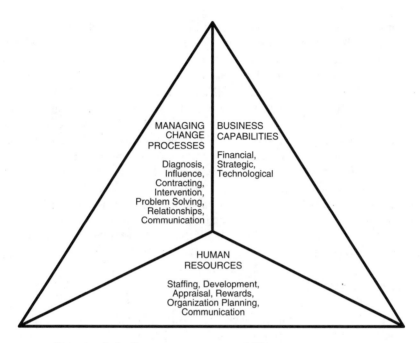

FIGURE 1-1. COMPETENCIES OF HR PROFESSIONALS.

reports is a reflection of the status and influence of the function. Human resources executives have gradually moved their reporting relationship to higher levels. In the early 80s, human resources managers usually reported to a chief administrative officer, chief operating officer, or chief financial officer. Currently, they usually report to the chairman, president, or CEO. An analysis of the *Personnel Journal 100,* which is a listing of the top 100 HR executives, reveals that 76 percent of them report to a person with the title of chairman, CEO, or president—a tremendous improvement in just a few years. Also, in the same list, at least three HR executives serve as members of the board of directors.[18]

Accounts of the importance of HR appear regularly in the newspapers. A reader doesn't have to venture very far into a newspaper to uncover a major story involving human resources. From massive loss of jobs to labor disputes, many of the major stories dominating business headlines have been directly related to human resource issues. These situations underscore what leaders in the nation's most progressive organizations have been saying for years: organizational success is inextricably linked to effective HR strategies. The popular press's treatment produces some interesting twists, particularly in the finance and investment field. There is some evidence that human resource organizational practices are one of the items mutual fund investment managers use to pick stocks for their portfolio. With greater emphasis being placed on customers, quality, employee empowerment, and flattened hierarchies, mutual fund managers are beginning to include the HR factor in fund selection.[19]

Finally, looking to the future, HR skills and issues will become more and more critical. A major study of 1,500 senior executives conducted by Columbia University revealed some insight into the knowledge and skills required of CEO's in the future. This study focused on what skills and knowledge they have now and will need for the year 2000. Among the current skills, human resource management was ranked third behind strategy formulation and marketing and sales. By the year 2000, human resource management skills will be second behind strategy formulation and will be followed by marketing and sales and accounting and finance. This trend shows the increasing importance of the HR function, not only among those who are involved in the field full-time, but for those top executives who must also devote time to this important function.[20]

Increased Accountability

The trend toward accountability can be illustrated in many ways and has been referred to by many different labels, as Figure 1-2 illustrates. These terms appear regularly in HR literature. Almost any professional HR publication devotes a tremendous amount of print space to HR accountability issues. Articles, presentations, and interviews all make a pitch for HR professionals to embrace the bottom line.[21] The accountability issue is illustrated by hundreds of published examples of HR programs that present their successes in measurable improvements and, in many cases, show monetary values. Some articles show that the connection between HR practices and the bottom line is quite clear and evident.[22] Organizations are offered numerous strategies to help move them from an activity-oriented process to a results-based orientation, usually by providing prescriptions to add value and measure the success of programs.[23] Fortunately, some of these strategies are working because evidence has been published of significant moves toward increased accountability in HR. In one survey, HR executives were asked how often the HR function was evaluated and in what ways. Thirty-two percent of the executives indicated that their HR department is evaluated at least annually. Unfortunately, 29 percent say they seldom or never conduct such an evaluation.[24]

Numerous empirical studies are conducted that attempt to relate the effectiveness of the HR function to organizational outputs. One study compared the HR practices of organizations identified as the top 100 rapid growth companies.[25] In this study, companies were divided into two groups, those that were engaged extensively in HR practices and those with moderate or low HR involvement. The profitability of the two groups was compared and the results indicated a strong

FIGURE 1-2. LABELING THE CONTRIBUTION OF THE HUMAN RESOURCES FUNCTION.

relationship between HR practices and the bottom line. The statistically significant results showed a tremendous difference in average net income between the two groups. A three-year study sponsored in part by the Society for Human Resource Management examined the relationships between sophisticated HR practices and productivity, turnover, and financial and accounting performance criteria. This study showed a strong correlation between the use of sound HR practices and increased firm performance by examining the gross rate of return on capital, total shareholder return, and price-cost margins. Sound HR practices are also associated with lower turnover and increased productivity measured as sales per employee. The study's author, Dr. Mark Huselid, of Rutgers University, states that "HR is the last great unrationalized area of business. Gains in production and performance won't be found in new financial and accounting methods. They probably won't be found in marketing. It's the HR area that has been overlooked."[26]

Another study, conducted by Hewitt Associates, a human resources consulting firm, shows the impact of the HR function in both financial and productivity performance. The study examined the effect of programs that focus on worker performance. It compared 205 companies with performance management programs to 232 companies without programs. Table 1-2 shows the results of this study. The companies with these programs posted higher profits, better cash flows,

TABLE 1-2
THE IMPACT OF HR ON FINANCIAL PERFORMANCE

	COMPANIES WITHOUT PERFORMANCE MANAGEMENT	COMPANIES WITH PERFORMANCE MANAGEMENT
Financial Performance: Return on Equity	4.4%	10.2%
Return on Assets	4.5%	8.0%
Productivity and Sales Per Employee	$126,100	$169,900
Income Per Employee	$1,900	$5,700

Source: "Effective People Management Helps the Bottom Line," Personnel Journal, December 1994, p. 17.

stronger stock market performance, and higher stock values. As the table shows, significant gains in productivity and financial performance were realized. According to the study's author, Edward L. Gubman, head of the HR consulting practice at Hewitt, "The study has broad implications for top management and human resource executives. In essence, this study proves that good human resource management practices produce a payoff in terms of bottom-line financial performance.[27] Programs that relate HR practices to bottom-line contributions are not limited to compensation programs such as incentives and gain sharing. They cover a broad range of programs. Even areas difficult to evaluate, such as diversity training, are now being linked to organizational success.[28]

Another interesting way in which HR accountability is being recognized is through awards presented to individuals and organizations for their HR programs that connect to the bottom line. One particular award is designed expressly for that purpose. The American Management Association annually provides HR awards of excellence to honor HR professionals who have demonstrated innovative programs and initiatives that positively impact the bottom line. For example, the 1994 award winner went to Thomas DuPree, policy manager for IBM's ideas department. DuPree was honored for technologically enhancing IBM's 63-year-old suggestion plan. The result: IBM ideas, an online computer application that makes it easier for the company's 124,000 employees to submit suggestions and have them evaluated and implemented faster.[29] The program's response increased by 25 percent with the new online process, and actual savings realized by IBM in

1993 reached $140 million. Program costs related to the ideas program has been reduced to 5 percent of savings accrued, down from 14 percent under the previous method.

Finally, the ultimate way in which HR accountability can be demonstrated is by gradually shifting the HR function to the profit center concept. Although this concept is controversial, there has been some movement toward the profit center concept in a few organizations.[30] Several companies are converting programs and services to a profit center internally and externally. In some cases, HR services are sold to outside firms.

Organizational Change and Quality Programs

A third dramatic trend related to HR contribution is the proliferation of a variety of organizational change and quality programs. These programs are sometimes referred to as re-engineering, restructuring, total quality management, continuous process improvement, employee empowerment, and customer focus. For many of the programs, the HR department implements the program. The role of HR in the process has never been more evident than in the survey of the *Personnel Journal 100.*[31] This survey asks the top 100 human resource executives what was their most challenging human resource issue in 1994. Of the total, over 70 percent said managing change, and another 30 percent indicated re-engineering.

Presently, the most common change program has been total quality management, sometimes labeled continuous process improvement or quality assurance. Recently the editors of *HR Focus,* a practitioner publication from the American Management Association, asked its readers in a random poll to identify the issues that would demand most of their time in the near future. The top three issues were promoting employee involvement, improving customer service, and supporting total quality management. According to the survey director, Sherri Brown, of the American Management Association, "These definitely are key concerns. In order for America to be competitive, companies must focus on employee involvement, be more aware of customer concerns and needs, and of course enhance the quality of their products and services."[32]

HR's significant role in managing change has brought about a re-examination of its own function. In short, human resources must increase its value to the organization by becoming consultative rather than administrative, automated rather than paper driven, and lean rather than layered. That's exactly what happened to American Express.[33] As the HR executive became the leader in the company's organizational change effort, the HR department reexamined its mode of operation and the way it was perceived in the organization.

The quest for quality continues to be an obsession in corporate America. For the vast majority of progressive firms, Total Quality Management (TQM) has become a way of life in the 90s. The extent of publicity and media coverage for this concept has been overwhelming. TQM has been given credit for turning companies around, increasing market share, increasing or creating significant growth rates, and more importantly, producing top quality products while increasing profitability. Much of the hoopla over TQM comes from the Malcolm Baldrige National Quality Award. Created in 1987, this award has become the most important catalyst for transforming American business, and more than any other initiative, public or private, it has reshaped manager's thinking and behavior. The Baldrige Award does more than signify the principles of quality management in clear and assessable language. It provides companies with a comprehensive framework for assessing their progress toward the new paradigm of management and such commonly acknowledged goals as customer satisfaction and increased employee involvement.[34] The relationship of HR to the Malcolm Baldrige Award is very clear. Of the seven categories, otherwise known as the Seven Pillars of Baldrige, human resource development and management ranks third highest in point value, having a total of 150 out of 1,000 possible points.[35] In addition, HR activities such as training and development can influence other categories such as leadership, strategic quality planning, and customer focus and satisfaction. When evaluating the HR function, Baldrige's judges examine how companies enable the workforce to develop its full potential. In doing so, they ask companies to describe their approach and proof of positive results in five categories:

1. HR planning and management
2. Employee involvement
3. Employee education and training
4. Employee performance and recognition
5. Employee well-being and satisfaction

The advent of TQM foreshadows great and positive change for corporations and for human resource professionals in particular. In the past ten years, the most forward thinking corporations in the United States have began a cultural shift that will transform work. HR can and will play a key role in this significant change.[36] The role of human resources can evolve into one of several possibilities. The HR director may be a passive receiver of a TQM effort initiated by another key manager. The HR manager may become part of a quality improvement project team or may be a member of a quality steering committee. Increasingly, however, the HR manager may be tapped to spearhead the total quality effort and belong to the quality council, a group of senior managers who direct the quality initiative.

The role of the human resources department in the quality effort is subject to much debate. Some researchers do not think that HR should lead the quality effort because staff groups rarely lead any key strategic initiative successfully. Ed

Lawler, professor at the Center for Effective Organizations at the University of Southern California in Los Angeles, believes that line management should lead the effort, but HR has to be involved as a partner from the beginning. In the early stages of the quality effort at Xerox, one of the pioneers of total quality management, the decision was made to exclude the human resources department. Previously, HR had managed all cultural change strategies and management felt that if HR led the quality effort, it would be perceived as just another flavor of the month. Instead, line managers and vice presidents carried the quality torch. It wasn't long, however, before Xerox managers realized they had made a mistake. The company had to align its HR systems with its quality goals for the effort to be successful. Xerox invited the HR department to the table and asked HR professionals to share, among other things, their expertise in training, rewards, and recognition.[37] Regardless of the approach, the HR manager should be involved in the process and there is evidence to indicate that HR's role is increasing.[38]

Unfortunately, not all change efforts are working. In fact, many of them are coming under fire. Consider this example. After $700,000 and 18 months of analysis, meetings, and recommendations, a midwestern company suspended its TQM efforts. Its CEO actively supported the process, trained the employees, participated in the quality council, and surveyed customers and employees, yet concluded that he had missed the boat. Business was flat, the market share was unmoved, and employee morale was back where it once was. Although he could point to some process improvements, the payoff was illusive.[39] *The Wall Street Journal* reported that two-thirds of all quality improvement efforts ultimately fail because organizations simply do not understand what quality means or how to attain it.[40]

Regardless of the outcome of TQM and organizational change programs in the workplace, three important conclusions emerge:

■ The process continues to expand to all types of businesses. There has been significant growth in its application to government and nonprofit organizations.
■ The role of human resources continues to increase with the implementation of these programs. More HR departments are driving the TQM process and other change programs in their organizations.
■ The greatest challenge is to continue to reap the initial results achieved in the early stages of implementation. The process of continuous improvement must produce results on a long-term basis.

The third conclusion provides a challenge for HR professionals. They must be poised to make the most of the process. A strong measurement and evaluation process is essential in every program implementation and may be the most important ingredient to the program's success.[41]

Improvement in Productivity

During the decade of the 1980s, the United States struggled to understand the erosion of its position as the world's economic power. International competition, particularly from the Far East, made deep inroads into the steel, automobile, electronics, rubber, and other industrial segments of the United States. Declining productivity was singled out as the root of the competition problem. This conclusion has led to a profusion of productivity improvement programs emphasizing issues such as participative management, commitment to excellence, empowerment, self-directed work teams, innovation, value added programs, entrepreneurship, automation, and Japanese management techniques.

With the consensus that there is a productivity problem in the United States economy, American management's interest in productivity reached dramatic proportions. So much has been said and written about the problem that many organizations joined the effort to reverse this trend simply because it appeared to be the thing to do. An important part of this trend is the increasing role of the HR function in productivity improvement programs. The HR department now plays a vital role in initiating, implementing, monitoring, and evaluating these programs. The role and impact of the HR function on productivity improvement are underscored by examining the causes of productivity problems, the barriers to improvements in productivity, and the elements necessary for a successful productivity improvement program. At the top of almost any HR practitioner's list of critical issues are those relating to competitiveness or productivity.[42]

The types of productivity improvement programs vary considerably. Some are strictly based on pay-for-improved productivity while some integrate cost savings, incentives, and participation. Others provide nonfinancial incentives, such as time off for improvements in productivity. Some plans operate on improvements in productivity based on changes in management style and philosophy to encourage participation in the workforce and the empowerment of employees. Still other programs will rely strictly on behavioral concepts, such as organizational behavior modification, to realize important productivity improvements. It appears that productivity improvements can be linked to almost any organizational variable.[43] Productivity improvement programs have spread through all types of settings including nonprofit and government organizations. One report shows that the productivity growth rate of the federal government is slightly ahead of the private sector.[44]

The important aspect about productivity is that, before it can be effectively improved, it must be measured, and this is where the HR function is actively involved. Measurement can be accomplished by isolating output by division, department, work team or by individual. The cost that went into producing the output has to be determined including labor and capital costs. Using a previous year as a baseline period, the HR manager must compare the current year figures with those of the previous years.[45] Standard productivity reporting methods must be integrated with generally accepted financial reporting practices. Actual productivity results should be included in regularly published financial and operational reports and should be an integral part of the goal setting and budgeting process in any business.

Some observers question the motivation and work ethic of the U.S. worker. Critics point to the declining role of work in the U.S. coupled with the rising demands for more leisure time. Many firms, however, proudly point to their productivity increases and claim that increases are due to employees working smarter, not harder.[46] The most powerful tools for productivity improvement often lie within management control, but the tools have to be applied consistently and within the framework of an overall strategy for performance improvement. Many HR programs are designed to improve productivity or performance. Training, compensation, motivational programs, employee relations practices, and organization development usually focus on performance improvement. A combined strategy must coordinate all the elements of human resource management.

Successful stories are reported regularly in the press. Consider an IMPROSHARE plan for example in which workers are essentially paid bonuses equal to ½ of any increase in productivity. A study of its use in manufacturing firms found that defect and downtime rates fell by 23 percent in the first year of its introduction. In the median firm, the overall increase in productivity was more than 5 percent in the first three months and more than 15 percent by the third year. By comparison, productivity increased by only 2 percent, on average, in these manufacturing sectors as a whole.[47] Improvement in productivity results from all types of HR programs. Consider for example, a program at Xerox where changes in work schedules produced impressive results. Xerox found its rigid 8:00 to 5:00 work schedule created stress among the employees and difficulties for employees who needed more flexibility with child care and family problems. When Xerox announced that employees could determine their own hours, they obtained some interesting results. Ten months after the announcement, about ½ the employees chose new starting times or compressed work weeks, while continuing to cover the work. Absences fell by ⅓, teamwork improved, and surveys show that morale rose. Other companies such as GTE, Stride Rite Corporation, and Chicago's Harris Bank have reported similar results. In fact, GTE managers are constantly astounded at the creativity employees bring to make nontraditional arrangements work.[48]

From all indications, it appears that the HR function will continue to play an integral part in productivity improvement efforts. In addition, because of their impact on the organization's bottom line, productivity improvement programs provide a means for the HR function to make a significant contribution to overall organizational effectiveness.

Adoption of Human Resources Strategies

Perhaps one of the most intriguing trends in recent years is the adoption of HR strategies by organizations. Strategic planning is critical to an organization's growth and prosperity when it attempts to gain or retain a competitive advantage. The growing importance has significant implications for both corporate strategy and HR management. The HR planning strategy is fundamental to measuring and evaluating the contribution of HR toward organizational effectiveness. Because it is tied to business success, it must be data based. While every planning process involves many subjective and expert judgments, the more relevant facts and information used, the greater the chances are that the plan will be appropriate, realistic, and effective.

Human resource strategies are essentially plans and programs to address fundamental strategic issues related to human resource management. Randall Shuler has defined strategic human resource management in this way:

> Strategic human resource management is largely about integration and adaptation. Its concern is to ensure that 1) human resources management is fully integrated with the strategy and the strategic needs of the firm, 2) HR policies are both across policy areas and across hierarchies, and 3) HR practices are adjusted, accepted, and used by line managers and employees as part of their everyday work.[49]

The importance of the human resource function to an organization's strategy is underscored by reviewing the overall functions of strategic planning. These include periodic forward scanning, analysis based on longer time frame, communication about goals and resource allocation, framework for short-term plan evaluation and integration, institutionalizing longer term time horizons necessary for investments, and decisional criteria for short-term decision making.[50] It is impossible to address these critical issues without bringing in the human resources factor at each element of the process.

In the early development of strategic planning and strategic management, there was little concern about the human resources function until the actual implementation began. Rarely was the human resource function brought into the planning process. Now this is changing. Strategy and human resource planning are integrated early in the process.[51] As shown in Table 1-3, there are several benefits of integrating human resource planning with strategic planning, making it imperative for this integration to be regularly pursued.[52] This issue is so important that

TABLE 1-3
BENEFITS OF INTEGRATING HUMAN RESOURCE PLANNING WITH
STRATEGIC PLANNING

1. Generates more diverse solutions to complex organizational problems.
2. Ensures consideration of human resources in organizational goal-setting processes.
3. Ensures consideration of human resources in assessment of the organization's abilities to accomplish goals and implement strategies.
4. Reciprocal integration prevents strategy formulation based on personnel rigidities/preferences.
5. Facilitates concurrent consideration of strategic plans and managerial succession.
6. Ensures that a comprehensive measurement system is in place.

Source: Adapted from Greer, C. R. Strategy and Human Resources: A General Managerial Perspective. *Englewood Cliffs: Prentice Hall, 1995.*

some experts have suggested that the human resource manager be labeled Director of People Strategy.[53]

Because of the importance of strategy in the success of firms and the critical ingredient of human resources in the strategic plan, human resource managers are finding themselves heavily involved in the strategic planning process. Because strategy is related to the organizational goals, the ultimate opportunity to show the contribution of human resources begins in the strategic planning arena.

Growing Use of Human Resources Information Systems

During the last decade, no trend has been more visible than the growing use of computers in the HR function. Advancements in the computer and data processing industry have expanded the use of HR information systems. These advances allowed HR managers in all types and sizes of organizations to tap the capabilities of computers. It is now possible to automate the HR function with a complete information system for under $10,000. Powerful microcomputers are changing the way managers and professionals work. In the early 1980s, there were only a few dozen software programs for the HR field. Now there are over 600 micro-based programs for personnel applications with more than 200 vendors.[54]

The vast capability of systems allows greater amounts of data to be analyzed, monitored, and reported, and ultimately leads to more accurate measures of performance at the organization, division, and department level. It is not uncommon for typical data elements in a human resources information system (HRIS) to include 150 variables on employees. These data represent a tremendous potential in developing measures, analyzing results, and reporting them to management. This trend alone has a tremendous influence on the organization's ability to measure the contribution of the HR function.[55]

With the tremendous pace of technological changes, this part of the HR function has changed more rapidly than any other element. There have been remarkable advances in the way massive amounts of information are collected, processed, and manipulated. As a result, the human resource function now pivots on the capability of the information system. In the late 80s, it was the norm to request information on a monthly basis and expect a week's delay to generate that information manually. Today, that information can be obtained instantly.

An effective HRIS system has altered senior management's expectations of the HR function. Because benefits and compensation costs represent huge investments with a major impact on the bottom line, senior management is keenly interested in HR costs and the ways to calculate and control them. Senior management is becoming accustomed to calling on HRIS to generate data and conduct "what-if" calculations and make projections. This information is needed on a timely basis to make proactive decisions about business strategy. Historical information is examined so that the organization can learn from past errors and successes.

It would be impossible to think of administering benefit and compensation programs without HRIS. It has become an important and essential tool for the human resource function managing a growing database for the organization. While the principal focus of HRIS in the past has been to keep records and analyze data in a variety of ways, emerging applications now make it possible for HR functions to accumulate and analyze data related to specific HR programs. Thus, the computer in the HRIS system will become the principal tool to track and monitor data to show the overall contribution of the human resource function.[56]

Reliance on Partnership Relationships

A final important trend related to the HR contribution is the movement toward, and reliance on, partnership relationships in organizations. There is no doubt that organizations change, particularly in the way they work internally. As part of this rapid change, many HR professionals have aligned themselves with key managers of functions in the organizations. In simple terms, the HR profession is desperately trying to collaborate with line management. HR executives have watched their roles shift from the reactive to the proactive and now to the collaborative role where they work hand-in-hand with key managers in anticipating problems and planning the strategic direction for the organization.[57]

Building this relationship is not easy. It takes a tremendous amount of time and a deliberate plan for HR managers. A critical ingredient to a partnership arrangement is that the HR manager must be knowledgeable of the business and contribute to business decisions. Also, HR managers must take the time to develop individual relationships; however, doing so takes precious time from other important activities.[58] But the investment can reap tremendous dividends, as many HR managers have experienced. An important part of the partnership relationship is convincing line management of the bottom-line contribution of HR. When line managers see the contribution and understand it, they are less reluctant to enter a partnership relationship. Because of the importance of this trend, it will be presented in more detail later.

THE IMPORTANCE OF THESE TRENDS

There are other important trends in HR such as global expansion, diversity management, and the implementation of work teams; however, the unique feature of the seven trends described here is that they are tightly integrated and are directly related to HR's contribution to the organization's bottom line. Changes in the HR function in the last decade have focused more attention on these trends because they have a significant impact on HR's ability to improve organizational performance. Clearly, the human resources function has taken on new dimensions and has become a valuable business partner in any organization. Still, there is much progress to be made. Increased concern for HR accountability has surfaced, and top management, as well as the other constituencies served by the HR function, are expecting significant contributions from human resources. It appears that the HR function must meet this demand with new and improved measurement and evaluation strategies.

CHALLENGES

The seven trends presented here set the stage for the development of concrete links between HR performance and organizational performance. Three important challenges are identified:

■ **The human resources function should be integrated into the strategic planning and operational framework of the organization.** It is essential that human resources become involved in the overall strategic direction of the organization. Also, it must be an active participant in the organization's operational planning. Otherwise, the important link between human resources and the organization's bottom line will not be clearly identified nor fully realized. It is no longer acceptable for organizations to develop strategic plans without considering all the ramifications of the employee costs or the potential contribution of employees to strategic initiatives. HR must be an integral part of the planning and not an add-on part of the process.

■ **The human resources staff must build relationships with other key managers in the organization, with a particular focus on the line organization.** The line function has a responsibility for achieving major organizational goals, and it must have the support of the HR department to achieve those goals. In many cases the extent of the combined contribution of the line organization and the HR staff depends on the quality of their relationship. The challenge is for the HR staff to refine and improve this relationship.

■ **The HR staff must improve techniques and processes in order to measure the effectiveness of the function.** This important challenge is relatively new to the field. For too many years the cost of human resources has been recognized and not challenged. Employee contributions have been forced, not inspired, and organizations are now faced with the consequences. Programs have been added, but the return on the investment has not been developed. The HR staff must implement specific processes appropriate for the organization to measure the contribution. The remainder of this book will focus on these three challenges with a particular emphasis on the second and third challenges.

PARADIGM SHIFTS

Many HR managers are inadequately prepared to make the shift from traditional HR function to a more results-based approach demanded in today's environment. As depicted in Table 1-4, the movement represents a significant paradigm shift for the HR manager and staff. In the traditional approach, new programs were initiated by request or suggestion from any significant manager or group. This led to a tremendous proliferation of programs, often too many to manage effectively. The new approach requires the HR staff to initiate programs only after a legitimate need is established and to focus its effort on a manageable number of programs that have a significant impact in the organization. In the traditional approach, existing programs were rarely, if ever, eliminated. Once established, they appeared to be set in concrete. The new approach means that there is a systematic review and adjustment of programs. If one is no longer needed, or if it is not making a contribution, then it has to be eliminated.

The basis of accountability has shifted significantly. In the traditional approach, activities, such as number of programs, hours of involvement, and the number of participants, are counted. In the results-based approach, specific measures of contribution are developed for each program. In the traditional approach, limited

TABLE 1-4
PARADIGM SHIFTS NECESSARY FOR A RESULTS-BASED APPROACH

TRADITIONAL APPROACH	RESULTS-BASED APPROACH
New programs initiated by request or suggestion of any significant manager or group.	New programs initiated only after a legitimate need is established.
A multitude of programs in all areas.	Fewer programs with greater opportunity to make an impact.
Existing programs are rarely, if ever, eliminated or changed.	Existing programs are regularly reviewed and eliminated when necessary.
Count activities, hours of involvement, number of employees involved, etc.	Measure the impact of programs on the organization.
Limited management involvement in the HR process.	Extensive involvement and collaboration with management.
HR viewed as cost center.	HR is viewed as an investment in employees.
HR staff unfamiliar with operations issues.	HR staff very knowledgeable about operations issues.
HR staff lack knowledge of finance and business concepts.	HR staff versed in basic finance and business concepts.

opportunities for management involvement in the HR process were possible. Both sides seemed to be comfortable with this arrangement. Relationships were not very productive. In the results-based approach, there is extensive involvement and collaboration with management, particularly at the middle and upper management levels. In the traditional approach, HR is viewed as a cost center and it is reported as such in all company documents. In a results-based approach, HR is viewed as an investment in employees. Some programs are undertaken to actually enhance the organization and thus produce a return on the investment.

In the traditional approach, the HR staff is unfamiliar with the basic issues, goals, and concerns of the operations of the organization. They also lack the knowledge of basic business and finance concepts. The results-based approach requires the staff to be knowledgeable in all of the key operational areas of the business and be versed in the basic finance and accounting concepts.

This is a tremendous shift for many HR managers who still cling to the traditional mode of operation. All the evidence in this chapter underscores the critical need to make this shift to the results-based approach.

CONCLUSION: PAYOFF OF MEASURING THE HR CONTRIBUTION

This chapter described an important movement toward accountability in the HR field. Central to this movement is the increased attention to the measurement and evaluation of HR. At least six important payoffs will result from a more formal approach to evaluation.[59] These payoffs are as follows:

- **Evaluation makes good economic sense.** Every HR program should provide an appropriate return on the investment. It makes good business sense to show a program's worth by providing convincing evidence that can only be obtained through a formal measurement and evaluation process. Accountability is a basic business principle.
- **Evaluation shows proof of results.** The HR staff need to see the results of their efforts. The staff should know how well they are performing, and management must see how well the function is progressing. This is difficult to accomplish without a formal approach to measurement and evaluation.
- **Results from evaluation encourage the HR staff to focus on important activities.** Evaluation brings into focus those activities that will make a difference in the contribution to organizational effectiveness. When program outcomes are tied to a bottom-line contribution, the HR staff can identify which programs have the most impact and concentrate on them. Otherwise, the HR staff may devote too much time on activities that may have little impact on organization success, wasting time and financial resources.
- **Data collected for evaluation isolate the causes of problems.** The HR staff often focuses on problem areas and implements new programs and policies to solve those problems. Sometimes they may attempt to solve problems that are beyond the scope of HR. A formal measurement and evaluation effort provides data necessary to clearly identify the causes of problems and to measure progress toward problem resolution when the problem can be corrected by HR.
- **Results from measurement and evaluation can lead to additional resources.** As the HR function continues to make contributions, additional resources are needed for new programs, services, and policies. One of the most effective ways to justify additional resources is to show the results from previous programs through the evaluation process.
- **Evaluation increases personal satisfaction and position.** An important sense of personal satisfaction comes from seeing the results of one's work. Evaluation allows the HR staff to judge their success much the same way as production or sales employees view their output. This not only increases per-

sonal satisfaction, but it can increase the influence and respect enjoyed by the HR function. As the function's importance grows from positive contributions, its influence will grow as well as the personal position of HR employees.

Together, these important payoffs should provide the incentive for HR departments and HR executives to pursue an ambitious, formal program of measurement and evaluation. To do otherwise, may lead to disappointment and frustration.

A SELF-ASSESSMENT TOOL

Evaluating the HR function and specific HR programs involves more than developing performance measures and administering evaluation instruments. It is a results-based philosophy that the organization must adopt at all levels if evaluation efforts are to be effective. Assessing current attitudes about measurement and evaluation in the organization poses difficult problems for HR practitioners. The instrument shown in Table 1-5 has been developed to assess the current sta-

Text continued on page 28

TABLE 1-5
HOW RESULTS-BASED ARE YOUR HUMAN RESOURCES PROGRAMS?
A QUICK CHECK FOR THE HUMAN RESOURCES MANAGER

Select the response that best describes the situation in your organization and circle the letter preceding the response. See Appendix 1 for scores.

1. Performance measurements have been developed and are used to determine the effectiveness of:
   A. All human resources (HR) functions.
   B. Approximately half of the HR functions.
   C. At least one HR function.

2. Major organizational decisions are:
   A. Usually made with input from the HR function.
   B. Usually made without input from the HR function.
   C. Always made with input from the HR function.

3. The return on the investment in HR is measured primarily by:
   A. Intuition and perception by senior executives.
   B. Observations by management and reactions from participants and users.
   C. Improvements in productivity, cost savings, quality, etc.

(continued on next page)

4. The concern for the method of evaluation in the design and implementation of HR programs occurs:
   A. Before a program is developed.
   B. After a program is implemented.
   C. After a program is developed but before it's implemented.

5. New HR programs *without* some formal method of measurement and evaluation are:
   A. Never implemented.
   B. Regularly implemented.
   C. Occasionally implemented.

6. The costs of specific HR programs are:
   A. Estimated when the programs are implemented.
   B. Never calculated.
   C. Continuously monitored.

7. The costs of absenteeism, turnover, and sick leave for the organization are:
   A. Routinely calculated and monitored.
   B. Occasionally calculated to identify problem areas.
   C. Not determined.

8. Cost/benefit comparisons of HR programs are:
   A. Never developed.
   B. Occasionally developed.
   C. Frequently developed.

9. In an economic downturn, the HR function will be:
   A. Retained at the same staffing level, unless the downturn is lengthy.
   B. The first to have its staff reduced.
   C. Untouched in staff reductions and possibly beefed up.

10. The cost of current or proposed employee benefits are:
   A. Regularly calculated and compared to national, industry, and local data.
   B. Occasionally estimated when there is concern about operating expenses.
   C. Not calculated, except for required quarterly and annual reports.

(continued on next page)

TABLE 1-5 CONTINUED
HOW RESULTS-BASED ARE YOUR HUMAN RESOURCES PROGRAMS?
A QUICK CHECK FOR THE HUMAN RESOURCES MANAGER

11. The chief executive officer (CEO) interfaces with the senior HR officer
   A. Infrequently, it is a delegated responsibility.
   B. Occasionally, when there is a pressing need.
   C. Frequently to know what's going on and to provide support.

12. On the organizational chart, the top HR manager:
   A. Reports directly to the CEO.
   B. Is more than two levels removed from the CEO.
   C. Is two levels below the CEO.

13. Line management involvement in implementing HR programs is:
   A. Limited to a few programs in their area of expertise.
   B. Nil; only HR specialists are involved in implementing programs.
   C. Significant; most of the programs are implemented through line managers.

14. The HR staff involvement in measurement and evaluation consists of:
   A. No specific responsibilities in measurement and evaluation with no formal training in evaluation methods.
   B. Partial responsibilities for measurement and evaluation, with some formal training in evaluation methods.
   C. Complete responsibilities for measurement and evaluation, even when some are devoted full time to the efforts; all staff members have been trained in evaluation methods.

15. Human resources development (HRD) efforts consist of:
   A. Full array of courses designed to meet individuals' needs.
   B. Usually one-shot, seminar-type approaches.
   C. A variety of education and training programs implemented to improve or change the organization.

16. When an employee participates in an HR program, his or her supervisor usually:
   A. Asks questions about the program and encourages the use of program materials.
   B. Requires use of the program material and uses positive rewards when the employee meets program objectives.
   C. Makes no reference to the program.

(continued on next page)

TABLE 1-5 CONTINUED
HOW RESULTS-BASED ARE YOUR HUMAN RESOURCES PROGRAMS?
A QUICK CHECK FOR THE HUMAN RESOURCES MANAGER

17. Pay-for-performance programs (bonuses, incentive plans, etc.):
   A. Exist for a few key employees.
   B. Are developed for all line employees.
   C. Are developed for most employees, line and staff.

18. Productivity improvement, cost reduction or quality of work life programs are:
   A. Not seriously considered in the organization.
   B. Under consideration at the present time.
   C. Implemented with good results.

19. The results of HR programs are communicated:
   A. Occasionally, to members of management only.
   B. Routinely, to a variety of selected target audiences.
   C. As requested, to those who have a need to know.

20. With the present HR staff and management's attitude toward results, the HR function's impact on profit can:
   A. Be estimated but probably at a significant cost.
   B. Be estimated (or is being estimated) with little additional cost.
   C. Never be assessed.

Note: An earlier version of this instrument was first published in Phillips, J. J. "How Does Your HR Department Rate? A Self Test," The Human Resources Professional Vol. 1, No. 6, Sept./Oct. 1989, pp. 12–17.

Text continued from page 25

tus of measurement and evaluation efforts and measure progress in the future. The instrument examines 20 issues related to a results-based philosophy that should help organizations assess the extent of success of their HR programs. It should also provide a means to compare one organization's efforts to another. The instrument is appropriate for all professional HR staff members, although the target audience is the individual responsible for the function. Responses should be candid and anonymous. After responding to all statements, the instrument should be scored using the guidelines provided in Appendix 1. The rationale for determining the correct responses is briefly outlined, and an interpretation of scores is also presented. Completing and scoring the instrument is usually an enlightening exercise that could alter the approach to program implementation.

REFERENCES

1. Caudron, S. "HR Leaders Brainstorm the Profession's Future," *Personnel Journal,* Vol. 73, No. 7, August 1994, pp. 54–61.
2. Halcrow, A. "The HR Budget Squeeze," *Personnel Journal,* June 1992, pp. 114–128.
3. Loomis, C. J. "Dinosaurs?" *Fortune,* May 3, 1993, pp. 36–42.
4. Carroll, P. *Big Blues: The Unmaking of IBM.* New York: Crown Publishers, 1993.
5. Dubnicki, C. and Williams, J. B. "Using Competency-Based Human Resources Planning to Improve the Bottom Line," *The Human Resources Professional,* Winter 1990, pp. 56–61.
6. Pechter, K. "Great Expectations," *Human Resource Executive,* June 1992, pp. 34–39.
7. Vines, L. S. "A Foot in the Boardroom Door," *Human Resource Executive,* November 1992, pp. 29–31.
8. Lehrer, R. N. (Ed). *White Collar Productivity.* New York: McGraw-Hill, 1983.
9. Fisher, L. M. "Sears Auto Centers to Hart Commissions," *New York Times,* June 23, 1992, p. D1.
10. Thornburg, L. "The White Knight of HR Effectiveness," *HRMagazine,* November 1992, pp. 67–73.
11. Drucker, P. F. "How to Measure White-Collar Productivity," *The Wall Street Journal,* November 26, 1985, p. 28.
12. Levering, R. and Moskowitz, M. *The 100 Best Companies to Work for in America.* New York: Doubleday, 1993.
13. Shetty, Y. K. and Buller, P. F. "Regaining Competitiveness Requires HR Solutions," *Personnel,* July 1990.
14. Halcrow, A. "Optimas Awards Recognize Triumphs in HR," *Personnel Journal,* January 1995.
15. Ulrich, D., Brockbank, W., and Yeung, A. "HR Competencies in the 1990's," *Personnel Administrator,* November 1989.
16. Bowlin, M. R. "HR Vet Leads ARCO," *HRMagazine,* December 1994, pp. 46–51.
17. Vines, L. S. "A Foot in the Boardroom Door," *Human Resource Executive,* November 1992, pp. 29–31.
18. Sunoo, B. P. "No Business As Usual," *Personnel Journal,* December 1994.

19. Ettorre, B. "HR Isn't a Factor for Mutual Funds . . . Yet," *HR Focus,* December 1994, p. 15.

20. Filipowski, D. and Halcrow, A. "HR Leaders Are Powerful," *Personnel Journal,* December 1992, p. 48.

21. Rhodeback, M. J. "Embrace the Bottom Line," *Personnel Journal,* May 1991.

22. Radford, J. and Kove, S. "Lessons from the Silicon Valley," *Personnel Journal,* February 1991.

23. Nathansonn, C. "Three Ways to Prove HR's Value," *Personnel Journal,* January 1993.

24. Cashman, M. E. and McElroy, J. C. "Evaluating the HR Function," *HRMagazine,* January 1991.

25. Albert, M. "HR Profit Power," *Personnel,* February 1990.

26. Thornburg, L. "Yes, Virginia, HR Contributes to the Bottom Line," *HRMagazine,* August 1993, pp. 62–63.

27. "Effective People Management Helps the Bottom Line," *Personnel Journal,* December 1994, p. 17.

28. Majors, G. and Sinclair, M. J. "Measure Results for Program Success," *HRMagazine,* November 1994, pp. 57–61.

29. Smith, B. "Winning Innovations in HR Management," *HR Focus,* June 1994, p. 7.

30. Pauly, D. "HR: The New Profit Center," *Human Resource Executive,* August 1993, pp. 36–41.

31. Sunoo, B. P. "No Business As Usual," *Personnel Journal,* December 1994.

32. Mattes, K. "A Look Ahead for '93," *HR Focus,* January 1993, p. 1, 4.

33. Overman, S. "Big Bang Change," *HRMagazine,* June 1994, pp. 50–53.

34. Garvin, D. A. "How the Baldrige Award Really Works," *Harvard Business Review,* November–December 1991.

35. Caudron, S. "HR Is One Pillar of the Baldrige Award," *Personnel Journal,* August 1993, p. 48J.

36. Carter, C. C. "Seven Basic Quality Tools," *HRMagazine,* January 1992.

37. Caudron, S. "How HR Drives TQM," *Personnel Journal,* August 1993, pp. 48B–48I.

38. Shadovitz, D. "Joining the Revolution," *Human Resource Executive,* April 1993.

39. Leibman, M. S. "Getting Results from TQM," *HRMagazine,* September 1992.

40. Caudron, S. "Keys to Starting a TQM Process," *Personnel Journal,* February 1993.

41. The Price Waterhouse Change Integration Team. *Better Change: Best Practices for Transforming Your Organization.* Burr Ridge: Irwin Professional Publishing, 1995.

42. Lewin, D. and Mitchell, D. J. *Human Resource Management: An Economic Approach,* 2nd Edition. Cincinnati: South-Western College Publishing, 1995.

43. Wilson, T. B. *Innovative Reward Systems for the Changing Workplace.* New York: McGraw-Hill, Inc., 1994.

44. U.S. Bureau of Labor Statistics, Productivity Measures for Selected Industries and Government Services, Bulletin 2406 (Washington: GPO, 199), pp. 106–110.

45. Ivancevich, J. M. *Human Resource Management.* Chicago: Irwin, 1995.

46. Cascio, W. F. *Managing Human Resources: Productivity, Quality of Work Life, Profits,* 4th Edition. New York: McGraw-Hill, 1995.

47. Kaufman, R. T. "The Effects of IMPROSHARE on Productivity," *Industrial and Labor Relations Review,* 45, 311–322, 1992.

48. Shellenbarger, S. "The Keys to Successful Flexibility," *The Wall Street Journal,* January 13, 1994, pp. B1, B2.

49. Schuler, R. S. "Strategic Human Resources Management: Linking the People with the Strategic Needs of the Business," *Organizational Dynamics,* 21, no. 1, 1992, 18–32.

50. Quinn, J. B. "Strategic Change: Logical Incrementalism," *Sloan Management Review,* 30, no. 4, 1989, 45–55.

51. Anthony, W. P., Perrewe, P. L., Kacmar, K. M. *Strategic Human Resource Management.* Fort Worth: The Dryden Press, 1993.

52. Greer, C. R. *Strategy and Human Resources: A General Managerial Perspective.* Englewood Cliffs: Prentice Hall, 1995.

53. Morin, W. J. "HR as Director of People Strategy," *HRMagazine,* December 1994, pp. 52–54.

54. Noe, R. A., Hollenbeck, J. R., Gerhart, B., and Wright, P. M. *Human Resource Management: Gaining a Competitive Advantage.* Burr Ridge: Irwin, 1994.

55. Flynn, G. "A New HRIS in Wake County Streamlines HR," *Personnel Journal,* May 1994, pp. 137–142.

56. Stright, J. F., Jr. "Strategic Goals Guide HRMS Development," *Personnel Journal,* September 1993, pp. 68–78.

57. Sujansky, J. G. *The Power of Partnering: Vision, Commitment, and Action.* San Diego: Pfeiffer & Company, 1991.

58. Moravec, M., Juliff, R., and Hesler, K. "Partnerships Help a Company Manage Performance," *Personnel Journal,* January 1995, pp. 104–108.

59. Fitz-Enz, J. *How to Measure Human Resource Management,* 2nd Edition. New York: McGraw Hill, 1995.

CHAPTER TWO

Measuring the HR Contribution: A Survey of Approaches

The concern for the contribution of the HR function dates back to the 1920s when personnel research set the stage for the development of measures of the function's activities and performance. In the 1940s and 1950s, about the time the function became a legitimate and essential part of organizations, practitioners and researchers began to explore ways of measuring its contribution. In the years that followed, HR practitioners wrestled with this difficult problem. By the late 1970s, evaluation became a part of some HR departments. Considerable advancements in measurement and evaluation took place in the 1980s, but it is still far from being widely practiced. The decade of the 1990s is seeing tremendous growth in this area.

A milestone was achieved when the Society of Human Resources Management (SHRM) in the early 1980s identified the evaluation process as one of the ten specialty areas of the HR field. By being classified in this way, the specialty areas of review, audit, and research are considered major functions of human resources along with such functions as training and development, staffing, compensation, and labor relations.

There is little question that the HR function, which includes a variety of activities, should be evaluated in some way and linked to the success of the organization. The difficulty in doing this lies in selecting the right combination of approaches to develop an adequate evaluation system. The approaches are varied, with some clearly more effective than others. The trends outlined in Chapter 1 presented an overview of these strategies. This chapter describes twelve approaches that have been used to evaluate the HR function. Each one is presented separately, although there is overlap in the techniques, processes, and focus of some approaches.

SURVEYS

Several organizations use attitude of climate surveys to evaluate the effectiveness of their HR department. These surveys attempt to link employee attitudes to the organizational performance. For example, Federal Express created a fully automated survey program in 1993 and considers it a key ingredient in the company's success.[1] Another study designed to determine the impact of surveys on an organization compared the use of employee surveys with the profitability of the company. As expected, those organizations responding as more profitable than most of the industry were high users of employee surveys. On the other hand, those organizations describing themselves as less profitable rarely used surveys.[2]

A major study conducted by the Hay Group examined the attitudes of employees in two groups of companies, high performers and low performers, based on performance data such as revenue and asset growth. Not surprisingly, in the higher performing companies, the attitudes of employees were more favorable.[3] The cause and effect of this relationship is not completely clear, but suggests that either positive attitudes could have enhanced organizational performance or the environment of a successful organization could have created positive attitude.

Some organizations have taken surveys a step further and have developed a Human Resources Index (HRI) that enables an organization to compare its progress over time and with other organizations. The Mayflower group, which consists of over 30 companies including Xerox, General Electric, IBM, and Prudential Insurance, have done pioneering work in cross-organizational exchange of attitudinal data.[4] According to its developer, the HRI is proven to be effective in many organizations for measuring attitudes, overall satisfaction, and commitment to organizational goals as well as pinpointing trouble spots and issues requiring concentrated efforts. One flaw with the use of this index is in the validity of its questionnaire. It was not possible to determine predictive validity through correlation with a criterion measure. Although this method of evaluation is intriguing and its developer claims that it represents the proven connection between people and profits, there is little evidence of any direct connection with organizational performance.

HR REPUTATION

Some HR professionals suggest that the effectiveness of the HR function should be judged by the feedback from those it is designed to serve, often referred to as constituencies or clients. Constituencies depend on, or exert control over, the HR function. Proponents of this approach argue that effectiveness is a value judgment. Even objective criteria are only one step removed from subjectivity. Someone has to determine what level of objective performance is considered effective and what level is considered ineffective. For these proponents, it is more important to measure the perception of the function in the mind of constituents.[5] After conducting three major studies on this approach, one researcher found some evidence, although moderate, to suggest that HR effectiveness, as perceived by constituents, is positively related to overall organizational performance.[6]

Another major study focusing on the constituency or reputational approach was sponsored by IBM. In this study, 785 opinion leaders, presumed to have well informed perspectives of current HR practices, were interviewed. Among those included were corporate officers, HR executives, faculty members, placement directors, leading consultants, and disseminators of business information.[7] Collectively, they determined what they perceived to be effective HR policies and practices. They were asked to rate the importance of 25 specific factors that they might use in judging the overall effectiveness of an organization's HR policies and practices. The factors rated as most important by these experts were:

- open communication
- high-performance standards
- rewards to employees based on performance
- effective use of employee skills and abilities
- encouragement of employee participation in work decisions
- advancement opportunities
- identification and development of high potential managers.

It is important that the HR function is perceived as effective and its clients and users are satisfied. However, there is little concrete evidence of a relationship between levels of satisfaction among constituencies and overall organizational performance. This process ignores HR outcomes that may have a direct impact on the bottom line.

HUMAN RESOURCES ACCOUNTING

A somewhat novel approach to evaluation, which gained popularity in the late 1960s and early 1970s, is Human Resources Accounting (HRA). Although its interest seemed to diminish in the early 1980s, it has recently obtained renewed emphasis. This concept attempts to place a value on employees as assets in an organization and to measure improvements or changes in these values using standard accounting principles. HRA was originally defined as the process of identifying, measuring, and communicating information about human resources to facilitate effective management within an organization.[8] It is an extension of the accounting principles of matching cost and revenues and of organizing data to communicate relevant information in financial terms. With HRA, human resources are viewed as assets or investments of the organization. Methods of measuring these assets are similar to those for measuring other assets. However, the process includes the concept of accounting for the condition of human capabilities and their value as provided by the measurement tools of the behavioral sciences.

From a practical standpoint, the concept is very sound. Consider, for example, a large consulting firm where the quality of service lies in the strengths and capabilities of the consulting staff. If, at one point in time, 30 percent of the consulting staff resigned, a tremendous drain on the organization as well as a devaluation of its assets would result. However, in standard accounting principles, the exit of the consulting staff would not be taken into consideration. The human resources accounting process attempts to show the value of these human assets. HR literature records many case studies of organizations, ranging from manufacturing firms to professional baseball teams, that have used this concept. The Upjohn Company for example, uses HRA principles to measure and forecast the return on its investment in people.

HRA is not without its share of critics. The concept developed very slowly, primarily because of controversies surrounding three important questions: are human beings assets, what costs should be capitalized, and what methods are most appropriate for establishing a value for employees with the eventual allocation of such value to expense. There are legitimate problems concerning the concept that employees can be owned or controlled by an organization, which is a prerequisite for defining them as assets. Many professionals question the source of the information provided by HRA, particularly when it is measured against the cost involved in developing an adequate and equitable system.[9]

Because of its negative image, the potential users of HRA (HR managers) have not realized the many possible uses of this concept and have not pressed accounting professionals to join them in developing this potentially useful idea. Promising signs indicate that many corporations will begin listing the financial value of their human assets on the balance sheet, and that action can lead to benefits that greatly outweigh the cost of implementing an HRA system.[10] The U.S. Department of Labor is also encouraging changes to accounting rules to allow companies to treat training expenditures as investments rather than expenses.[11]

In the context of measuring the HR contribution, HRA does not focus on the performance of the HR function but instead reflects the value and contribution of all employees. Thus, it falls short in linking HR performance to organizational performance.

HR AUDITING

A human resources audit is an investigative, analytical, and comparative process that attempts to reflect the effectiveness of the HR function. It undertakes a systematic search that gathers, compiles, and analyzes data in depth for an extended period, frequently a year, instead of with daily formal and informal reports. The use of HR audits has increased significantly. One reason for this is a commitment to moving the HR function from service to the strategic arena.[12]

HR auditing is an extension of traditional auditing, which until recent years was limited to the financial practices of the organization. There has been a tremendous expansion in the extent, scope, and types of information being audited. In addition to human resources, auditing has now moved into production, operations, sales, quality, data processing, and engineering. It has become a critical analytical tool to assess how well—or how poorly—an activity is performed. HR auditing provides the necessary baseline data so that actions can be taken to improve HR performance. The scope of the HR audit is increasing. A survey of 200 HR professionals yielded 16 categories to be measured, as shown in Table 2-1.[13]

A variety of methods can be used to conduct audits including interviews, surveys, observations, or a combination of these. The survey is the most preferred

TABLE 2-1
HR AUDITING CATEGORIES

■ Department Mission	■ Compensation
■ Department Organization	■ Human Resources Planning
■ Department Personnel	■ Organizational Planning and Development
■ Labor Relations	■ Equal Employment Opportunity
■ Recruitment and Selection	■ Safety
■ Training and Development	■ Security
■ Employee Relations	■ Facilities
■ Employee Benefits	■ Documentation

Source: McConnell, J. H. "How Are You Doing? Designing an Audit of the HR Function," Human Resources Professional, March/April 1989, pp. 61–64.

approach. In a typical audit, several questions would be developed for each cate-gory in Table 2-1.

In some cases, HR audits focus on the efficiency of internal functions. These functions include the types of activities or processes performed by the HR depart-ment and the degree of efficiency in administering those activities. Examples of internal efficiency measures include items such as the number of counseling ses-sions conducted, the length of time to fill job vacancies, and the number of com-plaints from employees. Although these are important activities that need to be monitored and addressed, there is no assurance that performing these functions efficiently will increase the overall contribution to the organization.

The major difficulty with auditing is that there is little direct connection between the information in the audit and the overall effectiveness of the organi-zation. Auditing is an important process that can help to improve the efficiency of the HR function and ensure that all components of an effective HR program are in place and fully functioning. In short, it is essential and important, yet falls short of a valid approach to measuring the contribution of the function.

HR CASE STUDIES

Another attractive approach to evaluation is to examine the success of individ-ual programs, policies, or practices and report the results of these successes to selected audiences. For example, an organization may report outstanding results with a physical fitness program and may summarize the program in case study for-mat for distribution to all key managers. Another company may describe a suc-cessful labor-management participation program in a booklet for all employees.

Success cases have significant value and can be presented with little cost. Also, this approach can be used to gain support for HR and help justify additional resources for the function. Case studies are developed using data on HR perfor-mance, reaction from individuals, or interviews with participants involved in HR programs or services. Interviews coupled with actual results create very convinc-ing case studies. One of the most successful efforts to use the case study approach to show HR contribution is a new publication of the American Society for Train-ing and Development.[14]

The case study approach as an evaluation process has some weaknesses. It does not represent a balance of the performance of the HR function or a program, but instead provides some evidence that certain programs are successful. It usually does not represent an ongoing evaluation of any particular program or the over-all function, only a one-shot examination. Also, it is often subjectively based and a program's success is usually judged by those participating in the interview, completing the questionnaire, or providing other input. Quantitative data are not always a part of these studies. However, even with its weaknesses, the success case approach should be an important part of an organization's overall measurement and evaluation program.

HR COST MONITORING

While most executives are aware of the total cost of payroll and benefits, they do not understand that changes in HR practices can result in a tremendous increase in costs. One approach to evaluate HR performance is to develop HR costs and use them in comparisons with cost standards. Some organizations compare these costs with other internal costs; however, these comparisons could possibly reinforce complacency. Comparisons with other, similar organizations may be more effective.

Data on HR costs per employee represent a common measure that was actually calculated and reported more than 50 years ago. The Bureau of National Affairs and other organizations regularly reports HR costs per employee and as a percent of both payroll and company budget. In one important project, the Saratoga Institute developed standards for key measures and costs that allow organizations to compare their performance with others.[15] Some common HR costs include training costs per employee, benefits costs as a percent of payroll, and compensation costs. Table 2-2 shows a typical listing of HR costs monitored by organizations.

TABLE 2-2
TYPICAL HR COSTS MONITORED BY ORGANIZATIONS

Employment	**Fair Employment**
■ Cost Per Hire	■ Cost Per Complaint
■ Orientation Cost	■ Cost of Litigation
Training and Development	**Labor Relations**
■ Cost Per Employee	■ Cost Per Grievance
■ Total Cost as a Percent of Payroll	■ Cost of Work Stoppages
Compensation	**Safety and Health**
■ Compensation Expense as a Percent of Operating Expense	■ Accident Costs
■ Total Compensation Costs	■ Costs of Citations/Fines
Benefits	**Overall HR**
■ Benefits Costs as a Percent of Payroll	■ HR Costs as a Percent of Operating Expenses
■ Health Care Costs Per Employee	■ Turnover Costs

This process does have its weaknesses. Tracking costs alone is no assurance of a direct link with organizational performance. Also, while cost comparisons are helpful, standard HR cost data are not yet available. From a practical approach, HR cost monitoring is necessary as input for other approaches to evaluation. For example, in the benefits/costs analysis, HR cost data are required for comparisons.

COMPETITIVE BENCHMARKING

A few organizations developed key measures that represent the output of the HR function. The measures are compared to measures from other organizations that are regarded as having the best industry practices. This process is known as competitive benchmarking. Benchmarking began as an important development in the American quality movement and examples of companies using benchmarking include such competitive giants as Xerox, Motorola, Kodak, Milliken, and Texas Instruments. These companies have used benchmarking as an important vehicle for improving their internal processes while improving quality and reducing costs. Despite the surge of interest in the process, few companies know what they are doing when they undertake a benchmarking study. To some managers, even in the human resources area, benchmarking just means a process similar to industrial tourism where a department or a few executives make superficial plant visits to assure themselves and others that they are par with the host company.[16] Other managers take the process more seriously and view it as a learning process that can improve overall HR effectiveness.

While benchmarking has proven successful in quality and other areas, it has been slow to develop with the human resources function. Benchmarking data are often collected in an organizational-wide project. However, if benchmarking is to be used to improve the HR process, a separate HR benchmarking study should be implemented. Although the process shows great promise, there are many hazards along the way. Because of this, a later chapter provides HR practitioners with a step-by-step guide to implement a benchmarking project.

KEY INDICATORS

In some HR evaluation efforts, key measures are developed that reflect the major efforts of the HR function. In some cases, these measures are linked to organizational performance. The key indicators approach is perhaps the best known and established method of HR evaluation. It uses a set of quantitative measures such as the accident frequency rate, absenteeism rate, turnover rate, and average time to fill requisitions. Table 2-3 shows the key indicators and gives two

TABLE 2-3
SELECTED KEY INDICATORS USED IN HR EVALUATION

Employment
- Average days taken to fill open requisitions
- Ratio of offers made to number of applicants

Equal Employment Opportunity
- Ratio of EEO grievances to employee population
- Minority representation by EEO categories

Training
- Percentage of employees completing training programs per job category
- Training hours per employee

Employee Appraisal and Development
- Distribution of performance appraisal ratings
- Reliability of appraisal ratings

Careers
- Ratio of promotions to number of employees
- Average years/months between promotions

Salary Administration
- Percentage of overtime hours in straight time
- Ratio of average salary to midpoint by grade level

Benefits
- Percentage of sick leave to total pay
- Average length of time taken to process claims

Work Environment/Safety
- Frequency/severity ratio of accidents
- Ratio of OSHA citations to number of employees

Labor Relations
- Percentage of grievances settled
- Average length of time to settle grievances

Overall Effectiveness
- Turnover rate
- Absenteeism rate

Source: Adapted from Gómez-Mejía, L. R., Balkin, D. B., and Cardy, R. L. Managing Human Resources. *Englewood Cliffs: Prentice Hall, 1995.*

examples of each one.[17] One study in a specific company developed three measures reflecting the HR department's contribution:

- productivity, as reflected in cost
- quality, as reflected in repair rates
- employee relations, as reflected in absenteeism and suggestions[18]

On a broader scale, another study assessed the effects of several variables on organizational performance involving 25 manufacturing plants in one company.[19] The study linked the attitudinal climate, absenteeism rate, grievance rate, disciplinary action rate, and overtime ratio to two measures of organizational performance: direct labor efficiency and quality of product. Each measure was significantly related to organizational performance except that absentee rate was not related to the quality of product.

A major study, conducted by the U.S. Department of Labor, examined the research on dozens of studies concerning high performance work practices.[20] These studies indicate a positive correlation between high performance work practices and productivity and long-term financial performance. The evidence shows that specific practices such as training, alternative pay systems, and employee involvement are often associated with higher levels of productivity. Industry studies show that these and other practices can have a greater impact when implemented together in systems.

One problem that has hampered evaluation of the HR's contribution to organizational performance is the lack of appropriate databases. While it is sometimes easy to examine one firm's HR practices and compare them with organizational success, it is difficult to secure consistent and standardized information across several organizations. Fortunately, efforts are being taken to develop these databases. Representatives from the Strategic Planning Institute, Hay Associates, and the University of Michigan recognized the need to integrate strategy and organizational practices into databases. These three partners formed a joint venture called Organization and Strategic Information Service (OASIS). OASIS is intended to provide business managers, strategic planners, HR specialists, and organizational researchers with an improved and factual base for designing and implementing strategies for business success. One problem with the use of OASIS and other databases is the lack of extensive HR data.

Although this approach of tying key measures to organizational performance seems to be sound, there is still little empirical evidence to show this direct connection. Indeed this is an area that needs additional support, research, and study.

HR EFFECTIVENESS INDEX

A few organizations have attempted to develop a single composite index of effectiveness for the HR function. One of the first examples of such an index was developed and used by the General Electric Company in the 1950s.[21] This Employee Relations Index (ERI) was based on eight indicators selected from a detailed study of employee behavior. Among the indicators were absenteeism, initial dispensary visits, terminations, grievances, and work stoppages. The indicators were combined by means of a multiple regression formula with the variables receiving different weights. Constants were added depending on the level of the variable in a plant and for the particular plant or group in question. According to its users, the ERI was intended to help managers evaluate policies and practices, trace trends in employee relations, find trouble spots, perform human relations duties more effectively, and control personnel costs. Index values were compared with plant profitability (ratio of net income before taxes to capital investment). Although the plants with the higher ERI's were the more profitable ones, the relationship was not statistically significant.

Another index attempt was the Human Resource Performance Index (HRPX) that uses massive data banks made available by human resource systems.[22] According to its developer, the HRPX has been successfully used to evaluate HR functions such as selection, compensation, development, and retention. No attempt was made to validate this index against organizational performance. In selection, the HRPX measures the effectiveness of college-recruiting activities in terms of success of recruits within the company and their retention rates. Recruiting success is measured by the annualized compensation growth. Because of its construction and suggested use, this index raised more questions than it answered.

Another example is the Employee Relations Index (ERI) that was developed in the late 1970s for use in an electric utility. The ERI provided a means to measure the status of employee relations and compare one department with another. The index contained weighted factors for measures such as absenteeism, turnover, safety, grievances, complaints, and motor vehicle accidents. Apparently, no attempts were made to relate the index to any organizational performance measures such as profitability or growth.

Atlantic Richfield Company (ARCO) developed a comprehensive index composed of eight items and used to predict union activity, or in a unionized plant, to predict a strike.[23] The index items are shown in Table 2-4. For each measure, the categories were established on a four-point scale. A score of 4 meant that the human resource problems were pronounced. Another effort, a research project funded by the Society for Human Resource Management, attempted to link the presence of sophisticated HR practices with financial measures of an organiza-

TABLE 2-4
INDEX ITEMS

- Absenteeism (Days)
- Absenteeism (Times)
- Separations
- Visits to the Dispensary
- Disciplinary Actions
- Grievances
- Retirement Plan Enrollment
- Group Life Insurance Enrollment

Source: Miner, J. B. and Crane, D. P. Human Resource Management: The Strategic Perspective. New York: HarperCollins College Publishers, 1995.

tion's performance. The ten areas are shown on Table 2-5.[24] In addition to linking these practices to financial performance, the researcher found these practices have a dramatic effect on turnover and productivity.

TABLE 2-5
SOPHISTICATED HR PRACTICES LINKED TO FIRM PERFORMANCE

- Employment tests for selection
- Formal performance appraisals
- Appraisals linked to compensation
- Participation in variable pay or company incentive plans
- Formal job analysis
- Nonentry jobs filled from inside the organization
- Access to a formal grievance procedure
- A formal information sharing program
- Attitude surveys
- Some form of labor/management cooperation

Source: Thornburg, L. "Yes, Virginia, HR Contributes to the Bottom Line," HRMagazine, August 1994, pp. 62–63.

The most comprehensive study on this issue was recently conducted to develop and test a Human Resources Effectiveness Index (HREI).[25] The study, involving 71 organizations from eight industry segments, provided additional empirical evidence of the relationship between HR performance and organizational effectiveness. Six measures of HR department performance were identified for use in the study:

- HR expenses/total operating expenses
- total compensation/total operating expenses
- total cost of benefits/total operating expenses
- training and development expenses/total employees
- absence rate
- turnover rate

The HREI represented a composite of the six measures and significant correlations were developed with revenue/employees, assets/employee costs, operating income/employee costs, and operating income/stockholders' equity (ROE).

An index is appealing because it is simple to compute and easy to understand. The indices described here, as well as other indices such as the HRI described earlier, have been useful for comparing one organization to another and can be used for internal control and goal setting.

HR MANAGEMENT BY OBJECTIVES

Perhaps the oldest approach to measuring HR performance is HR management by objectives. Based on the assumption that the major emphasis of human resources should be to improve performance on certain measures, an evaluation process of measuring progress toward objectives gained popularity in the 1960s because of the widespread use of management by objectives (MBO).[26] With this approach, the personnel department, as well as other departments, develops specific objectives and evaluates performance against those objectives. Typical objectives in those early years included personnel budgets, grievances, accidents, and turnover. The approach is still used by many organizations and is factored into their budgeting or goal setting processes.

The objective-setting process uses the characteristics of all sound objectives and must be measurable, dated, challenging, achievable, realistic, and understood by all parties involved. Objectives are based on what management wants accomplished or what is perceived to be necessary to achieve an adequate level of performance. Measures of turnover, absenteeism, job satisfaction, employee health, and compensation expenses are quantifiable and could be potential objectives for the HR function. However, these measures must be related to organization performance in order to represent meaningful approaches to reflect the HR contribution.

HR PROFIT CENTERS

According to some researchers and practitioners, the ultimate approach to evaluation is the profit-center approach. This concept requires a shift from the traditional view of the HR department as an expense center in which costs are accumulated to a view of HR as an investment that can achieve a bottom-line contribution and, in some cases, actually operate as a profit center. Increases in the investment in HR, through additional staff, programs, and resources, are expected to improve the performance of the organization. This is an important shift in the perception of the HR function.[27]

With the profit-center arrangement, the HR department operates as a profit center and charges the organization for the services and programs it offers. It establishes competitive rates for services provided to users within the organization. In some cases, outside firms may also compete with internal HR services. Typical examples of programs or services "sold" to user organizations are training and development programs, benefits administration, recruiting, safety and health programs, relocation programs, administration of compensation programs, and the implementation of union avoidance programs.[28]

The underlying premise of this approach is that user departments such as production, operations, sales, and engineering are charged for the services of the HR department and in some cases, have the option of using external services in lieu of those offered by the HR department. In effect, the HR department either makes a profit, breaks even, or experiences a loss. Assuming the services are priced on a competitive basis, the profit represents a financial return on the investment allocated to the HR function.[29]

Adoption of this approach requires the HR department to become client-oriented and quality conscious in delivering services and programs. Some organizations have expanded this concept to include selling HR services to outside clients, thus generating additional income for the organization. Control Data, Dupont, General Motors, Xerox, and Westinghouse are only a few of the organizations now selling their programs to the public. A profit-center approach to evaluation is in its embryonic stage of development but is generating considerable interest. It represents a significant departure from the traditional HR management practices, and because of this, it may never be fully implemented in most organizations.

RETURN ON INVESTMENT

An intriguing and probably most convincing approach to HR evaluation is to compare the cost of HR programs to the benefits derived from them. On an individual program basis, this has been used successfully in both the private sector and the public sector. In most cases, the cost of HR programs can be developed or monitored. Although confusion sometimes exists concerning ways to allocate specific costs, overall program costs can usually be pinpointed. The difficulty lies in determining program benefits. In many cases, subjective input is used to assign monetary values to benefits derived from programs, particularly for those benefits that are intangible in nature. Consequently, this approach is sometimes avoided as an evaluation tool. However, there are some reliable techniques that can generate accurate estimates that will be presented later.

While this approach may be effective with an individual program, it is difficult, if not impossible, to evaluate the entire HR function with this approach. However, many of those managers responsible for programs will not be satisfied with the results achieved until benefits are compared with the costs. This approach should be an integral part of an HR department's effort to show its contribution. Because of its importance, this concept is presented in more detail in later chapters.

SUMMARY

While there are many approaches to HR evaluation using a variety of tools and based on a variety of assumptions, HR departments still have difficulty achieving success with current approaches. Unfortunately, there are few success stories about comprehensive HR evaluation programs that show the contribution of the function. Many researchers question the quantitative approach to evaluation, suggesting that a return on investment in employees must be approached cautiously and judiciously, and that any such return may be the result of activities initiated by others than the HR staff. Some professionals even question the requirement of bottom-line results from HR programs on the premise that it is not possible to isolate monetary benefits an organization may receive from an HR program. Although there is an important trend toward HR accountability, a major problem is that evaluation approaches have been unable to deliver what top management and even HR practitioners want it to deliver: objective data showing the contribution of the HR function to organizational effectiveness.

No one best way exists to evaluate the contribution of human resources. This chapter presented twelve approaches, each with its specific advantages or disadvantages. Collectively, these approaches provide an array of useful tools to help the HR department develop a comprehensive strategy to show its contribution. Table 2-6 summarizes and compares these approaches. The measurement focus

TABLE 2-6
COMPARISON OF APPROACHES TO MEASURE THE HR CONTRIBUTION

APPROACH	MEASUREMENT FOCUS	RELATIVE COST	RELATIVE VALUE OF INFORMATION
Surveys	Attitudes/Perceptions	Moderate	Moderate
HR Reputation	Attitudes/Perceptions	Moderate	Moderate
HR Accounting	Value of Skills/ Capabilities	High	Moderate
HR Auditing	Efficiency/Existence of Practices	Low	Low
HR Case Studies	Qualitative Description with Data	Low	Low
HR Cost Monitoring	Program/Function/ Behavior Costs	Low	Low
Competitive Benchmarking	Performance Measures/Practices	High	High
HR Key Indicators	Program/Function Performance Measures	Moderate	Moderate
HR Effectiveness Index	Multiple Key Indicators	High	High
HR Management by Objectives	Goal Setting for HR Performance Measures	Low	Moderate
HR Profit Centers	Profit Contribution of Programs/Services	High	High
ROI	Benefits vs. Costs	High	High

describes the types of data collected and/or the focus of measurement. As the table illustrates, a wide range of possibilities exists, from perceptions to hard data involving monetary values. The relative cost category attempts to indicate the cost of implementing the evaluation process, when it is implemented properly. Some approaches are very low cost, such as conducting an internal audit; whereas others, such as the HR profit center, represent a tremendous investment. A final comparison shows the relative value of the information ranging from low value, such as the HR audit, to high value with the return on investment approach. The approaches with high values deserve additional attention and are presented in more detail in this book.

Although it is possible to use all the approaches to measure the contribution of an HR department, such a comprehensive effort would be redundant, expensive, and potentially confusing. A more realistic effort would be to select a few manageable approaches shaped by top management's expectations of the HR function.

From a business results viewpoint, those approaches that link HR performance with organizational effectiveness or focus on benefits vs. costs comparison appear the most credible and valid. However, successful efforts with these approaches have been sparse, and the reactions have been mixed. There is an important need to continue to develop and refine approaches that will create this link. This book meets this challenge by providing techniques for the HR staff to develop this critical link.

REFERENCES

1. Smith, B., "FedEx's Key to Success," *Management Review,* July 1993, pp. 23–24.

2. Wymer, W. E. and Parente, J. A., "Employee Surveys: What Employers Are Doing and What Works," *Employment Relations Today,* Winter 1991/92, pp. 477–484.

3. Cooper, M. R. *Employee Commitment in the Eighties.* Presentation at the Annual Meeting of the American Society for Personnel Administration, June 29, 1987.

4. Schuster, F. E. *The Schuster Report: The Proven Connection Between People and Profits.* New York: John Wiley, 1986.

5. Gómez-Mejía, L. R., Balkin, D. B., and Cardy, R. L. *Managing Human Resources.* Englewood Cliffs: Prentice Hall, 1995.

6. Tsui, A. S., "Defining the Activities and Effectiveness of the Human Resource Department: A Multiple Constituency Approach," *Human Resource Management,* 26, No. 1, 1987, pp. 35–69.

7. Alper, S. W. and Mandel, R. E. "What Policies and Practices Characterize the Most Effective HR Departments?" *Personnel Administrator,* 29, No. 11, 1984, pp. 120–124.

8. Flamholtz, E. G. *Human Resource Accounting,* 2nd Edition. San Francisco: Jossey-Bass Publishers, 1985.

9. Cascio, W. F. *Managing Human Resources: Productivity, Quality of Work Life, Profits,* 4th Edition. New York: McGraw-Hill, Inc., 1993.

10. Crawford, R. *In the Era of Human Capital.* New York: HarperBusiness, 1991.

11. Geber, B. "A Capital Idea," *Training,* January 1992, pp. 31–34.

12. Ivancevich, J. M. *Human Resource Management.* Chicago: Irwin, 1995.

13. McConnell, J. H. "How Are You Doing? Designing an Audit of the HR Function," *Human Resources Professional,* March/April 1989, pp. 61–64.

14. Phillips, J. J. (Ed.) *Measuring Return on Investment.* Alexandria: American Society for Training and Development, 1994.

15. Fitz-enz, J. *SHRM/Saratoga Institute Human Resource Effectiveness Survey: 1994 Annual Report.* Saratoga, CA: Saratoga Institute, 1995.

16. Overman, S. "In Search of Best Practices," *HRMagazine,* December 1993, pp. 48–50.

17. Gómez-Mejía, L. R., Balkin, D. B., and Cardy, R. L. *Managing Human Resources.* Englewood Cliffs: Prentice Hall, 1995.

18. Frohman, M. A. "Human Resource Management and the Bottom Line: Evidence of the Connection," *Human Resource Management,* 23, 1984, pp. 315–334.

19. Katz, H. C., Kochan, T. A., and Weber, M. R. "Assessing the Effects of Industrial Relations Systems and Efforts to Improve the Quality of Working Life on Organizational Effectiveness," *Academy of Management Journal,* 28, 1985, pp. 509–526.

20. U.S. Department of Labor, Background material for the Conference on the Future of the American Workplace, July 1993.

21. Merrihue, W. V. and Katzell, R. A. "ERI—Yardstick of Employee Relations," *Harvard Business Review,* 33, No. 6, 1955, pp. 91–99.

22. LaPointe, J. R. "Human Resource Performance Indexes," *Personnel Journal,* No. 62, 1983, pp. 545, 553.

23. Miner, J. B. and Crane, D. P. *Human Resource Management: The Strategic Perspective.* New York: HarperCollins College Publishers, 1995.

24. Thornburg, L. "Yes, Virginia, HR Contributes to the Bottom Line," *HRMagazine,* August 1993, pp. 62–63.

25. Phillips, J. J. *The Development of a Human Resources Effectiveness Index.* Ph.D. Dissertation, April 1988.

26. Odiorne, G. S. *Personnel Administration by Objectives.* Homewood, Il: Irwin, 1971.

27. Pauly, D. "HR: The New Profit Center," *Human Resource Executive,* August 1993, pp. 36–41.

28. Ball, L. P. "Take Charge: Be An Intrapreneur," *Personnel Journal,* August 1990, pp. 40–44.

29. Kromling, L. K. "CalComp Considers HR a Business Unit," *Personnel Journal,* February 1993, pp. 36–41.

CHAPTER THREE

Developing a Results-Based Approach and a New Model

Developing a results-based approach is more than developing and implementing a new technique, instrument, or computer software program. It represents a change in philosophy, with new understandings and attitudes, and a sharing of responsibilities. This chapter focuses on the elements necessary to develop a results-based approach. It begins the process by outlining specific purposes of HR evaluation. It explores the various myths and barriers that can inhibit the implementation process. The various levels of evaluation are presented as a useful framework to develop an understanding of the process. The attitudes of the HR team are discussed because they are so difficult to change. Various levels of responsibility are clearly defined. Most importantly, the chapter presents a new model for initiating, developing, and implementing programs along with a detailed example. All of these elements are necessary for a results-based approach to HR programs.

THE OPPORTUNITY TO INFLUENCE RESULTS

Although the statement, "People are the most important assets," has been used so often as to become a cliché, it still reflects the importance of human resources to an organization. However, too many organizations simply pay lip service to the statement. When asked about the potential for contribution from the human resources function, almost every CEO provides glowing remarks about its important impact on the organization, but few executives actually explain this tremendous impact in specific terms.

Figure 3-1 presents a simplistic view of this unique opportunity. The output of the organization (depicted as total revenue divided by the total expense) is derived from the product of the output volume times the unit price, divided by the total input volume times the unit cost. This concept is useful for both manufacturing or service industries because output can be a product or service.[1]

Although this is a simplified portrayal, it illustrates an important point about the HR function's impact. For example, consider a manufacturing firm with four essential functional components: sales and marketing, operations, finance and accounting, and human resources. The sales and marketing function can have a significant impact on output (in terms of the unit sales price and output volume). It has little or no impact on the input portion of the formula. The operations function has a direct influence on output volumes, unit cost, and input volumes. The

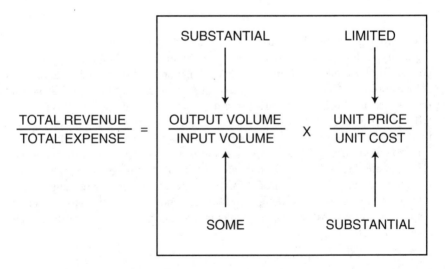

FIGURE 3-1. HUMAN RESOURCES' OPPORTUNITY TO INFLUENCE.

finance and accounting function has little effect on either the total revenue or expense except for its ability to establish the controls and reporting requirements that assist sales and operations to accomplish their missions. Human resources can impact both the total revenue and total expense. It can have a significant impact on output volume, both in sales and items produced, since HR programs are often designed to improve productivity and output. HR has some impact on the input volume through programs that improve employee recruiting practices. HR can have a major impact on unit costs because many HR programs focus on cost control and cost reduction. Costs are a fundamental measure of success of many HR programs. As this brief analysis shows, the HR function has a tremendous opportunity to influence the bottom line of an organization.

PURPOSES OF MEASUREMENT AND EVALUATION

Evaluation is usually undertaken to improve the HR function or measure its contribution to organizational effectiveness. However, there can be other purposes for evaluation and an understanding of each purpose can be helpful in planning the evaluation strategy. The following represent the six most common reasons for evaluating the HR function:

■ **To determine whether a program is accomplishing its objectives.** The most important purpose of HR evaluation is to determine the extent to which objectives are met. Properly designed HR programs should have objectives, stated in generally accepted terms (i.e., challenging, achievable, written, measurable, and dated).

■ **To identify the strengths and weaknesses of HR processes.** An evaluation effort can help to determine the effectiveness of the content and administration of HR programs or services. Typical processes evaluated include such items as time to fill a job vacancy, method of presentation for a training program, response time to process medical claims, and perceived effectiveness of an employee assistance program. These variables make a difference in the success of HR programs and should be evaluated to make improvements.

■ **To calculate the return on investment in an HR program.** An increasingly common reason for evaluation is to determine if a program justifies the expenditure. This type of evaluation compares the costs of the HR program to its economic value. For example, an absenteeism control program is implemented for retail sales associates. Absenteeism is monitored before and after the program. The resulting benefit (absenteeism reduction) is converted to a monetary value which is then compared with the cost of the pro-

gram to develop the return over a defined time period. This type of evaluation provides management with data to eliminate an unproductive program,
to increase support for programs that yield a high payoff, or to make necessary adjustments in programs to increase results or value.

■ **To gather data to assist in marketing future programs.** In some situations, HR departments are interested in knowing why employees participate
in specific programs. This type of evaluation is appropriate for programs in
which participants have an option for participation. Examples include career
development activities, flexible benefits plans, physical fitness programs,
employee assistance programs, savings plans, profit sharing plans, employee suggestion programs, and educational programs. In most organizations,
several options are offered and the HR department does not always know
why someone chooses to participate in a specific program or program
option. Questions are developed to provide insight into how employees
make choices and the results they have experienced. When integrated with
other evaluation data, this information is useful for program planning and
future promotional efforts.

■ **To determine if the program was appropriate.** Sometimes an evaluation
can determine if the original problem or issue that necessitated the program
was solvable by the HR staff. Too often an HR program is implemented to
correct problems that cannot be corrected by the program. Other reasons for
performance deficiencies may exist, such as systems, procedures, work flows
or supervision. An evaluation may yield insight into the actual need for HR
staff action. For example, in one organization, the evaluation of outcomes
from a career resource center indicated that the center was not utilized appropriately and actually resulted in employees leaving the organization.

■ **To establish a database that can assist management in making decisions.** The central theme of most evaluations is to make a decision about the
future of an HR program. A comprehensive evaluation system builds a database to help managers make these decisions. This information can be useful
to program coordinators and the HR management, as well as top executives
who must approve resources for future programs. For example, an ongoing
evaluation of an employee assistance program provides management with
information necessary to determine whether it should be continued and, if
so, whether any changes are needed.

HR EVALUATION MYTHS

Several faulty assumptions often surround the mysterious process of HR evaluation. These myths have hindered HR professionals from measuring their con-

tributions and have slowed the adoption of sound practices in this responsibility area. Nine common myths are presented here, along with a few reasons why they should be discarded.

■ Myth #1: **Evaluation should not be undertaken if the HR staff is not motivated to pursue it.** Although HR professionals are interested in implementing effective programs and achieving desired results, they often run into difficulty in defining acceptable results. To some, results may be in the form of self-satisfaction of seeing a program function smoothly with few problems. For others, only bottom-line results are acceptable. HR professionals do not often view evaluation as part of their job. It is perceived as a responsibility of other individuals or another section within the HR function. Also, HR professionals sometimes resist efforts to evaluate programs because their individual performance may be scrutinized. They do not want to expose their weaknesses, problem areas, and inefficiencies.

The need for evaluation must be convincingly presented to the HR staff. They must understand why evaluation is important and, most of all, they must perceive it as an essential responsibility of their department. Not unlike other professionals, the HR staff resists change, and the intrusion of evaluation responsibilities may represent a change that is unwanted. As with any change effort, thorough explanations and gradual implementation are important to having the process accepted and implemented by the staff. After the system has been operational, the staff will usually see the importance of evaluation, particularly when HR staff members achieve measurable results from their programs.

■ Myth #2: **Evaluation is difficult.** Evaluation is often perceived as a complex activity because it involves data collection and analysis. For a variety of reasons, HR professionals have a fear of data analysis and they are reluctant to develop an understanding of the process. The methods for collecting data are basic and the techniques for analyzing data are fundamental, within the grasp of understanding of every HR professional. The difficulty often lies in determining what type of data must be collected and how it will be analyzed and presented.

■ Myth #3: **The least important HR activities are measurable, while the most important HR activities are not.** HR professionals sometimes see measurement and evaluation as more adaptable to the least important activities of the HR function. Collecting data on items that may have little impact on overall organizational performance, such as the number of grievances or the number of employee complaints, seems relatively easy, while more important items such as those that cause declines in productivity, employee morale, or efficiency are more difficult to measure. Although this may be the perception, many of the important variables affecting morale, job satisfaction, productivity, and efficiency can easily be measured and monitored. An appropriate system to monitor the most significant performance data is needed, coupled with the discipline to follow through on the process.

■ Myth #4: **Evaluation is needed to justify the HR department's existence.** Some HR professionals perceive evaluation as a way to justify HR's existence. Fortunately, the HR function is here to stay; an organization cannot survive without it. A formal measurement and evaluation effort is unnecessary to justify the department's existence. It will, however, enable the department to demonstrate to top management its contribution in order to expand or maintain services and programs. In a few cases, evaluation may provide the basis for keeping the HR staff intact during periods of decline. Also, evaluation can improve the reputation of the department and enhance the influence of the HR staff.

■ Myth #5: **There is no time for evaluation.** Evaluation can be time-consuming if it is not integrated into each functional area or new program. One of the most time-consuming activities in HR evaluation involves recording information at various stages of program or service delivery. When planned and implemented properly, information needed for evaluation is frequently tabulated by clerical staff and the incremental time required to collect the required information is minimal.

■ Myth #6: **Evaluation is too expensive.** Because it is perceived to be complex and time-consuming, evaluation appears to be expensive. However, when integrated into program conception, design, development, and delivery, the evaluation process can be inexpensive and not time-consuming. It will represent only a small part of the total cost of a program. The consequences of not evaluating must be considered here. If evaluation is necessary to determine a payoff from a new HR program, how then can an HR department afford *not* to allocate funds for it?

■ Myth #7: **If top management does not require it, evaluation should not be pursued.** It is difficult to find time for a project that is not a priority of top management. Evaluation can be easily ignored when top management does not require evidence of HR contribution. Unfortunately, without data to show contributions, top management will make its own judgment about HR contributions and this judgment may be based on inaccurate perceptions or subjective assessments. Often, the focus will be on costs, and the consequences could be disastrous. This situation is changing as more chief executives and top managers demand results from all staff departments, including the HR function. The demand for accountability usually intensifies during a recession. A new top executive may also require evaluation, where the previous one did not. If the current trend continues, more top executives will require measurement and evaluation in the future. Prudent HR managers will be prepared for this eventual shift to increased accountability. HR professionals ignoring this trend are likely to be left out, possibly becoming victims of restructuring, downsizing, or layoffs.

■ Myth #8: **Unless a return on investment (ROI) is calculated, evaluation will be useless.** Some HR managers have the mistaken belief that when a program is evaluated, a benefit/cost ratio or ROI must be developed. ROI is only one approach to evaluation. It is not only difficult to produce, but in some cases it is impossible. For example, it is almost impossible to calculate the ROI for an affirmative action program implemented to meet federal regulations. At best, administrative effectiveness could be evaluated along with an assessment of progress toward goals. In still other programs, it is not economical to calculate an ROI, although it may be possible. For example, suppose a new low cost employee benefit is added to keep the benefits package competitive and improve job satisfaction. Through attitude surveys and detailed interviews, it may be possible to determine the improved job satisfaction as a result of a new benefit. A value can also be assigned to the increased job satisfaction with a reasonable degree of accuracy. However, the expense of collecting and analyzing the data may be greater than the cost of the additional benefit.

Quite often, it is sufficient to implement a new program or service because it is needed, management wants it, or a government regulation requires it. In these cases, it makes little sense to calculate ROI. A fundamental question about economic feasibility should always be asked: Should we spend this much time and money to evaluate this particular program?

■ Myth #9: **There are too many variables affecting HR program performance to measure and evaluate the function.** Some HR managers believe the HR process is a very complex and mysterious art that can be judged only by those who perform the work. Even then, the assessment is sometimes bounded by subjective criteria. They argue that business results measures cannot be applied to the HR function. Some even believe that the HR function is not a business activity, although often it exists in, and is funded by, the business organization.

In a work environment, several variables can affect an individual's performance including personal drive, the work environment, reinforcement, policies and practices, and external factors. While these are significant factors not directly under the control of the HR department, they should not be used as a basis for discarding evaluation. Some evaluation designs isolate the impact of HR programs on organizational performance by using control groups and other techniques. With this approach, it is possible to measure the impact of variables for which the HR department has primary control.

Waiting for a simpler job performance model with fewer variables is anal-ogous to waiting for taxes to go away. It will never happen. Jobs and work environments are becoming more complicated and require the analysis of many interrelated variables. Although measurements may not be precise and completely isolated, they are better than no measurements at all.

Obstacles to Measuring the Contribution

Not all problems connected with measuring the HR contribution are mythical. Some are realistic and represent genuine obstacles to a full implementation and adoption of a results-based HR philosophy. They must be recognized and addressed early in the process. Six common obstacles are outlined below.

■ **Evaluation cost.** Each additional stage in the process of designing and implementing an HR program increases cost, regardless of the complexity and necessity of the stage. The additional step of measurement and evalua-tion will increase costs, ranging from minimal costs for basic measures to significant costs for an extensive, formal evaluation effort. An HR depart-ment, stretched to provide a variety of programs under tight budget restraints, may have difficulty in allocating additional resources for mea-surement and evaluation. However, with proper planning, measurement and evaluation can be incorporated into the design of new systems and pro-grams, minimizing costs. An important consideration is to always examine the cost of evaluation when compared to the perceived value derived from the process. In some cases, an evaluation may not be worth the added cost.

■ **Lack of top management commitment.** Strong top level commitment to evaluation must be present for the process to be successful. A lack of com-mitment usually stems from executives not fully understanding the HR function and the potential contribution it can make to organizational goals. They do not see HR's opportunity to influence organizational performance and fully understand the HR goals, activities, and processes. One reason for this situation is that few top executives have actual experience in the human resources field.

■ **Lack of evaluation knowledge.** A major stumbling block to measuring the HR contribution is a lack of knowledge about the process. Many HR man-agers do not know how to measure the success of programs. The literature has been void of practical information in measurement and evaluation when compared to other parts of the HR field. Until recently, only a few articles were devoted to HR measurement and evaluation. Success stories were hard to find. Proven evaluation techniques were even more difficult to identify. This void has helped create an apparent lack of evaluation efforts, particularly in smaller organizations.

This problem has been amplified by the U.S. higher education system. Although the newer generation of HR managers has had an opportunity to study human resources in college, only a few courses are available that focus on measurement and evaluation. Unfortunately, statistical courses are usually based in financial, economic, or behavioral science programs, and are not part of the human resources curriculum. Statistical procedures seldom are used to measure the results of the human resources function. Although some researchers have developed a few measures, there has been little effort to communicate the results.

■ **Attention to evaluation in program design.** The design, development, and implementation of HR programs have not always followed logical steps, leaving efforts to evaluate results futile and inconclusive. To be effective, evaluation should be planned as one or more steps in program design. These steps should focus on planning the evaluation scheme, collecting data, analyzing data, interpreting the results, and communicating them to appropriate target audiences. A results-based model that includes these steps will be described later in this chapter.

■ **Fear of evaluation.** In some cases, HR program evaluation can reflect unfavorably on those who designed or administered the program, if it is not effective. All HR program results will not be positive, particularly when reactions and observations are obtained. Unless the HR staff is ready for criticism, evaluation should not be undertaken. Many HR managers have a fear of exposing what they do and letting others know the results of their efforts. Obviously, if a program or specific function is not working, the last thing the staff wants to do is to publish a report about it. This fear becomes even more pronounced when HR managers track the cost of programs with the benefits. Program costs should be compared to results, which can only be pinpointed through a properly designed and implemented measurement and evaluation system. Otherwise, costs alone can be frightening.

■ **Lack of standards.** The last important obstacle to measurement and evaluation is the lack of standards for judging the success of HR programs. In fields such as accounting, manufacturing, engineering, quality control, and data processing, generally accepted evaluation standards have been developed. Unfortunately, standards have not been developed for the HR field. Although most HR executives generally know when a measure represents acceptable performance, there have been only a few attempts to develop measures, standards, and indices. This obstacle may be minimized in the future because more organizations are beginning to adopt measurement and evaluation schemes and report their results publicly or through benchmarking projects.

LEVELS OF EVALUATION

Although it is important to develop objective measures to evaluate the HR function, some programs are difficult to measure objectively and other, more subjective measures may be appropriate to provide evidence of success. As shown in Table 3-1, it is helpful to view HR measurement and evaluation as consisting of three levels: measures of perceived effectiveness, measures of performance, and measures of return on investment. Each can be appropriate for a specific evaluation situation.

TABLE 3-1
LEVELS OF HR MEASUREMENT AND EVALUATION

LEVEL	FOCUS	EXAMPLE
1. Measure of Perceived Effectiveness	Feedback from stakeholders	Employees have a positive opinion of their benefits package
2. Measures of Performance	Key indicators of HR performance	Employee turnover has been reduced by 35%
3. Measures of Return on Investment	Monetary value of program benefits compared to costs	Safety incentive program yields 150% ROI

Measures of perceived effectiveness. All stakeholders involved in an HR program need to perceive it as effective. Stakeholders include participants in the program, supervisors of participants, team members of participants, and managers who must support HR efforts. Measures of perceived effectiveness are usually reactions and attitudes obtained from surveys, questionnaires, interviews, or observations.

In some cases, it is more appropriate to use this level of evaluation instead of other levels. For example, it may be difficult to measure the financial impact of the changes to an employee relocation program. However, it is easy, and possibly more appropriate, to measure the increased satisfaction of those involved in relocation and compare responses with previous measures.

Measures of performance. Many programs are implemented to improve performance and appropriate measures are usually available from which to judge success. The performance of an HR program can be compared to previous performance, the performance with groups (either within the same organization or same industry), or the expected performance level.

In some cases, this level of evaluation is just as important as an actual calculation of a return on investment. For example, consider the implementation of a program designed to reduce turnover. The measure of success is the reduction in the turnover rate that is caused by the HR program. The turnover rate could be compared to other similar work groups in the organization or in the same industry. Still another comparison is in terms of what management expects from the program. Targets are often established for this type of program and success depends on how the post-program turnover compares to what management expects. In this example, a cost/benefit analysis is not developed because some credibility may be lost with the assumptions required to calculate the value of the reduced turnover.

Measures of return on the investment. The ultimate level of evaluation is the actual value of the return on the investment (ROI) in an HR program. This is considered the ultimate measure of the HR function by many top executives in an organization. As more HR managers become bottom-line oriented and produce business results with their efforts, an evaluation in terms of the money saved or profit added is appropriate. This is the level of measurement that will attract the attention of top management. While this measure is desirable for reasons outlined earlier, it is not always possible.

Measures of return on investment are appropriate for many HR programs. For example, in a gainsharing plan where employees receive a portion of the savings generated below a predetermined cost target, the return of investment can be easily calculated. The savings after the plan has been implemented is compared with the cost associated with implementing the plan. The return can be calculated and monitored over specified time periods, providing management with objective, investment-oriented data on the payoff of an HR effort. The ROI is usually considered the most important and desired level of evaluation.

In addition to the ROI calculation, other levels of evaluation, taken simultaneously, may be appropriate. For example, it might be useful to monitor changes in performance variables after the gainsharing plan has been implemented. Absenteeism rates, turnover rates, and safety records are important measures that are appropriate to the overall evaluation of the gainsharing plan. Also, with this program, it might be useful to consider measures of perceived effectiveness. Surveys conducted before and after the program provide feedback on participants' perception of the program.

THE ATTITUDE OF THE HR TEAM

The success of HR measurement and evaluation will depend on the attitude of the professional HR staff. Evaluation goes beyond surveys, record keeping, measuring output data, and presenting statistical analyses of improved performance. It is a process and a philosophy that must be understood and supported. The staff's perception of the evaluation process determines the relative priority placed on evaluation and dictates the amount of time they will spend on the effort. HR team members who question the decision to develop evaluation procedures for HR programs are not convinced of the importance of measurement and evaluation. They do not have an appropriate attitude necessary for a successful evaluation effort. Without a commitment to the process, measurement and evaluation will not be very effective.

A key to developing an appropriate philosophy is the continuous involvement of the HR staff in the policies and procedures for evaluation. Involvement can lead to commitment and improved techniques for measurement and evaluation. Staff training will help them understand why evaluation is necessary and, more importantly, build the skills necessary to make the process work. Also, they need to see the payoff of their own programs. This provides reinforcement that the process is a value-added activity.

The staff must be familiar with the implementation model presented in this chapter that governs the process of introducing new programs in the organization. Ideally, they should assist in developing a customized model for the organization. Moreover, they should be challenged to apply the model and committed to make it work. Shortcuts can easily destroy an otherwise effective measurement and evaluation program. Staff professionals caught up in daily pressures and facing deadlines for implementation are likely to leave out important steps necessary to evaluate the overall impact of that program or service. Quality control checks should be in place to ensure that the entire team is working toward the same goal.

SHARING RESPONSIBILITIES FOR HR MEASUREMENT AND EVALUATION

While achieving results with HR programs is a goal of the HR department, it is a responsibility shared with others. In addition to being the responsibility of the HR staff who must design, develop, implement, and monitor programs, three other groups of stakeholders share in the ultimate responsibility.

Top management shares in the responsibility for achieving results with HR programs. They should, and often do, demand excellence from the HR function and require evidence of its contribution. Expectations from top management should be clearly communicated to the HR staff, and there should be some mechanism to provide top management information on program results.

The middle management group also shares the responsibility for achieving results. Usually they supervise the employees who participate in HR programs and represent an important link necessary for achieving the desired results. Their encouragement to employees to participate in programs often makes the difference in employee participation rates. Their reinforcement, or lack of reinforcement, can have a significant impact on results. Also, their direct involvement, or lack of involvement, can be critical to program success.

Finally, the participants themselves often have an important role in achieving results. They need to have a thorough understanding of what each program is intended to accomplish and have the skills to make it work. With proper motivation and understanding, they can maximize their participation and contribution to help achieve desired outcomes.

HR program results must be a multiple responsibility. It is only through a shared responsibility for results with each party accepting their respective roles that maximum results can be achieved.

A RESULTS-BASED MODEL FOR PROGRAM IMPLEMENTATION

In the last 50 years, the human resources function has evolved slowly and incrementally from a basic administrative function to a very complex and challenging part of an organization. In its early development, there were only a few specific functions. Gradually new programs or services were added to satisfy internal demands as well as external requirements. Most new programs were implemented to meet justifiable needs while others evolved for less credible reasons. The net result of this growth of the HR department is a cumbersome and complex function that may include a patchwork of 50 or more specific programs or services. Efforts to streamline the department often fail because HR professionals rarely discontinue obsolete programs. Also, new programs are not often implemented systematically except at some progressive organizations where HR departments implement new programs only after they justify the need for them and develop methods to measure their contribution.

The results-based human resources model, shown in Figure 3-2, places emphasis on achieving results and involves nine steps necessary to fully analyze, develop, and implement HR programs. Three of the steps (three, four, and five) make up the traditional model where objectives are established and the program is developed and implemented. The other steps, which have received more emphasis in recent years, are necessary to place the proper emphasis on measuring the

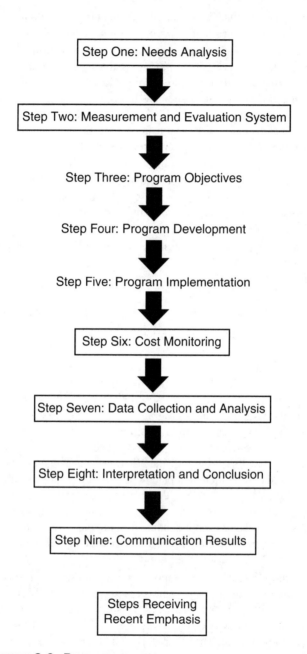

FIGURE 3-2. RESULTS-BASED HUMAN RESOURCE MODEL.

contribution of the new program and thus prevent unneeded programs from being implemented.

Step One: Needs Analysis

Before a new program is implemented, a needs analysis should be conducted to determine if the program is necessary. Table 3-2 shows that at least eight influ-

TABLE 3-2
INFLUENCES THAT SHAPE CREATION OF NEW HR PROGRAMS

INFLUENCE	EXAMPLE
Government Intervention	Affirmative Action Plan
Other Organizations	Team Building
Interference from Outside Groups	Labor Management Cooperation Program
Performance Improvement	Gainsharing Plan
Employee Satisfaction	Wellness/Fitness Center
Top Management Requests	Total Quality Management
Problem Solving	Employee Assistance Program
Strategic Planning	Employee Empowerment

ences shape the creation of most of the new programs offered by HR departments. Probably the most significant influence in recent years has been government intervention. Local, state, and federal laws, and subsequent regulations, created dozens of programs, including complete departments and sections within the HR function. Every functional area in HR is affected by government regulations. In some organizations, the top HR manager's job title has been changed to reflect the influence of government regulation.

A second influence has been other organizations. In their quest to remain competitive, HR executives have attempted to keep up with the other organizations. The WEED (What Everyone Else Does) factor has created a significant number of programs. A unique approach to compensation, a new type of employee benefit, or an improved training program are often borrowed from other organizations and implemented in an attempt to meet competition or take the lead in a competitive environment.

Interference from outside groups represents a third influence. Heading this list are unions, which have organized employees and create the need for elaborate labor relations staffs to negotiate and administer labor contracts. The threat of unions has caused other organizations to develop a variety of programs to maintain a non-union status.

The desire to improve performance and fine tune the organization is a fourth influence and is probably the most productive reason for establishing a new program. Alternative reward systems, productivity improvement programs, team building programs, and employee suggestion systems are only a few of the efforts used by HR departments to improve the profitability, quality, or efficiency of the organization.

A fifth influence is the never-ending desire of HR managers to make employees happy. With this intention of boosting morale, improving job satisfaction, or inspiring cooperation, many new programs have been developed to make employees feel good about their jobs, supervisors, and employer. These programs are based on the assumption that a happy employee is a productive employee.

The sixth influence has been top management's request to implement a program, project, function, or service because they want it to be implemented. Many of the current total quality management programs and re-engineering programs are developed and implemented because of top management's interests. Most HR professionals will respond to the demands of top management, even if the program is not needed.

The seventh influence is a desire for HR managers to solve problems or avoid future problems. This stems from their reactive and proactive roles of HR. In a reactive mode, many HR managers are brought problems or observe problems in the organization and implement programs to solve them. In a proactive role, they anticipate problems and implement programs to avoid them. Most employee relations programs are aimed at preventing future problems.

The final influence comes from the long-range planning process in which strategic planning is used to identify a specific need or change for the organization in the future. In this scenario, management scans the environmental threats and opportunities, determines the organization's strengths and weaknesses, and develops specific plans to position the organization for success in the future. Some specific HR program needs usually evolve from this process that are long-term in nature and are aimed at gradual and continuing improvement. In the past, only a few programs have been initiated from this process because of the lack of involvement of HR in the strategic planning process. As discussed in Chapter 1, this situation is changing.

A more systematic approach to developing new programs requires that some type of needs analysis be conducted to compare the benefits of a program with the projected costs and determine the long-term implications of the program. When a program is implemented to meet regulatory needs, little analysis is required. The program must be implemented and the focus should be on the efficiency of the program's operations. In areas where a program's need is questionable or where there could be alternatives, the needs analysis step becomes essential. This step also focuses on the impact of adding to the HR workload.

Typical questions that might be appropriate for a detailed needs analysis are:

■ Are we attempting to avoid a problem or potential deficiency?
■ How important is this problem?
■ Is there a performance problem? If so, what evidence is there?
■ Is there a lack of skill or attitude?
■ What happens if nothing is done?
■ Is this program required by government regulation?
■ Is this program designed to satisfy an external influence? If so, what is it?
■ What is our competition doing with this issue? Why?
■ Are there alternative solutions?
■ Who will be required to administer this program?
■ Will the employees involved in the new program need to be trained? If so, by whom and how?
■ To what extent will other departments be involved?
■ Are there natural barriers to accomplishing this program?
■ Who supports this new program?

These and other questions help HR professionals focus on the need for the new program and consider all of the ramifications of its implementation. A needs analysis involves questionnaires, interviews, surveys, group meetings, observations, or examination of performance records. Additional information on conducting a needs analysis is found in other publications.[2]

It is tempting to implement a suggestion system or install a management succession plan because others have them. A hard look at why the program is necessary may keep an unnecessary program from being a cost burden on the organization. This step is extremely important because it may cause the HR department to scrap its plans for a new program if there is not a legitimate need for it. The remaining steps will help to determine what contributions this new program will provide to the organization.

Step Two: Measurement and Evaluation System

Before a contribution can be determined, there must be some basis for measuring the impact of the program. Usually, measurements are taken before program implementation and compared with measurements after program implementation. This step involves three important areas:

■ Establishing baseline data
■ Selecting the evaluation strategy
■ Designing data collection instruments.

Baseline data are usually available in most situations. It is often the analysis of this data that leads to the development of the new program. Data may exist in a variety of forms and should be collected for a period of time necessary for a realistic comparison. This step becomes difficult when a program is designed to improve a situation in which there is no clear evidence of the current status. When this is the case, it may be appropriate to return to step one and to determine if the program is really needed. If the current performance level cannot be clearly defined, then it is important to ask if there is a need to improve, and more importantly, to ask if anyone will know if there has been any improvement.

Much progress has been made in establishing baseline data for performance in human resources programs and functions. Specific types of measurements are covered in another part of this book. When appropriate baseline data do not exist, the organization may have to collect data for a brief period. For example, suppose management senses that employee complaints are increasing, yet there is no way to know exactly how many complaints are being made. If this is perceived to be a serious problem, it may be appropriate to ask supervisors to note the frequency and type of complaints received from employees over a specified time period. With adequate data, a program can be developed and implemented to reduce complaints and its impact can be monitored.

The second area to consider is the overall evaluation strategy that outlines how the data will be collected and how comparisons are to be made. Pre- and post-program comparisons are common, while in some cases data is collected only after the program is implemented. In some cases, control groups are used. (This process is described later.) Specific plans for data collection should be formulated at this step. Data collection may simply involve tabulating costs, counting employees, or measuring employee output. Or it may involve the use of attitude surveys, interviews, and other data collection instruments to measure the change caused by the new program. This process also includes identifying who will collect the data and where it will be collected. These responsibilities are important and must be clearly defined early in the process.

The third area for consideration in this step is the actual design of data collection instruments, which range from a simple record keeping system to detailed questionnaires, attitude surveys, or structured interviews. Instrument design is important to ensure adequate and reliable data collection.

These three areas make up the formal steps of designing the data collection and evaluation systems, which may be simple or complex depending on the type of data needed. For example, it is a relatively easy task to measure and evaluate the impact of a minority recruitment program. It is a matter of keeping track of the progress of candidates and the costs incurred in recruiting those candidates. Other programs are more difficult to measure. For example, a program designed to boost employee morale may have a number of measurements obtained from a variety of instruments and may result in a more complex evaluation and data collection scheme.

Step Three: Program Objectives

Too often, new HR programs are implemented without objectives. And when objectives are developed, they are often vague and established after the program was implemented. With the results-based approach, specific objectives are developed at the beginning of the process. Tentative objectives are usually drafted during the needs analysis and are finalized in this step after reviewing planned data in the previous step. Data must be available to judge progress toward objectives and should be centered around the data developed in the previous step of this model.

Two examples will help clarify the types of objectives described here. In the first example, an organization embarks on a new college recruiting program. Previously, it relied on other sources for new professional employees, including referrals and former summer employees. These sources are now unable to furnish the required number of candidates. As a result, a recruiter will visit a select group of colleges to recruit professional employees. The following objective was developed.

> College recruiting will supply at least 40 qualified professional candidates each year at a cost not to exceed $3,000 per new recruit.

The objective clearly identifies measurable targets with a cost factor, which is a very important consideration. With this objective, the individual responsible for the college recruiting program can more clearly focus on the expected results.

In another example, an organization considers implementing a sales incentive plan for sales representatives. Previously, sales representatives were compensated with a base salary and no bonus. A specific objective for the new plan is

> Increase the sales volume by 15% while meeting the target price goals in each quarter of its operation.

The objective clearly sets the target for participants in the plan. The new plan should be designed to achieve an average of 15% of additional volume.

Setting specific and measurable objectives is a fundamental process, but still is not common in all HR departments. Objectives should meet the following criteria. They should be:

- challenging for the participants and program
- measurable and dated so that all stakeholders will know if the program is working
- achievable with the proper determination and focus
- developed with input from all stakeholders
- understood by all stakeholders

Overall, objectives should provide the clear direction for program developers, program implementers, and participants.

Step Four: Program Development

The most time-consuming step of the model is the development of the new program. This effort varies considerably with the type of program and includes the development of program guidelines, program materials, administrative procedures, and special requirements. It is developed with the best input available and requires a careful review by the appropriate management. In some situations, the program material is purchased from an outside vendor, and this step involves making the purchasing decision. For additional information on evaluating vendor products and consultants, see other references.[3] There is little need for additional detail on this step other than to stress that completion of the first three steps will help keep program developers clearly focused on the purpose and intent of the new program or service. As a result, this process eliminates the development of unimportant or unnecessary materials.

Step Five: Program Implementation

Implementation is another traditional step for new HR programs, involving timing, communication, and responsibilities. Timing is usually critical because external influences have dictated implementation dates. For example, a new program, developed to respond to a government regulation, must be ready on or before the date the regulation becomes effective. In situations where a program is implemented to improve the organization, implementation immediately follows program development. In still other situations, the timing relates to a trigger date such as the beginning of the quarter or the first day of the fiscal year. For example, a new benefit may be implemented at the beginning of the plan year.

Proper implementation requires communication with all stakeholders in the program so they will have a clear understanding of its purposes, how it will be administered, and more importantly, the expected results. A common understanding of expectations will improve the program's chances of success. Communication pieces come in a wide variety and include items such as press releases (if appropriate), memos to participants, introductory videos, program descriptions, guidelines, and progress reports.

Implementation also includes assigning responsibilities to all individuals involved in the program. Many individuals in the organization are usually involved in program coordination, including line and staff management. In some cases, all employees may have specific responsibilities in a program, as is the case with a company-wide quality improvement effort. Responsibilities must be clearly defined and accepted by those involved.

Step Six: Cost Monitoring

An often overlooked step is the calculation of costs of a new program. Although a brief estimate of proposed costs is part of the needs analysis, this step involves more detailed and accurate tabulations of program costs over a predetermined time period. This step is essential if costs are compared to benefits and the ultimate impact is to be calculated. For some efforts, it may be inappropriate to develop a detailed cost/benefit analysis. In these cases, costs should be monitored to improve efficiency. For example, it might be difficult to develop a cost/benefit analysis in the implementation of an affirmative action program. The organization is likely responding to a requirement or a perceived need to rectify a past practice of under-utilization of employees in minority groups. However, tracking costs of the program is necessary to plan for future budgets and to properly manage the affirmative action effort. In another example, a new program implemented to improve attendance should be subjected to a cost/benefit analysis so that anticipated benefits can be compared with actual program costs. If the benefits do not outweigh the costs, the program probably should not be undertaken.

Costs can be classified in several ways, and usually the most logical approach is to use the organization's cost accounting systems. Costs should be reported on a program basis and classified by convenient categories such as analysis, development, implementation, operations, and evaluation costs. Additional information on developing and tracking costs is presented in a later chapter.

Step Seven: Data Collection and Analysis

This step involves three phases: data collection, isolating influences, and data analysis. Because of the concern about analysis, some HR staff members view this as the most difficult step of this model. It is important that data be collected as planned in step three. While this seems obvious, in a busy setting with day-to-day job pressures, it is easy for someone to neglect recording and tabulating data for program evaluation. Data should be reviewed to make sure it is being collected properly and that it reflects the original intentions outlined in step three.

As an early step in the process, some attempt should be made to isolate the effects of the HR program when compared to the influence of other factors. In most HR programs designed to improve performance, several variables will influence the improvement. Specific techniques for accomplishing this are covered later.

All data must be tabulated and summarized for comparison and presentation. In some cases, data analysis might result in a simple comparison expressed as a percentage. In others, a more detailed statistical analysis is usually needed. Three types of statistical techniques useful for analyzing data are (1) measures of central tendency, (2) measures of dispersion, and (3) measures of association. In some situations, hypothesis testing is used to determine whether improvement occurred as a result of chance or as a result of the new program. Also, an analysis may be conducted to see if other variables entered the situation. Each of these techniques will be discussed in more detail in a later chapter.

Data analysis includes converting an improvement to monetary values if it is appropriate for the evaluation. Judgmental factors may be involved in arriving at the conversion, and these factors must be clearly explained. The analysis and interpretation of the data may be done at different stages to be meaningful. For example, data collected early in the program might show one level of results, while data collected at a later period may show another.

Step Eight: Interpretation and Conclusion

After analysis, the results are tabulated and prepared for presentation to appropriate target groups. In this step, specific contributions of the program are clearly determined. If a benefit/cost analysis is planned, it is developed in this step. Another approach includes the calculation of a return on investment, with investment defined as the expenditures for the program. Although economic justification is difficult, it is appearing more frequently as part of an increasing trend of accountability in human resources. An example clearly shows the rationale for this type of analysis. The Tennessee Valley Authority implemented an employee suggestion program to encourage cost-saving ideas. TVA received nearly 1,000 suggestions over a period of 10 months that collectively saved about $580,000. Ten percent of that saving was paid to employees as suggestion awards. However, the program cost more to administer than it saved. In total, TVA spent $700,000 on the program, including $514,000 for staff expenses. "The idea of the program was good, but what we ended up with was a bureaucratic, convulted system that took so long to review suggestions that it proved to be ineffective," said Sue Wallace, acting director of TVA's human resources department.[4]

In some cases, the results of evaluation may simply include reporting on how well the program is operating. For example, in a salary administration program, a report on the number, frequency, and amount of merit increases in a particular time period, possibly with some comparisons with previous results, may be appropriate. This step also involves pinpointing the causes of unacceptable or unexpected results. If the desired results are not achieved, the reasons should be identified.

Step Nine: Communicating Results

One of the most important steps in the implementation of a new program or service is communicating the results to the appropriate individuals. While there are many audiences that should know about the results of the program, four important groups stand out as essential targets. One of the most important is the HR staff members who need this information to make improvements in the program. This refinement will ensure that programs are modified to secure improved results in the future. A second important group is senior management, who must make decisions regarding the future of the program. Should funds be expended to continue the effort, or should it be discontinued? Without sufficient information about results, the decision could be faulty. The employees involved with the new program are the third group. They need to know how well the program is working, and especially the extent to which their efforts helped achieve the results. Without this communication, participants may be concerned about the success of the program. The supervisors of participants are the fourth group who should know about the results. Sometimes the magnitude of the results is a reflection of the efforts of these supervisors and this communication provides appropriate recognition of the efforts. This communication will help to secure needed support in the future.

Communicating results is an often overlooked final step in the results-based model. Although results are usually reported to someone, problems occur when individuals or groups who need the information do not receive it or they receive incomplete or distorted information. All information must be presented in an unbiased, effective way, using a variety of methods. Because of its importance, additional information on communicating results successfully is presented later.

AN APPLICATION OF THE MODEL

The following example illustrates how the results-based human resources model works. It is based on an actual implementation of a safety incentive program aimed at reducing accidents and their related costs. A major division of a large construction materials firm experienced higher than acceptable accident frequency rates, accident severity rates, and total accident costs. For a two-year period, costs hovered around the $200,000 to $300,000 range—much too high for division expectations.

1. *Needs Analysis.* The HR department met with managers and employees to seek solutions to the problem. They also analyzed accident costs and types of accidents. Their conclusions were:
   - Employees know and understand safety rules and practices. (Training is not needed.)
   - Employees are not focusing enough attention on safety.
   - A significant proportion of accidents and related costs involved "questionable" injuries.
   - Employees are likely to respond to some type of monetary incentive. (This approach had been successful in another division.)
   - Peer pressure could possibly be used to remind employees of safety practices and the need to avoid the costs of seeing a physician when it is not necessary.
   As a result, the division decided to implement a group-based safety incentive plan.
2. *Measurement and Evaluation System.* The following data were needed to analyze safety performance data:
   - Number of medical treatment cases
   - Hours worked
   - Number of lost-time accidents
   - Number of lost-time days
   - Accident costs
   - Incentive costs
   Each plant collected data on a monthly basis. Fortunately, the data collection system had been in place prior to the implementation of the safety incentive program. No additional data collection procedures were needed.
3. *Program Objectives.* The objectives of the program were two-fold:
   - To reduce the annual accident frequency rate from a level of approximately 40 to a much lower level of approximately 20.
   - To reduce the annual disabling accident frequency rate from a level of about 15 to a level of about 10.
4. *Program Development.* The program consisted of a simple cash award incentive plan designed to provide each employee in a work unit $50, after taxes, for each six months he or she worked without a medical treatment case. A medical treatment case is defined as an accident that cannot be treated by plant first aid and, therefore, must have the attention of a physician. Because of their small size of approximately 20 employees, each plant comprised a work unit. A team effort at the plant was important because the actions of one employee could impact the safety of another. Peer pressure was necessary to keep employees focused and to remind them to avoid unnecessary physician costs. For this reason, the award was not paid unless

the entire unit completed six months without a medical treatment case. When an accident occurred, a new six-month period began.

5. *Program Implementation.* The plant managers implemented the program at the beginning of a new year so that results could easily be monitored and compared with performance in previous years. They announced the program to all employees, and distributed general rules and guidelines. Thorough communication was necessary so that employees had a clear understanding of how the program functioned and what they had to accomplish in order to receive an award.

6. *Cost Monitoring.* Two groups of costs were monitored: the total accident costs and the incentive compensation costs. Total accident costs were monitored prior to the safety incentive program as part of the safety performance data. The additional costs related directly to incentive compensation were also tabulated. Because $50 cash was provided after taxes, the cost to the division was approximately $65 per employee for each six-month period completed without a medical treatment case. Additional administration costs were minimal because the data used in analysis was collected prior to the program and the time required to administer the program and calculate the award was almost negligible. No additional staff was needed and no overtime for existing staff could be directly attributed to the program. However, a conservative estimate of $1,000 per year of program administration costs was used in the tabulation of incentive costs.

7. *Data Collection and Analysis.* Data were collected over a two-year period after the program implementation to provide an adequate before and after comparison. Medical treatment injuries, lost-time injuries, frequency rates, and injury costs were all monitored to show the contribution of the safety incentive program. The data, shown in Table 3-3, reveal significant reductions in the two-year period following the implementation of the program.

TABLE 3-3
THE CONTRIBUTION OF A SAFETY INCENTIVE PROGRAM

	YEAR 1	YEAR 2	YEAR 3	YEAR 4
Medical Treatment Injuries	99	63	25	21
Lost-Time Injuries	27	18	6	7
Non-Disabling Frequency	54.8	35.2	15.5	16.2
Disabling Frequency	14.6	10.0	3.7	5.4
Injury Costs	$234,890	$322,128	$5,013	$24,892
Safety Incentive Costs	—	—	$53,125	$50,313
Total Costs (Injury Plus Incentive)	$234,890	$322,128	$58,138	$75,205

Plan implemented beginning in Year 3.

When comparing the average of years 3 and 4 with years 1 and 2 average, the non-disabling accident frequency was reduced by 65 percent, while the disabling accident frequency was reduced by 63 percent.

8. *Interpretation and Conclusion.* The bottom-line contribution of the safety incentive program is determined by adding injury costs to incentive program costs and comparing this total with the previous injury costs. As Table 3-3 shows, the total costs were reduced significantly. The average for total costs after the program was 76 percent less than the average for injury costs before the implementation. This improvement was attributed entirely to the incentive program because no other factors could be identified that could have influenced safety performance during this period. Also, the safety record at other similar divisions showed no improvement during the same time period.

9. *Communicating Results.* The results of the safety incentive program were communicated to a variety of target audiences to show the contribution of the program. First, the division president summarized the results in a monthly report to the chief executive officer of the corporation. Next, the HR department presented the results in their monthly report to all middle and upper division management. They then presented the results to all plant level personnel through a *Safety Newsletter* to all employees and a *Superintendent's Report,* which was sent to all plant superintendents. Finally, the results were distributed to all division employees through the division newspaper. Communications were positive and increased the awareness for the need for the program's continuation.

Although this example is very simple, it illustrates the step-by-step process used to implement a new program, where the contribution of the program is very important. In this example, the data analysis was void of any complicated statistical techniques and the results were convincing, assuming that no other significant factors influenced safety performance during this period.

REFERENCES

1. Fitz-Enz, J. *Human Value Management.* San Francisco: Jossey-Bass Publishers, 1990.

2a. Phillips, J. J. and Holton, E. F. (Eds.) *In Action: Conducting Needs Assessment.* Alexandria: American Society for Training and Development, 1995.

2b. Swanson, R. A. *Analysis for Improving Performance.* San Francisco: Berrett-Koehler Publishers, 1994.

2c. Moseley, J. L. and Heaney, M. J. "Needs Assessment Across Disciplines," *Performance Improvement Quarterly,* Vol. 7, No. 1, 1994, pp. 60–79.

3. Phillips, J. J. *Handbook of Training Evaluation and Measurement Methods,* 2nd Edition. Houston: Gulf Publishing Company, 1991.

4. Adapted from "It Cost Too Much to Save Money," Associated Press, August 27, 1988.

CHAPTER FOUR

Management Influence on HR Results

Several factors outside the traditional scope and direct control of the HR department have a significant impact on HR effectiveness. These factors primarily relate to the actions and attitudes of the management group and the operational environment where programs are implemented. Managers make decisions to allocate resources for HR programs, support HR programs, participate in program development and implementation, allow participants to be involved in programs, and reinforce program objectives. Although the HR department may not have direct control (i.e., authority) over these managerial activities, HR staff members can exert a tremendous influence on them. The fundamental premise of this chapter is that the HR department is not solely responsible for human resources utilization in the organization. The HR staff serves as the coordinator, advisor, facilitator, and partner for HR use. Management is ultimately responsible for human resources utilization through their commitment, support, reinforcement, involvement, and direct action. The extent of their influence will ultimately determine the success of HR programs.

Several terms used in this chapter may need clarification. Partnership relationship, line management, management commitment, management support, reinforcement, and management involvement are related terms that are sometimes confusing and overlapping in their definitions.

■ **Partnership relationship** describes the quality of interactions and supportive actions between the HR staff and key managers in the organization.

■ **Line management** consists of managers responsible for producing, selling, distributing, or delivering an organization's products or services.

■ **Management commitment** refers to the top management group's pledge or promise and includes the actions of top management to allocate resources and lend support to the HR effort.

■ **Management support for** HR programs and policies refers to the supportive actions of the entire management group, with emphasis on middle and first-line management. Supportive actions include a variety of activities that can influence the effectiveness of HR programs.

■ **Reinforcement** refers to actions that increase the probability of a desired behavior occurring after participating in the HR program. Reinforcement is more useful in HR programs designed to improve an organization, such as education and training, organization development, and performance management.

■ **Management involvement** refers to the extent to which non HR managers are actively engaged in the HR process and programs.

Because management commitment, support, and involvement have similar meanings, they are sometimes used interchangeably in practice and in the literature. Consequently, there will be some overlap in their use in this chapter. Table 4-1 summarizes the features and focus of these important items. This chapter provides a comprehensive description of effective behaviors, tools, and techniques that any HR staff person can use to increase overall effectiveness and success within the organization. Some strategies should yield short-term results, while others are more appropriate for a long-term payoff. Some are effective for one-on-one situations, while others are more appropriate in group settings.

This chapter also explores several other factors that will enhance relationships and increase HR's prospects for success. It also discusses the importance of

TABLE 4-1
COMPARISON OF KEY MANAGEMENT ACTIONS

MANAGEMENT ACTION	TARGET GROUP	SCOPE	PAYOFF OF EFFORT
Management Commitment	Top Executives	All Programs	Very High
Management Support	Middle Managers, Supervisors	Usually several programs	High
Management Reinforcement	Supervisors	Specific Programs	Moderate
Management Involvement	All Levels of Managers	Specific Programs	Moderate

achieving results and the various roles and responsibilities of the HR function. The chapter concludes with specific recommendations for improving HR's relationship with other managers, and presents a step-by-step guide to using the strategies presented throughout the chapter.

PARTNERSHIP RELATIONSHIPS

An important element in shaping management's influence on the HR function is the relationship between the HR department and key managers in the organization, particularly line managers. Developing partnership relationships is part of an important trend taking place in organizations throughout the world.[1] Effective partnerships are being developed between:

- organizations and their suppliers
- organizations and their customers
- managers and employees
- managers and consultants
- line managers and staff support functions

For too many years, HR managers ignored this fundamental, yet powerful, ingredient to HR success. HR managers operated in a vacuum and spent little time cultivating relationships with other managers, and encountered problems when implementing new programs. They overlooked the fact that when the relationship is not effective, it is difficult for HR programs to be effective.

An effective partnership is based on the principles of collaboration and empowerment. An extremely powerful tool for organizations, partnering provides a strategic approach for maximizing output. Highly successful HR programs that contribute significantly to the organization usually are based on this principle.

Line Manager Concern

A line manager's perception of the HR function is not always favorable, as several studies have shown. Table 4-2 summarizes one such study based on responses of 500 personnel managers that reveals line management images of the HR function.[2] Line managers perceive HR to be bureaucratic, expensive, unresponsive, and not focused on the major goals of the organization. In reality, most HR departments do not operate this way. Effective HR departments with supportive partnership arrangements with line managers exist in many organizations. The problem often lies in misperceptions and faulty communication between the two groups. The challenge for most HR managers is to find out exactly what line managers want from the HR function and respond appropriately. Surveys, questionnaires, interviews, or focus groups are all effective techniques to determine line

TABLE 4-2
LINE MANAGEMENT IMAGES OF THE HR FUNCTION

IMAGE	FREQUENCY OF MENTION
Human Resources is too costly	401
HR doesn't add value	287
HR is bureaucratic and unresponsive	184
We can do it ourselves	163
HR staff are time wasters	159
HR interferes with operations	155
HR staff does not know the business	118

Source: Based on a study by Jac Fitz-enz. Human Value Management, *San Francisco: Jossey Bass, 1990.*

manager perceptions of HR and their specific needs. Although the results from this type of exercise may vary, line management needs from the HR function will usually include items on the following list that was developed in one organization. Line managers want:

- results from their requests. They want some assurance that a program is going to work before it is implemented. After it is implemented, they want to know if it is contributing to the bottom line.
- quick responses to their requests. Often frustrated with delays and procrastination, they want action now and results "yesterday."
- HR staff members to understand operational functions and have a working knowledge of the business. Working in the mainstream functions in the organization, line managers are the driving forces who make, deliver, or sell the product or service. Without their efforts, the organization does not exist. Line managers want staff support employees to understand what they do and the importance of it.
- helpful and sincere service with positive approaches from HR staff members. Line managers view themselves as customers of HR, and consequently, they want to be treated as important customers. They want the HR staff to be resourceful and courteous with their requests.
- to work with HR staff members who have the necessary skills and motivation to help them achieve their goals. They want to work with a competent HR staff who can complete projects and assist them with core business activities.
- HR staff members who will stretch and extend themselves. A willingness to exceed expectations when assisting with projects, programs, and goals is desired.

■ HR staff members to be experts in the HR field. When line managers seek help from the HR department, they expect expert advice and credible technical assistance. Otherwise, they may lose respect for the HR staff.

■ a practical approach to help solve problems and resolve issues in the line organization. They have no time for theoretical issues, complex models, or the latest fad. They want proven and practical techniques and programs.

For most HR staff members, these line management needs should not come as a surprise. They represent typical demands placed on any support staff. The important issue is that, until there is a clear understanding of what the line managers want, it may be difficult to deliver it.[3]

Characteristics of a Successful Partnership

The key ingredients of successful partnerships between HR and line management are similar to other successful partnership arrangements, such as a business partnership or a marriage partnership. A successful partnership arrangement is based on several characteristics, outlined below:

■ **Mutual respect between the partners is necessary.** The HR staff must respect line management and line management must respect the HR staff. This fundamental ingredient is essential for productive and fruitful relationships.

■ **Common goals must exist.** HR goals should be consistent with, and supportive of, operational goals such as production levels, service targets, sales volumes, productivity improvement, quality enhancement, cost reduction, and customer satisfaction.

■ **Each partner should offer a unique contribution to the relationship.** Partnerships are usually formed on this principle. Often the contributions of each partner are complementary.

■ **Each partner's role should be clearly understood.** Partnerships function best when responsibilities, expectations, and activities are defined, discussed, and documented.

■ **Each partner should recognize the strengths and weaknesses of the other partner.** In many effective partnerships, the strength of one partner is a weakness of the other, thus making the combined relationship more effective. This brings synergy to the relationship.

■ **Time must be allocated to improve the relationship.** A relationship will not grow and mature unless sufficient time is allocated for the specific purpose of improvement. Social time allocated for this purpose may be just as valuable and effective as work time.

■ **A helpful attitude should permeate the relationship.** Each partner must be willing to help the other at all times, in all situations. An effective partner will support, encourage, and protect the other partner.

■ **Partners should adopt a results-based approach to meet goals and solve problems.** Partners must focus on desired outcomes, and develop appropriate strategies and tactics to achieve them. Sustained results are essential for the partnership to continue.

■ **Partners should share rewards and risks.** In a legal partnership, this is automatic; partners share in success as well as the risks associated with business failure. This should be an important ingredient in all partnerships.

The above factors represent the *ideal* arrangement in a successful partnership arrangement. Although in practice, all factors will not exist to the fullest extent, collectively, they provide a framework that the organization can use to improve the partnership arrangement. Consider, for example, the last item on the list. Ideally, the compensation of the HR manager (and other key HR staff) should be similar to the line manager's plan. When management goals are met and line managers receive incentive compensation, HR managers should receive a similar bonus, assuming that they have common goals. As the line manager's bonus compensation declines because of inadequate results, the HR manager should suffer the same consequences.

The remainder of the chapter provides other specific strategies to improve this partnership relationship. Some strategies are directed at top management, while others focus on middle managers or first level supervisors. Collectively they provide an important framework from which to develop, cultivate, and refine this important relationship that is essential for a results-based HR program.

TOP MANAGEMENT COMMITMENT

While the influence of the entire management group is important to HR success, no group will have more impact than the top executive group. This group allocates resources, initiates programs, assists in goal setting, and often provides a role model for program support. Without strong support and endorsement from top executives and administrators, HR programs will fall short of their potential and the HR function will not be very effective. Developing a supportive relationship with top executives is a critical challenge for the HR staff. The extent to which this is accomplished could separate the mediocre HR departments from the outstanding ones.

Each chief executive officer (CEO) or other top official has some degree of commitment to the HR function. (The term CEO is used to identify the top executive or administrator over the organization or major part of the organization.) The extent of this commitment usually varies with the style, attitude, and philosophy of the chief executive and to a certain extent may reflect the organization's historical use of HR. A heavy commitment to HR usually correlates with a successful organization. HR managers must show top management the payoffs of HR investment and convince those key executives that they should be strong supporters of HR efforts. With this approach, HR managers can actually change the role of top management and its relationship with the HR staff.

A Commitment Check

As a first step in exploring ways to improve top management commitment, it is useful to assess the extent of commitment currently prevailing in the organization. The commitment checklist presented as Table 4-3 contains a self-test for the

TABLE 4-3
CEO: CHECK YOUR COMMITMENT TO THE
HUMAN RESOURCES FUNCTION
(SEE APPENDIX 2 FOR RESPONSES)

Select the response that best answers the question.

YES NO

☐ ☐ 1. Do you have a corporate policy or mission statement for the HR function?

☐ ☐ 2. Do you occasionally question the need for your HR function?

☐ ☐ 3. Does your organization set goals for employee participation in and utilization of formal HR programs?

☐ ☐ 4. Do you periodically survey employee attitudes and make adjustments based on the results?

☐ ☐ 5. Is your involvement in the HR function more than introductory statements, memos, and approvals?

☐ ☐ 6. Is your top HR officer involved in key strategic planning sessions?

☐ ☐ 7. Do you require the HR department to monitor important performance measures related to their efforts?

☐ ☐ 8. Do you occasionally participate in an HR program or review parts of one?

☐ ☐ 9. Do you require your managers to be actively involved in HR programs?

☐ ☐ 10. Does your top HR officer have a title that reflects senior officer status?

(continued on next page)

TABLE 4-3 (CONTINUED)
CEO: CHECK YOUR COMMITMENT TO THE
HUMAN RESOURCES FUNCTION
(SEE APPENDIX 2 FOR RESPONSES)

☐ ☐ 11. Is the total compensation package for the top HR officer structured in the same way as packages for top functional executives in finance, sales operations, and other key areas?

☐ ☐ 12. Do you require your management group to support and reinforce HR programs?

☐ ☐ 13. Do you require the HR department to distribute performance data to division or regional managers?

☐ ☐ 14. Do you require that all new HR programs be justified in some way?

☐ ☐ 15. Is your top HR officer's job an attractive and respected executive position?

☐ ☐ 16. Do you encourage your line managers and HR staff to work together as a partnership to prevent problems and improve the organization?

☐ ☐ 17. Does the HR department have an annual budget and operating objectives?

☐ ☐ 18. Does the HR manager have access to you regularly?

☐ ☐ 19. Do you often suggest that the HR staff help solve performance problems?

☐ ☐ 20. Do you frequently meet with the HR officer to review HR problems and progress?

☐ ☐ 21. Do you require a formal top executive review and assessment of HR programs at least annually?

☐ ☐ 22. Do you require an assessment of needs and a proposal for new HR programs?

☐ ☐ 23. When business declines, do you resist cutting the HR budget?

☐ ☐ 24. Do you frequently speak out in support of the HR function?

☐ ☐ 25. Does the top HR officer report directly to you?

☐ ☐ 26. Do you require the HR department to have a cost-tracking system for each major program?

☐ ☐ 27. Is the HR department required to monitor the results of each HR program in some way?

☐ ☐ 28. Do you ask to see the results of major HR programs?

☐ ☐ 29. Do you encourage a cost/benefit calculation for major HR programs?

☐ ☐ 30. Do you require major HR program results to be linked to key organizational measure of productivity and efficiency?

top executive. In just a few minutes, a CEO or top executive can assess the level of commitment and identify ways in which commitment can be increased. When taken in the proper setting, this checklist can be a revealing exercise, resulting in a favorable impact on the attitudes and actions of a chief executive. The impact is often greater in organizations where there has been little effort to secure commitment for the function. While the interpretation of the number of "yes" responses to the test may vary with the organization, one approach is presented in Appendix 2.

The CEO self-test will usually reveal several areas where additional commitment is needed. By grouping the issues into general areas of emphasis, clear guidelines for strong top management commitment begin to emerge. The ten major commitment areas, shown in Table 4-4, need little additional explanation.

TABLE 4-4
TEN ESSENTIAL COMMITMENTS FROM TOP MANAGEMENT

For strong top management HR commitment, the chief executive officer should:

• Develop a mission for the HR function.
• Allocate the necessary funds for successful HR programs.
• Allow employees time to participate in HR programs.
• Get actively involved in HR programs and require others to do so.
• Support the HR effort and ask other managers to do the same.
• Place the HR function in a visible and high-level position close to the chief executive.
• Require that each new and existing HR program be justified in some way.
• Insist that HR programs be cost-effective and require supporting data.
• Involve the top HR officer in strategic management issues.
• Create an atmosphere of open communication between the chief executive and key HR personnel.

Some are obvious requirements for a successful HR effort and have been discussed previously as requirements for a results-based HR philosophy in the organization. The other items will be covered in other sections of this book.

Increasing Commitment

Now for the important question: How can top management commitment for HR be increased? This puzzling question represents a unique challenge for HR professionals who often operate under the assumption that they cannot influence commitment. The actual commitment to HR develops slowly over time and often varies with the size or nature of the organization. It is a derivative of how the HR department evolved in its role, the attitude and philosophy of the top management group toward the HR function, and how the HR function has been managed. The last two of the three items show promise for increasing commitment and are illustrated in the following actions:

■ **Results.** Top management commitment will usually increase when HR programs achieve or exceed desired results. This is an integral part of an important cycle. Commitment is necessary to build effective HR programs where results can be obtained. And when results are obtained, commitment is increased. Few things are more convincing to top executives than measurable results they can understand and perceive as valuable to the organization. When a new program is proposed, additional funding is sometimes based solely on the results anticipated from the program.

■ **Management Involvement.** Commitment is increased when managers are actively involved in HR programs. This involvement, which can occur in almost every phase of the HR process, reflects a strong cooperative management effort to use human resources effectively. Top executives want their managers involved because it reflects a team spirit and they assume the process will be more effective because of the participation. Specific techniques for increasing involvement are covered later in the chapter.

■ **Professionalism.** A highly professional HR staff can help improve commitment. Where the achievement of excellence is the goal of many professional groups, it should be a mandate for the HR department. The HR staff must be perceived as professional in all actions including welcoming criticism, adjusting to the changing needs of the organization, maintaining productive relationships with other staff, and setting the example for others. Professionalism will show up in the attention to detail in every HR program— detail that is often overlooked by non-professionals.

■ **Knowledge of Business.** A comprehensive knowledge of the organization's primary businesses is a key ingredient in building respect and credibility with the management group. Top executives and administrators want staff support groups to understand their core businesses and how they function, learn all about the organization, and show interest in operational goals. Top executives are more inclined to provide additional funds to an HR staff who understands the business and are willing to help the business reach its goals.

■ **Communications.** The HR department must communicate needs to top management and make them understand that HR is an integral part of the organization. Whether developing new program proposals, reviewing program progress with top management, seeking helpful advice, or reporting program results, communication is critical. When top management understands the results-based process, they will usually respond with additional commitment.

■ **Visibility.** The HR staff should position itself in a visible role, preferably alongside key managers, helping to solve operational problems. More than being "at the right place at the right time," this strategy includes a variety of actions that increase the presence of the staff and function. Top executives want staff members who "are involved," with a "hands-on" philosophy and a desire to be "where the action is." Top management will usually support those who meet this challenge.

■ **Generalist Approach.** The HR department should avoid being narrowly focused. HR programs should not be confined to those mandated by regulations, laws, or organizational necessities. While sometimes enjoying a favorable reputation in certain areas such as record keeping, benefits administration, or EEO compliance, the HR staff may not be regarded as problem solvers or performance enhancers. A progressive HR staff should be perceived as versatile, flexible, and resourceful, and utilized in a variety of situations to help make a contribution to organizational success.

■ **Practical Orientation.** The HR department must have a practical approach to program design, development, and implementation. An approach focusing on theories and philosophical ideas may be perceived as not contributing to the organization. While there is a place for theoretical processes and analyzes, much of the efforts of HR within the organization should focus on practical application of proven techniques. Programs should normally be useful and helpful and coordinated by experienced people who understand the needs and program.

While in some organizations there may be other factors that are contextual or unique to a particular setting, the above strategies apply in most settings. They represent actions or requirements that top management notices and recognizes as important to HR success. Taken individually, the above items may not have much effect on overall commitment. However, when the HR staff pursues excellence on every item, top management commitment will increase.

MANAGEMENT SUPPORT AND REINFORCEMENT

As defined in this book, management support for HR programs is concerned with actions for first and middle level managers. Before presenting techniques for improving support, it may be useful to present the concept of ideal management support. Ideal support occurs when a manager reacts in the following ways to the HR function:

- Encourages employees to be involved in HR programs.
- Volunteers personal services or resources to assist the HR function.
- When appropriate, makes an agreement with employees before they become involved in HR programs; this agreement outlines what changes should occur or what tasks should be accomplished after the program is implemented or completed.
- Reinforces the behavior change objectives of HR programs; this reinforcement may be demonstrated in a variety of ways.
- Meets all responsibilities and duties for making HR programs successful.
- Assists in determining the results achieved from HR programs.
- Provides rewards and recognition to participants who achieve outstanding accomplishments with HR program participation.
- Makes unsolicited positive comments about the quality and effectiveness of HR programs and services.

This level of support represents utopia for the HR profession. The following section explores ways to move closer to this idealistic supportive environment.

Support Prior to Implementation

Support is necessary before a program is implemented as well as after it becomes operational. One strategy is to secure pre-program agreements or commitments. Probably the most common type of agreement is formulated between the HR department and the participant's supervisor and outlines the responsibilities of both the supervisor and HR department. Usually developed in a meeting with supervisors of participants prior to the beginning of the HR program, this approach is particularly useful for training programs, total quality management initiatives, safety and health programs, employee benefit plans, and alternative reward systems. For example, in the implementation of a productivity improvement program, prior agreements covering expectations and roles of participants and supervisors are important to help maximize program success. Other variations of pre-program agreements involve commitments between the participant and the participant's supervisor or between the HR department, the participant, and the participant's supervisor. More information on the structure of these agreements is available in other references.[4]

Defining and documenting the responsibilities of both participants and supervisors of participants represents an effective type of pre-program activity. Some organizations develop program descriptions, program brochures, or other documents that provide specific duties for each party. Others define responsibilities in policy and procedure manuals. Timing becomes an issue with this tactic. Participant responsibilities are sometimes defined prior to, or at the beginning of, an HR program to ensure that participants are fully aware of expectations and to achieve desired results. For example, in the introduction of a new employee involvement program in one organization, participants and their supervisors were provided a copy of their respective responsibilities along with the requirements for program success.

Communication with participants prior to involvement in an HR program is an often overlooked but effective pre-program activity. This is particularly important when participation is not required of all employees. When selected to participate, the individuals are usually curious about the reasons for their involvement. Participants are interested in the purpose of the program and eligibility requirements. Much of this pre-program anxiety can be eliminated if the participants are provided the following information:

- The basis for their selection or eligibility requirements for participation.
- The purpose of the program, including a brief overview of the program content.
- The administrative details of the program (time, place, dates, etc.).
- Instructions about pre-program assignments, if applicable.
- Expected results.
- Follow-up plans, including program monitoring and tracking.

It is important to provide information on the last two items, program results and follow-up plans, because of their link to program success. Detailed prior information places the participant at ease and enhances the achievement of results. Participants will have a clearer picture of why they are involved in the program and how they can make it successful. Also, pre-program information may strengthen the relationship between the participant and those who administer the program.

Support After Implementation

Probably the most critical area of support involves activities after the program is implemented. In some HR programs, participants are expected to change habits or attitudes or improve skills after the program is implemented. Post-program support, in the form of follow-up assignments or planned actions, are important to assess what change has taken place. Otherwise, the program's ultimate success may not be accurately determined. In this context, the terms "support" and "reinforcement" are almost synonymous. When support is exhibited, it helps reinforce what the participants should accomplish to meet program objectives.

For most follow-up activities, the participant's supervisor is a key individual in the process. Supervisors must see the results achieved and understand the importance of participation. Some follow-up assignments require participants to funnel their new accomplishments through the supervisor who is asked to make comments about the significance of the improvement and the assistance the program provided to help produce the results. Follow-up actions are essential for HR programs that focus on improvement. For example, in a total quality management program in one organization, supervisors are required to provide follow-up information on several planned actions that focus on continuous improvement. A follow-up report is sent to the Quality Manager. Specific types of follow-up activities are presented in a later chapter.

Reinforcement

The results-based approach requires an effective work relationship between the HR staff, participants, and the participant's supervisor. This relationship can be viewed as part of a three-legged stool representing the major influences. One leg of the stool is the HR staff member who coordinates the program. Another leg is the participant who is involved in the program, and the third leg is the participant's supervisor who reinforces program objectives and follow-up activities. Without one of the legs, the stool collapses, as does the results-based approach.

The necessity of reinforcing actions from the participant's supervisor cannot be underrated. Too often participants face obstacles or barriers to successful implementation or application of the HR program and even the best participants fail to succeed. Regardless of how well an HR program is designed and implemented, unless it is reinforced on the job, most of its effectiveness is lost.

To improve reinforcement, the primary focus must be on supervisors of program participants. Collectively, this group can exert a major influence on the participant's behavior by providing reinforcement in the following ways:

■ Explain or clarify certain parts or features of the program.
■ Help participants diagnose problems related to the HR program.
■ Discuss possible alternatives for handling specific situations.
■ Coach participants to help them meet program objectives.
■ Encourage participants to use the HR program effectively.
■ Serve as a role model for the proper implementation of the HR program material.
■ Give positive recognition to participants when the HR program objectives are met.

A management reinforcement workshop is an effective approach to teach supervisors and managers how to develop the above skills to reinforce behavior changes desired from an HR program. The power of these combined activities to reinforce program objectives and ensure program success is impressive. This process is effective, whether the HR program focuses on training or health care cost containment.

Reinforcement can come from sources other than the supervisor. Sometimes, when participants achieve success with an application of an HR program, they will want to try it again. This self-reinforcement causes a few participants to excel with HR program materials even in the face of on-the-job obstacles that hinder program success. Participants may attempt to meet objectives if they feel an obligation to implement them or they may be curious to see if the program will actually work. The satisfaction of achieving success provides reinforcement for them to try it again. Sometimes there are tangible benefits for program application. Self-reinforcement is particularly effective in programs where new skills, attitudes, or work practices are required for programs such as skill base pay plans, employee involvement efforts, labor-management cooperation, total quality management, and training and development.

An often overlooked avenue for reinforcement is the peer group, which includes employees at the same level engaged in the same HR program. When participants achieve success with program applications, others are encouraged to make the program work. Subtle peer pressure is at work influencing group members to meet program objectives. Also, it can spawn intergroup coaching among the peer group where successful participants will sometimes show others how to achieve the desired results. Peer reinforcement can be enhanced when specific actions are taken to bring attention to the results achieved by group members. For example, in one program, a report on the progress made by each group member was distributed to each group member after three-month intervals. Peer reinforcement works best in group-based programs such as gainsharing, team building, group incentive plans, safety programs, and empowerment programs.

Recognition of Support and Reinforcement

A very effective strategy for building or enhancing a supportive relationship is to provide sincere, appropriate recognition to managers of participants when they show support or reinforcement for HR programs. Recognition can come in a variety of formats and must be both sincere and appropriate for the action or behavior being recognized. Among the techniques that have worked for organizations are the following:

- Provide praise in meetings to recognize managers who are supporting the efforts or have contributed to a successful HR program.
- Send a memo to managers who have supported HR programs or provided special input or assistance. Copy the manager's immediate superior. The memo should detail exactly what has been accomplished and express appreciation for the accomplishment.
- Provide input for the performance review process for those efforts that represent a significant accomplishment.
- Use an existing publication to bring attention to the accomplishments of managers when they assist, implement, and deliver HR programs. For organizational wide publications, the recognition should be contained in a general interest story. In special interest publications, such as an HR newsletter, recognition is more direct and specific.
- Arrange appreciation dinners for those who provide appropriate support and input into the HR function. These events are appropriately held at certain milestones to provide program updates to review of program performance as well as to provide appropriate recognition.
- Recognize managers in a formal awards program such as the manager of the year award or division manager of the month. These awards presented by the Human Resources staff should be made based on objective criteria reflecting the quality of the input and contribution of managers to HR programs.
- Provide specialty advertising items such as mugs, T-shirts, umbrellas, or briefcases to supervisors and managers who have provided assistance and support. These items should be useful while at the same time should bring attention to the HR efforts with appropriate logos, slogans, or messages.
- Send thank-you notes to managers who have made a difference. This simple gesture can be very effective.

Collectively, these techniques, plus others appropriate for the specific situation, can enhance and maintain the support of the HR staff.

MANAGEMENT INVOLVEMENT

Significant management involvement in the HR function leads to high levels of program ownership that helps increase HR program effectiveness.[5] In addition to this benefit, management's expertise can provide valuable assistance to enhance program quality. Although many opportunities exist for management's involvement in the function—as many as there are steps in designing and implementing an HR program—management's input and active participation will usually occur only in the most significant steps of the process. Determining needs, developing objectives, designing programs, conducting or coordinating programs, and evaluating program results are typical stages where management input is needed. Five widely used techniques to involve managers are presented here.

Managers as Advisory Committee Members

HR advisory committees offer an excellent opportunity to increase line management involvement in the HR function. Sometimes operating under other names such as councils or advisory boards, committees are developed for a variety of programs and specific functions, as shown in Table 4-5. Depending on the

TABLE 4-5
HR COMMITTEES

FOCUS	EXAMPLE
Individual program	New employee orientation program committee
	Account executive's training committee
	Job evaluation committee
	Profit sharing committee
	Employee suggestion committee
Specific function	Compensation committee
	Executive development committee
	EEO committee
	Collective bargaining committee
	Employment standards committee
Multiple functions	Employee involvement committee
	QWL committee
	Operating cost committee
	Communication committee
	Governmental compliance committee

duration of the HR program and the emphasis needed for the specific function, committees can serve as a one-shot assignment or a continuing process. Committees can be used in many stages of the HR process, from needs analysis to communication of program results. The HR department benefits from the expertise of management's input and from management's commitment to the process. It is unlikely that managers will criticize something of which they are a part. Typical duties of an advisory committee include:

 Explore the need for the program or review the results of a needs analysis.
■ Establish program objectives.

- Discuss alternatives for meeting program objectives.
- Approve a proposed program design.
- Recommend potential changes in a program.
- Review program results.
- Monitor program activity.

Committees can meet periodically or on an as-needed basis. In a typical meeting, a senior HR manager reviews specific issues to secure input, support, and endorsement of the HR program.

The selection of committee members is an important issue. Key managers or influential executives who are decisive, knowledgeable, and respected in the organization make the best members. A committee comprised of dysfunctional managers, commanding little respect in the organization, will be ineffective. It is also important that committee members not get bogged down in irrelevant and insignificant matters and thus lose the clout and credibility they could otherwise enjoy. Before deciding on whether a committee is appropriate, the HR department should determine if the potential benefits outweigh the time that must be given to make the committee process work. Some organizations have a committee for almost every program, while others manage to survive well without them.

Managers as Task Force Members

Managers should be considered for an HR task force assignment. A task force consists of a group of employees, usually managers or specialists, who are charged with the task of developing an HR program. Task forces are more useful for programs that are beyond the scope of HR staff capability and expertise. For example, a job evaluation task force has the responsibility for revising and updating all jobs. The task force members from each major functional area provide the needed expertise for the assignment.

A major difference between the functions of a task force and a committee is that the task force is required to produce something. It must devote a considerable amount of time and effort to researching, designing, developing, writing, testing, or implementing the program. Time requirements vary from a one-week assignment to a full-time project for several months. The time span, of course, depends on the nature of the program being developed and the availability of task force members. Examples of task force projects include:

- Designing an organization-wide suggestion system.
- Developing a recruiting strategy for new robotics technicians.
- Implementing a productivity improvement program for a specific area.
- Revising the salary administration system for all exempt employees.
- Designing a skill-based pay system for engineers.

■ Assessing the effectiveness of the employee benefits package.

■ Developing a technical training program for the engineering department.

The selection of task force members is more critical than the selection of committee members. The experience base of task force members is extremely important and should represent the range of skills needed for program development and implementation. Although a task force may include management or non-management members who have the expertise needed for the project, including management on the task force adds credibility and influence that can enhance the program's success. The drawback, however, is that managers may not have time to devote to the project.

In addition to increased credibility, an advantage of the task force approach to HR is usually a savings in time and money. A task force frees the HR staff from the time-consuming activity of program development and implementation. Another advantage is the teamwork example created by the task force. The target employees may accept the end product of a task force more readily than a program designed by the HR staff.

Managers as Discussion Leaders

A common and effective approach to involvement is the use of managers as HR program discussion leaders. For example, one organization, involved in a major effort to implement a gainsharing program in several plants, used managers as discussion leaders for monthly employee meetings. These meetings were designed to feed back results and teach employees how to control costs. This approach presents some unique challenges because not everyone has the flair for leading a discussion. Discussion leaders should be carefully chosen based on their expertise, presentation skills, reputation, and availability.

The expertise requirement is usually one of the most important reasons for soliciting outside assistance. The HR staff cannot provide expertise for all programs conducted. Although a subject matter expert is used in the program design, it may be more meaningful to participants to have a discussion leader knowledgeable in the subject matter. Good presentation skills are important as well. Even the most well-respected and knowledgeable manager can fail in this assignment if he or she cannot make an effective presentation. Discussion leaders should have a good reputation in order to bring credibility to the program. Similarly, managers who are considered substandard performers or improper role models will have a negative impact on the program. Finally, availability is important. While it may not be the norm in every organization, effective managers are usually very busy individuals and may not have the time to help conduct programs. However, other equally effective managers, because of some unusual circumstances, may not be fully challenged in their jobs and are likely candidates for an assignment as a discussion leader. Also, top management will sometimes insist that even the busiest line managers be involved in the HR effort. This stance makes HR a high priority and leaves a favorable impact on HR programs.

After the discussion leaders are selected, the main task is to prepare them for their assignments. Because this may be a lengthy process, the actual time involved in preparing others to conduct or coordinate a program may be greater than the time required for the HR staff to prepare for and present the program. Detailed objectives, prepared scripts, visual aids, and other items may need to be prepared. If appropriate, discussion leaders should have a chance to practice a session before presenting it to participants. The HR staff should offer suggestions. At a minimum, an HR staff member should attend the first presentation and provide feedback to the leader in an attempt to keep program quality at a high level.

Managers as Program Coordinators

Occasionally, it may be necessary to recruit managers, usually line managers, to represent the HR function in a particular division, plant, department, or work area. This action relinquishes the ownership of an HR program to line managers and removes the stigma that the program is a staff initiative. Program coordinators or administrators have specific duties to provide local representation and/or management of a specific HR program. The specific situations in which this is appropriate include programs where a high degree of HR expertise is not required, but the additional credibility, influence, and knowledge of a local manager is very important. Some typical examples of these types of programs are alternative reward systems, employee involvement efforts, employee relations programs and on-the-job training programs. In these situations, managers are briefed (and sometimes trained) on their specific roles as program coordinators and receive detailed descriptions of what they should do and when they should do it. An HR member may occasionally visit with the coordinator or attend a meeting conducted by the coordinator.

The extent to which outsiders are involved in coordinating HR programs can vary considerably. In some situations, the entire program is coordinated by the HR staff. In others, programs are coordinated entirely by line management. The right combination depends on factors such as:

- The nature, scope, and complexity of the HR program.
- The ability of other managers to coordinate the program.
- The value placed on having other managers identified with the HR program.
- The professional expertise of the HR staff to coordinate the program.

- The size and budget of the HR staff.
- The physical location of program developers when compared to the location of line managers.

The use of non-HR managers in HR programs creates an impressive display of teamwork. In one organization where manager coordination of a program was extensive, there were periodic "coordinator" meetings. In these meetings the results of the program were presented along with proposed changes and general information about the program's future. A team spirit was created and, at the same time, the gesture reminded managers that their contribution was necessary for program success.

Managers as Participants

While many HR programs require managers to participate along with their employees, others do not. For some programs, such as safety and health, employee benefits, organization development, employee involvement and training, it may still be important for managers of the participants to be involved even though their involvement is not required. Management participation, when feasible, enables managers to experience the program in the same way as other participants. Although they may be involved in separate sessions, managers are exposed to essentially the same material, either in a full program or a scaled-down version.

Managers are sometimes reluctant to become involved in HR programs designed for their subordinates and, in some situations, managers do not need full exposure to the program. A program description or a brief outline, along with an explanation of responsibilities, might suffice. However, this approach usually falls short of an optimum situation. It is difficult for managers to have a clear understanding of a program unless they experience all of it. As an additional benefit, managers have an opportunity to sharpen skills or enhance knowledge after participating in the program. Participation can range from attending the full program to auditing a portion to examine its content.

Manager attendance is appropriate when one or more of these conditions exist:

- A high percentage of the manager's employees will be involved in the program. Because of the broad coverage alone, managers need to understand program content and observe the dynamics of the program.
- Managers must have a clear understanding of why their employees are involved.

■ Support and reinforcement from the manager are essential to the program's success. Managers must know what role to assume to support the program and reinforce its objectives.

■ Managers need the same knowledge or skills the participants will obtain from the program. Although the program may not be designed for managers, it may be important for them to know and use the program information, and participation may be the most efficient way to obtain this information.

This approach may not be feasible for all types of HR programs. For example, in specialized programs designed for only a few individuals, managerial participation may not be practical nor desirable. Also, management participation may inhibit the involvement of other employees.

Why Managers Should Get Involved

As discussed earlier, management involvement can occur at any stage of the development and delivery of an HR program. Some strategies of involvement fit more appropriately into specific stages. Table 4-6 shows the steps in the results-based model and the level of potential management involvement in each step. High levels of involvement are possible in many steps. The most appropriate involvement strategy is listed.

TABLE 4-6
MANAGER INVOLVEMENT OPPORTUNITIES

STEPS IN RESULTS-BASED MODEL	OPPORTUNITY FOR MANAGER INVOLVEMENT	MOST APPROPRIATE STRATEGY
Conduct Needs Analysis	High	Task Force
Development Measurement/ Evaluation System	Moderate	Advisory Committee
Establish Program Objectives	High	Advisory Committee
Develop Program	Moderate	Task Force
Implement Program	High	Program Leader
Monitor Costs	Low	Program Coordinator
Collect/Analyze Data	Moderate	Program Coordinator
Interpret Data/Draw Conclusions	High	Program Coordinator
Communicate Results	Moderate	Participant

Seven major benefits are derived from manager involvement in the HR function:

- Added program credibility that might otherwise be lacking.
- Increased ownership of programs by managers when they are involved in developing, implementing, or evaluating HR programs.
- Improved working relationships, because program participants and HR staff have more interaction with other key managers.
- Enhanced managerial skills of managers who are actively involved in programs.
- Increased savings for the HR budget, in cases where it is more economical to use other managers than to add HR staff.
- Improved performance of HR programs because of an increased focus on results.
- Additional rewards for managers who contribute to the HR effort.

With these advantages more organizations should use the skills, expertise, and influence of management in the HR process and build effective partnerships. HR leaders will be challenged in the 1990s to tap the input of this important group, in particular, key line managers. Otherwise, HR programs may not achieve optimum results.

FOCUSING ON RESULTS WITH MANAGERS

When building relationships with other managers, and particularly line managers, a focus on results helps solidify and enhance the relationships, as discussed in the section on characteristics of successful partnerships. A focus on results involves specific actions of the HR staff throughout the different stages of the HR program development and delivery.

Regardless of whether a product is produced or a service is delivered, all HR programs should in some way tie into the organization's output. Some programs will be directly related to the bottom line and aimed at specific improvements, while others will be indirect, but still aimed at helping the organization meet its primary goals.

A concern for the bottom line should appear in the scope, nature, type, and content of HR programs. A review of the portfolio of products and services offered by HR will reveal the degree to which there is a concern for, and a relationship to, the bottom line. An important concern for bottom-line contribution is evidenced when programs are tied directly and indirectly to the bottom line. This relationship must be explained and communicated. For example, an employee benefits program involving cost sharing for medical costs can easily be linked directly to the organization's bottom line. Conversely, a new benefit designed to provide financial counseling to employees may have little connection to the bottom line. If only a few programs can make this connection, there may be problems in the future. The important point here is that a concern for the results helps build the partnership relationships with line managers, because line managers are primarily concerned with the bottom line of the organization. When line managers see the same concern from staff members, they are more interested in developing a partnership.

In some cases the staff can see problems on the horizon when line managers are unable to see them. Perhaps the HR staff sees increases in absenteeism, turnover, grievance rates, or accident frequency rates. These danger signals might escape the scrutiny of a line manager whose principle focus may be on the output variables such as productivity, quality, cost, and delivery schedules. Immediate attention by the HR staff with proposed programs, actions, and strategies to help alleviate problems before they become serious issues can win the support of most progressive line managers who welcome assistance to prevent future problems. Avoiding problems can be convincing evidence of concern for the bottom line to line managers and can help build an effective partnership.

While avoiding problems is the least costly approach, it is sometimes ignored. Too often HR managers wait, sometimes intentionally, until problems become serious and then charge to the rescue attacking and correcting the problem. While this might feed egos and make HR managers feel important, it does not serve the organization very well if the problem could have been avoided with preventive programs.

ROLES, RESPONSIBILITIES, RISKS, AND REWARDS

Another effective set of actions to improve the partnership relationship with line managers concerns HR roles, responsibilities, risks, and rewards. The last three decades have brought significant changes to the role of the human resources staff. Initially HR, or personnel as it was called, primarily performed an administrative role of keeping records, developing reports, and paying employees. Because the administrative role was essential and very critical at the time, it consumed most of the department's resources. Slowly, the reactive role emerged in which HR responded to requests for developing programs and providing services to meet realistic and perceived needs. The HR staff became known as helpful problem solvers, responding to requests from the organization or responding to environmental needs, particularly as they related to government regulations. Gradually, the proactive role evolved. HR began to realize that programs should be implemented to prevent problems and consequently, the HR staff began initiating programs, sometimes based on what others were pursuing at that time. In the '80s, HR was quite productive in initiating new programs, earning the label of being too proactive in some organizations. In the '90s, the newest role for HR staff is collaboration. Here, HR staff members, in concert with key managers, observe or anticipate problems or opportunities and jointly develop programs to prevent problems, boost efficiency, raise productivity, and increase customer satisfaction. In this role, the HR staff is truly an effective partner with line managers collaborating on important issues.

Currently, HR staffs are involved with administrative work, responding to requests, initiating new programs, and collaborating with line managers. The present emphasis, as illustrated in Figure 4-1, is on the roles of the initiator and col-

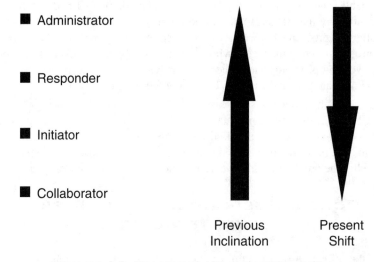

FIGURE 4-1. ROLES FOR HR RELATIONSHIPS.

laborator. This shift is sometimes accomplished by examining the current time spent on each of the four roles and setting targets for those percentages in the future. This translates into an HR staff focusing more quality time to the roles of collaborator and initiator.

For years HR managers have been trying to increase their power base by gaining control over issues, policies, and individuals. HR managers want approval authority for items such as staff additions, salary increases, and employee terminations. This "desire to control" increases resentment with line managers who think the HR staff has excessive influence. In some cases, it causes line managers to resist any involvement by HR in their efforts. What HR managers must learn is that in order to build effective partnership relationships, they must be willing to shift HR responsibility to the line organization. HR must be willing to let the line managers make critical decisions previously reserved for the HR staff. This is a dramatic and sometimes emotional shift. As one HR manager stated,

> I have worked too hard to build a power base to give up control now. It has taken years to get in the approval loops on critical issues. I do not trust line managers to handle these issues on their own. I need that control over them in order to get their attention on critical issues and have them work with me when I need them.[6]

While this approach may satisfy an ego, it does little for building partnerships. This shift is inevitable and should be initiated by the HR staff before top executives require it.

A critical issue must be addressed before responsibility can be shifted. Line managers must know how to deal with the issues and make effective decisions. Most progressive HR departments have found that when they relinquish responsibilities to the line, the partnership relationship is enhanced and line managers begin to consult with them more frequently. Teaching line managers to manage the human resources is a gradual process. It must be built into routine management training and become a part of job responsibilities, expectations, and department goals. It is an ongoing process that must be nurtured by the HR staff. Some organizations have identified this shift as a major organizational strategy. By design, these organizations want line managers to be knowledgeable of HR practices and skilled in handling HR issues so they can make quality decisions, consult with the HR staff on unresolved issues, or seek additional information for the HR process.[7]

This shift of responsibility requires the HR staff to view themselves as agents of change. They must clearly define responsibility for results and gradually shift it to the line organization, at least on a shared basis. For example, in one organization, before a responsibility shift, the HR staff was accountable for the consequences of excessive turnover. When turnover exceeded expectations, the HR staff had to explain variations and outline corrective action. Gradually, at the initiation of the HR staff, turnover became a shared responsibility where line managers were held accountable for their turnover statistics along with HR managers, forcing them to work together to keep the number as low as possible. Finally, after a complete shift, turnover was perceived as a primary responsibility of the line manager. The HR staff was there to provide advice and assistance as needed to reduce turnover or to keep it at a manageable level. Line managers had to report results and offer solutions to problem situations.

Most experts will agree that an effective partnership arrangement allows for reward and risk sharing. Some HR-line manager partnerships have this ingredient in existing arrangements. There is risk sharing when programs fail because responsibility is shared by both groups and there is a share in the rewards in terms of credit for both parties when programs are successful. This risk/reward relationship should be moved to the next level to include direct and indirect compensation. How often does the top HR executive in an organization have the same type of bonus plan as other top executives? When programs fail to meet objectives, is there a financial penalty assessed with the HR staff to the extent that line managers are penalized when they fail to achieve targeted results? In an effective partnership arrangement, key HR staff members should share the same type of compensation arrangement as line managers, although the magnitudes might not be as great. After all, line managers have more overall impact on the organization's bottom-line than do staff managers. This is an area that should command considerable attention in the future, particularly as new innovative pay systems are being developed by the HR staff.

IMPROVING RELATIONSHIPS WITH MANAGERS

Now for the big challenge: How are supportive relationships improved? Although a variety of strategies have been presented, this section brings them together in critical steps to improve this important relationship. It is possible to strengthen a supportive relationship significantly by implementing the steps presented later in this chapter.

Relationship Classification

Before pursuing specific steps for improving supportive relationships, it is useful to classify key managers into four different types according to their degree or level of support.

Supportive. A very strong, active supporter of all HR efforts, this manager wants to be involved in programs and insists that his or her employees take advantage of every appropriate program and HR opportunity. This manager reinforces the objectives of HR programs, requires participants to meet program objectives, publicly voices approval for HR efforts, provides positive feedback to the HR department, and frequently seeks the HR department's assistance, advice, and counsel. This manager is a very valuable asset to the staff. A typical comment from this manager is, "the HR staff is very effective and professional and they can help us meet our goals."

Responsible. This manager supports HR programs because it is a fundamental managerial responsibility, just as budgeting and planning are. Although support is not as strong as with the supportive manager, this manager allows employees to participate in HR programs, encourages participants to get the most out of the program, and occasionally voices support for programs, but will not go out of the way to show unusual interest in HR programs. With prodding from the HR staff, this manager will reinforce program objectives and become involved in HR programs. A typical comment from this manager is, "there is a strong commitment for HR at this organization, so we should support the effort."

Non-supportive. This manager will privately voice displeasure with HR programs and reluctantly allow employees to participate in HR programs, sometimes allowing participation only when it is required. Thinking that the organization is spending too much time and money on HR efforts, this manager, in private conversations, will usually criticize the HR staff and their efforts. When employees are involved in an HR program, there is very little (if any) reinforcement from this manager—even if the manager is instructed to provide reinforcement. Conversely, this manager's actions may destroy the value of the program. A typical comment about an HR program from this manager is, "Regardless of what HR says, this is the way we do it here."

Irresponsive. This manager will try to keep employees from participating in HR programs, will attempt to destroy the HR effort, and will openly criticize programs and the HR staff. This manager believes that most HR activities should be performed by the manager, on the job. When this manager's employees participate in an HR program, there is usually negative reinforcement. Fortunately, this type of manager is rare in today's setting; however, there may be enough of them to cause some concern for the HR staff. In seminars conducted by the author, HR managers have indicated about 5-10 percent of key managers are in this category. A typical comment from this manager is, "Stay away from the HR staff, they are destroying this organization."

Summary of Strategies

Several important strategies for improving the supportive relationship with other managers are available. Most of them were presented in this chapter. In summary, the specific strategies are outlined in Table 4-7. Collectively, these strategies are extremely effective in developing very productive relationships which allow the organization to achieve desired results from HR programs.

TABLE 4-7
STRATEGIES FOR IMPROVING RELATIONSHIPS WITH MANAGERS

1. Improve top management commitment for the HR function through a variety of tactics.
2. Show managers how to support HR programs, before and after program implementation.
3. Teach managers how to reinforce program objectives.
4. Involve managers in the HR process in one or more of the five different ways.
5. Provide recognition for managers who support and reinforce the HR programs.
6. Use a results-based approach when designing, developing, and delivering HR programs.
7. Identify potential problem situations and implement effective HR programs to prevent them.
8. Change the role of HR from the administrative and reactive nature to initiator and collaborator approaches.
9. Shift the control, influence, and responsibility for HR to line managers.
10. Provide mechanisms for HR staff and line managers to share in risks and rewards for program failures and successes.

Steps for Improving the Relationship

The degree to which management supports HR programs is based on their perception of the value of the HR function, role of the HR department, and the actions of the HR staff. To improve management support, commitment, and influence, the HR department should carefully analyze each opportunity to improve the relationship with an individual manager or a group of managers. This improvement requires a series of critical steps:

1. *Identify the key managers where support is necessary or improvement is needed.* This step involves selecting individual key managers (i.e., decision makers) from middle-management or senior management, where support is necessary or critical to the success of an HR program. Individuals selected should be effective leaders, either formally or informally.
2. *Analyze and classify the degree of support.* Following the descriptions in the previous section, managers should be classified according to their level of support for the HR function. Input from the entire HR staff may be helpful to classify all key managers.

3. *Analyze reasons for support or non-support.* Managers will usually show support (or non-support) of HR programs based on a series of facts, beliefs, and values related to HR. A fact is something that is indisputable and can be proven without doubt. A belief is an interpretation of the meaning of past or present experiences and is used to predict what will happen in the future. A value is the worth assigned to a particular belief. An example of a fact is a statement such as, "All of my employees participate in the total quality management program." An example of a belief is, "Progressive discipline does not work." The various levels of support outlined previously are usually based on facts, beliefs, or values assigned to the HR effort by individual managers. The key emphasis of this step is to attempt to uncover the basis for the manager's support or lack of support. Which facts, beliefs, or value systems have caused an individual's behavior? Once these are established, a strategy can be selected that may work with the individual manager to improve the supportive relationship.

4. *Select the best strategy.* The strategy appropriate for a particular manager depends on his or her level of support. Using the strategies presented earlier, this step involves selecting the best combination of strategies with the best chances to improve the relationship.

Supportive managers are a welcome sight to the HR department because there is little need for a concentrated effort other than to show appreciation for the support they provide. Possibly they should be involved in HR programs in the capacities described in this chapter. This involvement will usually keep them as strong supporters of HR in the future.

Responsive managers need to see the results from HR programs and understand the effectiveness of HR practices so they will remain responsible supporters. Because they view HR support as a responsibility, these managers seek a return on their investment, whether their investment is funds allocated to HR or the time for participants to be involved in HR programs.

The next two types of managers represent challenges to the HR department. Primary attention should be focused on non-supportive managers who in practice can represent a significant number of managers in the organization, in the range of 25-35 percent. The analysis in the previous step should reveal the basis for the non-support, either facts, beliefs, or values. Based on the analysis, the problem can be tackled by providing additional information, getting these managers involved in the HR effort, or showing them the results of HR programs. Current values or beliefs, if improperly based, need to be clarified and changed. Statements made about a value or belief can usually be refuted diplomatically by implementing several of the strategies outlined in this chapter.

Irresponsible managers are a serious threat to the HR department. Although there is no place in a professional organization for irresponsible thinking or behavior, they do exist and while their numbers are small, they cannot be ignored. If these managers are regarded as leaders in the organization, the HR department is in for real trouble. Dealing with these managers may require confrontations and possibly a few confidential sessions with the top management. Reminding top management of its commitment to the HR effort can possibly influence them to insist the manager refrain from working against the HR department. Otherwise, efforts to show results or get those managers involved in HR programs may be fruitless. These managers may require much candid and frank communication about the reasons for their actions.

From this brief assessment, it's easy to see that some strategies are more appropriate for a particular manager classification. For example, it makes little sense to have an irresponsible manager involved in the HR program. He or she might use the opportunity as a platform with which to destroy the program.

5. *Adjust the approach if necessary.* If an attempt to change a manager's behavior does not work, possibly another approach can be successful. If a manager's action is perceived to be based on a belief, but instead is based on a value, then an adjustment in approach is necessary. The key point is that each manager responds differently. The HR staff should assess their efforts to increase support and make adjustments in strategies to improve it. The primary concern is to move more managers from the less supportive to the more supportive categories.

SUMMARY

This chapter explored the critical influence of the management group on the success of the HR function. It is impossible for an HR function to be successful without the positive and supportive influence of the management group. The target groups for action include the top managers who must demonstrate its commitment to the function through resource allocation. Middle managers who support the functions in a variety of ways are ideal targets for partnership relationships with the HR staff. Supervisors of participants who may function as first or second level managers must support and reinforce the objectives of the program. Without this reinforcement, programs will not be as successful as they should. This chapter outlined a variety of strategies to work effectively with all of these groups, with specific blueprints for success through teamwork and collaborative efforts.

REFERENCES

1. Steinburg, C. "Partnerships With the Line," *Training & Development,* October 1991, pp. 28–35.

2. Fitz-enz, J. *Human Value Management.* San Francisco: Jossey-Bass Publishers, 1990.

3. King, A. S. and Bishop, T. R. "Functional Requisites of Human Resources: Personnel Professionals' and Line Managers' Criteria for Effectiveness." *Public Personnel Management,* Vol. 20, No. 3, Fall 1991, pp. 285–298.

4. Phillips, J. J. *Handbook of Training Evaluation and Measurement Methods,* 2nd Edition. Houston: Gulf Publishing Company, 1991.

5. Stuart, P. "HR and Operations Work Together at Texas Instruments," *Personnel Journal,* April 1992, pp. 64–68.

6. Comment from participant in a seminar on "Building Effective HR Relationships" conducted by the author, 1992.

7. Shimko, B.W. "All Managers Are HR Managers," *HRMagazine,* January 1990, pp. 67–70.

CHAPTER FIVE

Data Collection Techniques

DATA COLLECTION CONSIDERATIONS

While parts of the HR model presented in Chapter 3 focused on data collection, this chapter covers the most common techniques. A data collection technique is a data-gathering device or process administered at appropriate stages in the HR process. Sometimes referred to as evaluation instruments, data collection techniques may come in a variety of forms and are usually divided into the following categories:

- ■ Questionnaires
- ■ Surveys
- ■ Tests
- ■ Interviews

- ■ Focus groups
- ■ Observations
- ■ Organizational Performance Data

This chapter reviews data collection issues and general design considerations, and then presents each technique with specific applications and a few specific design considerations. Before exploring the various data collection techniques, it is helpful to distinguish between external and internal research. The material presented in this chapter focuses on internal research. Internal research includes data gathered within the organization concerning programs, events, and issues facing the organization. External research may involve the use of a literature search, case studies, field surveys, and other methods to collect data on a specific topic. The focus of this book is on the issue of whether or not a specific program, function, or overall HR effort is working as it was planned. To determine this, the research is internal, involving data that should change as a result of the programs.

Types of Data

An important part of evaluation is to collect data directly related to the objectives of the HR program. Sometimes, HR professionals make the assumption that appropriate data needed to show the HR contribution are not available. Fortunately, this is not the case. Most organizations collect the data needed to evaluate HR; they just don't recognize the evaluative potential of that data. The confusion sometimes stems from the variety of outcomes expected from HR programs. The evaluation process is easy for some programs, such as productivity improvement initiatives, where data are readily available. Other programs, with skill and behavioral outcomes, are more difficult to measure and evaluate. Demonstrating that a stress reduction program has decreased costs is much more difficult than demonstrating that assembly line employees are maintaining production and quality standards.

Because of this dilemma, a distinction is made in two general categories of data—hard data and soft data. Hard data are the primary measurement of improvement, presented in rational, undisputed facts that are easily accumulated. They are the most desired type of data to collect. Soft data are usually behaviorally oriented and less credible. In the long run, the ultimate criteria for measuring the effectiveness of management rests with hard data items, such as productivity, profitability, cost control, and quality improvement. Because changes in these data may lag behind changes in the condition of the human organization by many months, it is highly useful for management planning and control to supplement these measures with interim soft data measures of attitudes, motivation, satisfaction, and skills.[1] Although an HR program designed to motivate employees should have an ultimate impact on hard data items, it can be best measured by soft data items. Soft data are more difficult to collect and analyze but are used when hard data are not available.

Hard Data. Hard data can usually be grouped in four categories or subdivisions as shown in Table 5-1. These categories of output, quality, cost, and time are typical performance measures in almost every organization. When they are not available, the basic approach is to convert soft data to one of these four basic measurements.

TABLE 5-1
EXAMPLES OF HARD DATA

OUTPUT	TIME
Units Produced	Equipment Downtime
Tons Manufactured	Overtime
Items Assembled	On-time Shipments
Money Collected	Time to Project Completion
Items Sold	Processing Time
Forms Processed	Supervisory Time
Loans Approved	Break-in Time for New Employees
Inventory/Turnover	Training Time
Patients Visited	Meeting Schedules
Applications Processed	Repair Time
Students Graduated	Efficiency
Tasks Completed	Work Stoppages
Output Per Hour	Order Response
Productivity	Late Reporting
Work Backlog	Lost Time Days
Incentive Bonus	
Shipments	
New Accounts Generated	

COSTS	QUALITY
Budget Variances	Scrap
Unit Costs	Waste
Cost by Account	Rejects
Variable Costs	Error Rates
Fixed Costs	Rework
Overhead Cost	Shortages
Operating Costs	Product Defects
Number of Cost Reductions	Deviation from Standard
Project Cost Savings	Product Failures
Accident Costs	Inventory Adjustments
Program Costs	Time Card Corrections
Sales Expense	Percent of Tasks Completed Properly
	Number of Accidents

The most significant result that can be achieved by any HR program is that involving improvements in the output of the work unit. Every organization, regardless of scope, has basic measurements of work output. Output is measured in absolute terms (production) or as ratios (productivity). Because these measures are normally evaluated by organizations, changes can be easily evaluated by comparing before- and after-program output. The quality of output is probably the most critical variable to measure. Every organization is concerned with improving quality and, consequently, procedures are usually in place to measure quality. Many HR programs are designed to enhance quality, and the results can easily be documented. Costs are another significant item for HR evaluation. Reduction in operating costs, administrative costs, and capital expenditures are sometimes linked to HR programs. In addition, costs are needed to develop a benefits vs. costs analysis for evaluation. Finally, time can be an outcome of HR programs and can be just as critical as cost and quality. A time savings may mean that the product is shipped sooner than anticipated, a project is completed ahead of schedule, a new product is introduced earlier, or the time to repair equipment is reduced. These outcomes translate into additional output or lower operating costs.

The distinction between these four groups of hard data is sometimes unclear, because there may be some overlap. For example, accident costs may be listed under the cost category, the number of accidents listed under quality, and the lost-time days due to an accident listed under the time category. Accidents represent a cost that can easily be determined. Also, they are usually caused by someone making a mistake, a reflection of the quality of the employee's efforts. The days lost from the job represent time lost to the organization. The distinction between the groupings is not as important as developing an awareness of the vast number of measurements in these four areas, and the relative ease at which hard data can be converted to monetary values.

Soft Data. When hard, rational numbers do not exist, soft data may be more meaningful to use in evaluating HR programs. Table 5-2 shows typical types of soft data divided into work habits, skills, work climate, attitudes, and initiative. There may be other ways to classify soft data because there are so many types—the possibilities are limitless.

Employee work habits are important to the success of a work group. Ineffective work habits can lead to an unproductive and dysfunctional work group, while positive work habits can boost the output and morale of the group. HR programs often focus on improving work habits, which can be tied to cost savings. In some organizations, systems are in place to record employee work habits such as absenteeism, tardiness, visits to the first-aid station, and excessive lunch periods.

Skill building is an important area for many HR programs. While the successful application of new skills might result in hard data measurements such as improved production, new skills will usually involve soft data measurements. Examples of soft data skills include making decisions, solving problems, and resolving conflicts. Another potential measurement is the frequency with which the new skill is used. The success of many skill-building programs lies in the frequency of use after the program is completed.

TABLE 5-2
EXAMPLES OF SOFT DATA

WORK HABITS	SKILLS
Absenteeism	Decisions Made
Tardiness	Problems Solved
Visits to the Dispensary	Conflicts Avoided
First Aid Treatments	Grievances Resolved
Violations of Safety Rules	Counseling Problems Solved
Number of Communication Breakdowns	Listening Skills
Excessive Breaks	Presentation Skills
Follow-Up	Interviewing Skills
Disruptions of Others	Reading Speed
	Discrimination Charges Resolved
	Intention to Use New Skills
	Frequency of Use of New Skills

WORK CLIMATE	INITIATIVE
Number of Grievances	Brain Storming Ideas
Number of Discrimination Charges	Implementation of New Ideas
Employee Complaints	Successful Completion of Projects
Job Satisfaction	Number of Suggestions Submitted
Unionization Avoidance	Number of Suggestions Implemented
Employee Turnover	Work Accomplishment
Reduced Litigation	Setting Goals and Objectives

ATTITUDES
Favorable Reactions
Attitude Changes
Perceptions of Job Responsibilities
Perceived Changes in Performance
Employee Loyalty
Increased Confidence

Improving work climate is another important area of measurement. Excessive grievances, discrimination charges, and complaints, as well as increased job dissatisfaction are often the result of an inadequate work climate. Ultimately this climate lowers efficiency or output and increases unionization or turnover.

Some HR programs focus on attitudes of employees and are designed to change perceptions of the job, organization, other employees, or other aspects of the workplace. Attitudes are relatively easy to document with questionnaires and surveys.

A final category of soft data involves initiative. With some HR programs, employees are encouraged to offer new ideas and implement new techniques. The extent to which employees accomplish what they plan provides additional evidence of program success. Also, the employee's initiative to generate ideas and submit suggestions further indicates that improvement has occurred.

As with the hard data, these subdivisions have some overlap. Some items listed under one category could just as appropriately be listed in another. As with hard data, the distinction between the categories is not as important as the awareness of the wide variety of soft data available and the steps needed to convert a monetary value.

Soft Data vs. Hard Data. The preference of hard data in program evaluation does not mean that soft data are not valuable. A program's total success may rest on soft data measurements. For example, in a program to reduce turnover at a large fast food chain, four key measures of success were identified in the program evaluation—all soft data items: trainee turnover, participant's evaluation, interview-to-hire ratios, and reduced litigation.

A comprehensive evaluation would usually provide a combination of hard data and soft data measurements in the evaluation. For example, an HR program for maintenance at Travenol Laboratories used the following measures of success:

- A reduction of costs associated with specific maintenance activities
- Improvement in production equipment processes
- Changes in maintenance responsibilities and procedures
- Improvement in training of maintenance employees
- Changes in organization and personnel.

These changes included both hard data (production and costs) and soft data (increased training, changes in procedures, and changes in the organization).[2] Soft data are usually best when evaluating behavior and skill outcomes. For example, in behavior modeling, which has proven to be a very effective approach to building supervisory skills, the evaluation of behavioral and skill outcomes rests almost entirely on soft data.

Preliminary Design Considerations

Before developing data collection techniques, several issues should be addressed. The following questions can be used to determine the optimum design for the data collection technique.

■ **How will the data be used?** Prior to selecting the technique, the basic purpose(s) of evaluation must be reviewed. Will the data be used to calculate return on investment? Will it be used to strengthen the HR process? Will it be used to attract new participants? The answers can have an impact on the type of data collection technique needed.

■ **How will the data be analyzed?** Data are usually collected to be tabulated, summarized, and reported to others. The types of analyses, including statistical comparisons, should be considered before designing the appropriate technique.

■ **Who will use the information?** Another important consideration is the target audience for communicating results. Who will be reviewing the information in its raw state or in a summarized manner? Answers to this question can lead to specific data items on the data collection issue.

■ **What type of data are needed?** An effective evaluation requires different types of data, including soft and hard data. Which ones are best for the evaluation? While costs, output, time, and quality are usually desired, attitudes, reactions, or observations may be needed.

■ **Should the instrument be tested?** It may be appropriate to test a data collection instrument before using it in program evaluation, particularly in programs representing a significant investment. Testing provides an opportunity to analyze the data to see if there are problems with the design.

■ **Is there a standard instrument?** In some cases, standard instruments can be effective for data collection with less cost than custom-designed instruments. In these cases, program content and objectives must be consistent with the areas covered in the instrument. The measurement of broad-based skills such as communications, human relations, or leadership may be appropriate for standard instruments. For example, in an HR program designed to improve communications, a standard inventory on communications is used in the evaluation.

■ **What are the consequences of wrong answers or biased responses?** An often overlooked issue is the consequence of participants supplying biased information on the instrument. Evaluation data are sometimes supplied on a voluntary or anonymous basis, and biases may enter into the analysis. When opinions are sought, the information may not be reliable. Purposeful wrong answers can possibly influence outcomes.

Validity

Probably the most important characteristic of an evaluation instrument is its validity. A valid instrument measures what the individual using the instrument wishes to measure. The degree to which it performs this function satisfactorily is usually called the relative validity. The HR professional should be concerned with validity when the appropriateness of a particular instrument is questioned. The economics of design may dictate that little time is spent with the subject; whereas, the evaluation of elaborate programs will demand more attention to validity. Four basic approaches are available to determine if an instrument is valid. Adopted by the American Psychological Association, these approaches are: (1) content validity, (2) construct validity, (3) concurrent validity, and (4) predictive validity.[3] The actions taken to make the instrument valid are usually referred to as "defending" the validity of the instrument.

Before discussing validity, the term "correlation" should be briefly defined. Correlation refers to the strength of the relationship between two measures. It is expressed as a coefficient that can be positive or negative, ranging from -1 to +1. Methods for calculating the correlation coefficient are presented in a later chapter.

Content validity. Content validity refers to the extent to which the instrument represents the content of the program as a representative sample of the items in the HR program. Low content validity means that the instrument does not represent a true sample of the HR program; whereas, high content validity means that the instrument represents a good balance of the HR program. To ensure content validity, no important items, behaviors, or information contained in the program should be omitted from the instrument. Also, there should not be an imbalance of the material. The number of items or questions in the instrument should correspond roughly with the amount of time, exposure, or importance of the material in the program. A seven-step procedure for ensuring content validity is contained in another reference.[4]

Construct validity. Construct validity refers to the extent to which an instrument represents the construct it purports to measure. A construct is an abstract variable such as the skill, attitude, or ability that the instrument is intended to measure. Examples of constructs are:

- Attitude toward supervisor
- Ability to read a scale
- Skill in conducting an effective performance discussion

As a first step in defending construct validity, all parts of the construct are defined, and a case is made to show that the instrument is an adequate measure of that construct. The definition of the construct should be as detailed as possible to make it easy to understand. Then construct validity can be defended by expert opinion, correlations, logical deductions, or criterion group studies.

Expert opinion is a relatively easy approach. A group of experts state that the instrument, in their opinion, is an accurate measurement of the construct. Correlations are more complex. In this case, another instrument is used to measure the same or a similar construct, and the results are correlated with the first instrument. Positive correlations would show construct validity. Logical deduction is more subjective. The instrument designer must logically conclude, through a series of deductions, that the instrument does represent a measure of the construct. The criterion group studies can be more useful. The instrument is administered to a group of people possessing an abundance or deficiency of the construct in question. If the result agrees with the existing knowledge about the group, it can be used as a measure of construct validity.

Construct validity is a complex matter. Perhaps an example can help illustrate the process. An HR program is designed to improve organizational commitment for a group of employees. An instrument must be designed to measure the extent of commitment before and after the program. During the program analysis, the following conclusions are made. Employees with high levels of organizational commitment:

■ Have a desire to work hard for the organization (high productivity)
■ Become part of the organization's goals and values (high job satisfaction, job involvement)
■ Have a strong desire to remain with the organization (low turnover, low absenteeism).

The construct in this example is organizational commitment. The instrument is designed to measure job satisfaction and job involvement. Productivity is monitored directly. Data are also collected on absenteeism and turnover. The instrument is administered to employees who are perceived to have a high degree of organizational commitment. Data collected from the instruments show a positive relationship between organizational commitment and job satisfaction, involvement, and productivity and a negative correlation between organizational commitment and absenteeism and turnover. This information provides necessary support for the validity of the organizational commitment construct.

Concurrent validity. Concurrent validity refers to the extent to which an instrument agrees with the results of other instruments administered at approximately the same time to measure the same characteristics. For example, an attitude survey is conducted to measure employee attitudes about employee benefit programs. Another attitude survey, designed for the same purpose, is administered to the same group. If both instruments show the same results, then it can be argued that the instrument is valid based on concurrent validity. Concurrent validity is determined by calculating the correlation coefficient between the results of the instrument in question and the results of a similar instrument.

Predictive validity. Predictive validity refers to the extent to which an instrument can predict future behaviors or results. Although this approach has less application in program evaluation, it may be useful in some situations. For example, the results obtained from an employment test may be used to predict future behavior on the job. The predictive validity must be defended over a sufficient time period. If an instrument predicts a behavior, and a significant number of participants do exhibit that behavior, then the instrument possesses predictive validity. Predictive validity can be calculated and expressed as a correlation coefficient relating the instrument in question to the measure of the predicted results or behavior.

Improving Validity. There are no magic formulas to ensure than an instrument is valid when it is designed. However, a few simple guidelines may help improve validity.[5]

- ■ **Include an ample number of appropriate items.** Too few items on an instrument can hamper the validity, while too many can be cumbersome and time-consuming. A proper balance can improve the validity.
- ■ **Reduce response bias.** Participants responding to questions on an instrument may tend to say what they think administrators want them to say. This desire to please can make an instrument invalid. Participants should be encouraged to provide candid responses.
- ■ **Involve subject matter experts regularly.** One of the best ways to improve validity, particularly content validity, is to have subject matter experts review the materials, processes, steps, and procedures. Individuals who are experts with the topic can help ensure that our efforts are appropriate and the materials we develop are an accurate reflection of the real situation.
- ■ **Ensure accuracy, completeness, and thoroughness.** Every step of the process should be scrutinized to ensure that the instructions are followed, the data analysis is accurate, the collection is rigorous and thorough.
- ■ **Ensure objective instrument administration.** In some cases the staff administering the instrument may be biased in the expected outcomes. For example, if one group is expected to outperform another, the administrator can sometimes influence the results.

Reliability

Reliability is another important characteristic of a data collection instrument. A reliable instrument is one that is consistent enough that subsequent measurements of an item produce approximately the same results. For example, an attitude survey is administered to an employee. The same survey is administered to the same employee two days later. The results should be the same, assuming that nothing has occurred in the interim period to influence the attitude of the employee. A reliable instrument will have the same results. If there is a significant difference each time the instrument is used, then the instrument is unreliable.

The causes of potential fluctuations of results are called errors, and there are a number of sources of errors that affect the reliability of instruments.[6] They include:

- Fluctuations in the mental alertness of participants
- Variations in conditions under which the instrument is administered
- Differences in interpreting the results from the instrument
- Random effects caused by the personal motivation of the participants
- The length of the instrument. (With a longer instrument, more data are collected, but reliability may be increased at the expense of other factors.)

In pre- and post-program measurements where data are collected from participants before and after a program, it is essential to have reliable instruments; otherwise, the changes in responses cannot be attributed to the HR program. Four procedures are available to determine that an instrument is reliable: test/retest, alternate form, split half, and inter-item correlations.

Test/retest is a procedure that involves administering the same test or survey to the same group of employees at two different time periods and calculating the correlation between the two scores. If there is a high degree of positive correlation, then the test is reliable. An **alternate-form method** involves constructing two similar instruments and administering both to employees at the same time and analyzing the correlation between the two scores. A high positive correlation indicates that the instrument is reliable. Constructing a similar instrument is time-consuming, which may make this approach impractical. A **split-half procedure** divides the instrument into two equal parts and compares the results for each half. For example, it might be appropriate to compare responses to even-numbered questions with the odd-numbered questions. The scores of the two halves are compared, and correlations are developed. A high correlation indicates a reliable instrument. A fourth procedure, called **inter-item analysis,** develops correlations between each of the items on the instrument. For example, a survey with 25 items is divided into 25 parts. Correlations are developed comparing each item with all of the others. For more information on reliability, see other references.[7]

Administrative Issues

An instrument used for data collection should be easy to administer and should not be burdensome or difficult for the participant or the HR staff member. Directions and instructions should be simple and straightforward, increasing the likelihood that the instrument will be administered consistently with different groups. Written instructions to participants (as well as verbal explanations) will help to ensure consistent application.

Other characteristics of an effective instrument are simplicity and brevity. Readability levels should be appropriate for the target audience's knowledge, ability, and background. Whenever possible, short objective responses should be sought. Lengthy essay responses detract from the simplistic approach. The least number of questions necessary to cover a topic is recommended. Evaluators tend to over-survey (ask more questions than necessary), and this adds to the length and to the possible frustration of the participants.

As with every other stage of the HR process, economics must be considered in the design and/or selection of an instrument. An effective instrument will be one that is economical for its planned use. Costs must be considered in designing, developing, or purchasing an instrument. The time needed to administer an instrument as well as the time necessary to analyze the data collected and present it in a meaningful format are other cost considerations.

QUESTIONNAIRES

Probably the most common data collection technique is the questionnaire. Ranging from short reaction forms to detailed follow-up instruments, questionnaires come in all sizes. They can be used to obtain subjective information about participant reactions as well as to document measurable results for use in an economic analysis. With this versatility and popularity, it is important that questionnaires be designed properly to satisfy their intended purposes. Improperly worded questionnaires are a major cause of problems in research methods.[8]

Types of Questions

There are five basic types of questions. A questionnaire may contain any or all of these types of questions:

■ **Open-ended question** asks for an unlimited answer. The question is followed by ample blank space for the response.

- ■ **Checklist** presents a list of items. A participant is asked to check those items that apply to the situation.
- ■ **Two-way question** asks for alternate responses, a yes/no, or other possibilities.
- ■ **Multiple-choice question** presents several choices. The participant is asked to select the most correct one.
- ■ **Ranking scales** requires the participant to rank a list of items.

Table 5-3 shows examples of each of these types of questions.

TABLE 5-3
QUESTIONNAIRES: TYPES OF QUESTIONS

1. Open-Ended Question:
   What problems have you encountered in using the customer contact skills presented in the program?

   _____

   _____

   _____

2. Checklist:
   In the following list, check the items that are considered important and necessary for success in your job.

☐ Decisiveness	☐ Energy
☐ Initiative	☐ Sensitivity
☐ Stress Tolerance	☐ Oral Communication Skills
☐ Risk Taking	☐ Written Communication Skills
☐ Creativity	☐ Flexibility
☐ Leadership	☐ Independence

3. Two-Way Question:
   As a result of the new PRIDE program, I have a better understanding of the customer focus portion of my job.
   Yes _____   No _____

4. Multiple-Choice Question:
   The absenteeism rate for our company last year was:
   a. 2.0%   b. 2.8%
   c. 3.2%   d. 4.1%

(continued on next page)

5. Ranking Scales:

The following list contains five important aspects of our pay-for-performance program. Place a one (1) by the item that is most important, and so on. The five (5) will be the least important item on the list.

Objective Measures	_____
Frequent Payouts of Bonuses	_____
Results Based on Individual Performance	_____
Frequent Feedback on Results	_____
Opportunity to Help Establish Targets	_____

Questionnaire Design Issues

Questionnaire design can be a simple and logical process. A flawed design or an improperly worded questionnaire will be confusing, frustrating, and potentially embarrassing when it is administered. The following steps can ensure that a valid, reliable, and effective questionnaire is developed.

■ **Determine the information needed.** A first step in questionnaire design is to itemize the topics covered in the program or the topics that were in some way related to the program. Questions can be developed later. It might be appropriate to develop this information in outline form so that related questions can be grouped.

■ **Select the type(s) of questions.** Using the five types of questions described earlier, select the type(s) that will be best for the intended purpose, taking into consideration the planned data analysis and variety of data to be collected.

■ **Develop the questions.** Develop the questions based on the type of question(s) planned and the information needed. Questions should be simple and straightforward to avoid confusion or lead the participant to a desired response. Terms or expressions unfamiliar to the participant should be avoided or explained. Develop the appropriate number and variety of questions, taking into consideration validity and reliability issues.

■ **Test the questions.** After the questions are developed, test them for understanding. Ideally, questions should be tested on a group of participants in a pilot program. If this is not feasible, they should be tested on a group of employees at approximately the same job level and working environment as the potential participants. Critical input is very helpful to revise and improve questions.

■ **Develop the completed questionnaire and prepare a data summary.** Develop the questions into a neatly arranged questionnaire with proper instructions. In addition, prepare a data summary sheet so that the data can be tabulated quickly for summary and interpretation.

After completing the above steps, the questionnaire is ready for use.

Questionnaire Applications

Questionnaires have a place in the evaluation of almost every type of HR program. They are used to:

- collect reactions from program participants
- uncover specific problems in program design
- solicit recommendations for improvement
- outline plans for the application of program materials
- report successes from the application of program materials
- identify barriers to success
- suggest who should be involved in future programs.

Questionnaires can be administered before programs begin, during their implementation, or after the program is fully implemented or completed. They represent one of the most versatile and effective methods of obtaining important information about a program's design, effectiveness, and weaknesses. A few examples of specific HR applications are:

- Survey new employees for their reaction to the employment process in order to judge the effectiveness of the orientation program.
- Obtain feedback from new management trainees as they progress through a twelve-month training program.
- Gain input and suggestions for a new benefit program from a sample of employees.
- Obtain feedback from sales representatives on a new incentive program.
- Obtain feedback from employees and their supervisors on a new performance appraisal process.
- Gain input on program features and concerns from participants in a new wellness program.

The applications are varied, making questionnaires one of the most versatile data collection techniques. For additional information on questionnaire design see other references.[9]

SURVEYS

Surveys represent a specific type of questionnaire with several applications for measuring HR program results. An HR program may be designed to change employee attitudes toward the job, policies, procedures, benefits, pay, the organization, and the immediate supervisor. Periodic measurements show changes in attitudes that have an impact on a work group, department, division, or entire organization. One report estimated that over 45 percent of mid- and large-sized employers conducted a written employee survey in the last three years.[10]

Sometimes an organization will conduct a survey to measure employee attitudes. Then, based on the feedback, HR programs are undertaken to change attitudes in areas where improvement is needed. Sometimes referred to as attitude surveys, opinion surveys, feedback surveys, or employee surveys, this data-collection technique can help evaluate HR in a variety of ways. Surveys can be used to:

- Provide feedback to managers on how well they balance their various managerial and supervisory responsibilities.
- Build a database to inform the organization of the content and processes of selecting, developing, training, and retaining employees.
- Assist in the design and modification of HR policies, management systems, and decision-making processes, thereby improving overall organizational effectiveness.
- Provide a way to assess progress during periods of change.
- Assess the organization's internal employee relations climate and monitor the trends.[11]

Measuring attitudes is a complex task. It is impossible to measure an attitude precisely, because information gathered may not represent the participant's true feelings or planned actions. Also, the behavior, beliefs, and feelings of an individual will not always correlate. Attitudes tend to change with time, and there are a number of factors that form an individual's attitude. Even with these shortcomings, it is possible to get a reasonable measure of employee attitudes.

Survey Design Issues

The principles of survey construction are similar to questionnaire design discussed earlier. However, a few guidelines are unique to the design or purchase of an attitude survey.[12]

- **Limit statements to areas in which employees are capable of responding.** Employees should be capable of expressing an attitude or opinion on the subject. For example, suppose employees are asked about their attitude toward a job posting system in the company. If the system has just been initiated and little information has been provided, it will be difficult for the employees to respond with accurate information.

■ **Involve appropriate management.** Executives and administrators involved with this process must be committed to take action when survey results indicate that action is necessary. Management concerns, issues, and suggestions should be addressed early in the process, before the survey is conducted.

■ **Focus on the attitudes that must be measured.** While this may be obvious, it is very easy to stray into areas unrelated to the subject. "Let's check their attitude on this" is a familiar trap. While it may be interesting information, if it is not related to program objectives, it should be omitted.

■ **Keep survey statements as simple as possible.** Participants need to understand the meaning of a statement or question. Statements should be precise, straightforward, and easy to understand. Ambiguous or vague statements must be avoided.

■ **Ensure that participant responses are anonymous.** Participants should feel free to respond openly to statements or questions without fear of retaliation. The confidentiality of responses is of the utmost importance. Research indicates a link between survey anonymity and accuracy.[13] If data are collected that can identify a respondent, then a neutral third party should collect and process the data.

■ **Communicate the purpose of the survey.** Participants will usually cooperate in an activity when they understand the rationale for it. When a survey is administered, participants should be provided an appropriate explanation of its purpose and be told what will be done with the information. Also, they should be encouraged to provide correct and proper statements or answers.

■ **Plan and communicate survey comparisons.** Attitude measures by themselves are virtually meaningless. They must be compared to attitudes before or after the HR program or compared to other groups or organizations. The attitudes of a group of employees may be compared to all employees, a division, or a department. For purchased surveys, information may be available from similar industries in the form of norm data. Specific comparisons should be planned before administering the survey.

■ **Design for easy tabulation.** In an attitude survey, yes/no responses or varying degrees of agreement and disagreement are the usual formats. The two types of responses are illustrated in Table 5-4.

Uniform types of responses make it easier for tabulation and comparisons. On a scale of strongly agree to strongly disagree, numbers are usually assigned to reflect responses. For instance, a one (1) may represent strongly disagree and a five (5) strongly agree. An average response of 2.2 on a pre-program survey followed by a post-program average response of 4.3 shows a significant change in

TABLE 5-4
TYPICAL ATTITUDE SURVEY QUESTIONS

Yes/No Responses	Yes	No
My supervisor gives us credit for work well done	☐	☐
My supervisor solicits our ideas about our job	☐	☐

Agreement/Disagreement Responses

	Strongly Agree	Agree	Neutral	Disagree	Strongly Disagree
Our organization has too many policies that interfere with doing a good job.	☐	☐	☐	☐	☐
Management gives me support on my personal problems.	☐	☐	☐	☐	☐

attitude. Some experts argue that a five-point scale merely permits the respondent to select the midpoint and avoid making a choice. If this is a concern, an even-numbered scale should be used.

Vendor-Produced Surveys

Many organizations purchase existing surveys to use in HR program evaluation, and they have several advantages. They can save time in development and pilot testing. Most of the reputable companies producing and marketing surveys designed them to be reliable and valid for specific applications. Often these firms can easily tabulate the results, thereby saving additional time and expense. Also, externally developed surveys make it easy to compare results with others. For example, a company conducted a survey to determine what employees thought about an employee empowerment program. Based on the results, the company planned a communications program to reinforce the major elements where needed. They conducted a survey before and after the communications program and compared the results with other organizations within the same or similar industries.

Survey Applications

Surveys have a significant place in HR measurement and evaluation. In some organizations, surveys are the primary means to evaluate the HR function. A typical approach is to conduct surveys annually, feedback the results to employees, outline specific action plans, correct problem areas or deficiencies, and measure progress the next year.

In addition to overall measures, surveys can be used to measure attitudes toward a specific function of HR or an individual program. For example, employees may be asked to provide responses about compensation, benefits, or the affirmative action program. As with overall survey results, this information can provide feedback necessary to make changes, implement new programs, or discontinue old programs.

Specific programs can easily be evaluated based on attitude surveys. For example, when a company implements a new total quality management (TQM) program it can solicit employee attitudes to identify major problems, concerns, or successes connected with the program. Because surveys are a type of a questionnaire, their use is almost as widespread as questionnaires, making them an integral part of the data collection process.

TESTS

Testing is used to measure learning in program evaluations. It is important in HR functions such as education and training, organizational development and change, or in specific programs such as total quality management, gainsharing, or skill-based pay. Pre- and post-program test scores reveal changes in skills and knowledge attributed to the program. By any measure, the use of tests in the 1980s increased dramatically and is expected to continue to do so in the 1990s.[15]

Types of Tests

While there are several types of tests in use in HR, tests can be classified in three ways. The first classification is based on the medium used for administering the test. The most common media for tests is paper and pencil. However, performance tests use simulated tools or the actual equipment, and computer-based tests use computers and video displays. Written tests are the most common type of tests used in the HR process and represent a quick method for assessing knowledge. Most written tests are inexpensive to administer and to score for large groups.

Performance tests are usually more costly to develop and administer than are written examinations. Performance testing allows the participant to exhibit skills, knowledge, or attitudes. The skill can be manual, verbal, or analytical, or a combination of the three. Performance testing is used frequently in job-related training to allow the participants to demonstrate what they have learned. In supervisory and management training, performance testing comes in the form of skill practices or role plays. Participants are asked to demonstrate the discussion or problem-solving skills they have acquired. In selection, performance testing determines placement possibilities.

Computer-based tests and those using interactive video are relatively new developments in testing and hold great promise for the future. A computer monitor or video screen presents the test questions or situations. Test participants respond by typing on a keyboard or touching the screen.[16] Interactive videos have a strong element of realism because the person being tested can react to images—often moving pictures and video vignettes that reproduce the real job situation.

The second way to classify tests is by purpose and content. This classification divides tests into aptitude tests or achievement tests. Aptitude tests measure basic skills or innate or acquired capacity to learn. An achievement test assesses a person's knowledge or competence in a particular subject. It measures the end result of education and training.

A third way in which to classify tests is by test design. The most common designs are oral examinations, essay tests, objective tests, and performance tests. Oral examinations and essay tests have limited use in HR program evaluation. They are probably more useful in academic settings. Objective tests call for answers that are specific and precise, based on the objectives of a program. Attitudes, feelings, creativity, problem-solving processes, and other intangible skills and abilities cannot be measured accurately with objective tests. Performance testing is useful in training, selection, and promotion.

Test Design Issues

For a test to be effective, the following elements are necessary in the design and administration of the test.[17]

- **The test should be a representative sample of the HR program.** The test should allow the participant to demonstrate as many skills as possible related to the program. This increases the validity of the test and makes it more meaningful to the participant.
- **The test should be thoroughly planned.** Every phase of test administration should be planned—the timing, participant preparation, collection of necessary materials and tools, and evaluation of the results.
- **Thorough and consistent instructions are necessary.** As with other instruments, the quality of the instructions can influence test results. All participants should be provided with the same instructions, which should be clear and concise. Charts, diagrams, blueprints, and other aids should be provided if they are normally provided in the work setting.

■ **Procedures for objective evaluation should be developed.** Acceptable standards must be developed for the test. Standards are sometimes difficult to develop because there can be varying degrees of speed, skill, and quality associated with test outcomes. Predetermined standards must be developed so employees know in advance what has to be accomplished to be considered satisfactory and acceptable for test completion.

■ **Information that will lead participants astray should be omitted.** The HR program is designed to assess particular skills. Participants should not be led astray or tricked into obvious wrong answers unless they face the same obstacles in the real-world environment.

Following these general guidelines, tests can be effective tools for HR program evaluation.

Test Applications

Testing is appropriate in any situation where employees learn skills or knowledge. Primary applications are in training and development and employment functions.[18] The following is a sampling of some applications of testing in HR:

■ A large financial services company began a continuous process improvement program with its employees. Using a variety of processes including training sessions, team meetings, newsletters, posters, payroll stuffers, and other media, employees are taught fundamentals of continuous process improvement. The company administers tests at six-month intervals to measure the general level of knowledge among employees concerning different processes, terms, techniques, and principles in the program. This process provides a measure of progress from which the program planners and coordinators could make changes.

■ A large waste treatment company selects supervisors through a combination of an assessment process and a variety of tests. The assessment process uses exercises that allow supervisor candidates to demonstrate the skills and abilities needed to function in a supervisor job. Each exercise is validated through the content validity process. The tests are related to specific job dimensions and are validated in other settings for similar jobs. The candidate's performance on the assessment exercises and tests provides an overall rating to determine whether he or she should be part of the supervisory pool.

■ An engineering company requires newly employed industrial engineers to demonstrate time study skills. Participants are asked to conduct a time study on an actual job in a plant. An expert observes the participants and performs the same study and compares his results with participants. These comparisons provide an adequate reflection of the skills needed in the job.

■ As part of a management development program, managers at one company are trained to motivate average performers. Part of the evaluation requires managers to write a skill practice session in an actual situation involving an average performer in the department. Participants are then asked to conduct the skill practice (performance test) with another member of the group using the real situation and applying the principles and steps taught in the program. The instructor observes the skill practice and provides a written critique at the end of the practice. These critiques provide part of the evaluation of the program.

■ Potential aircraft assemblers participate in a pre-employment program on the basics of aircraft production assembly techniques. At the end of the program, participants are required to complete a special job-related project. They are provided a blueprint and a list of materials and are asked to build the item according to the specifications outlined on the blueprint. The time for completion, quality of the work, and the accuracy of the completed project are recorded. A successful combination is necessary for the candidate to be selected for the permanent job of an aircraft assembler.

These are only a few of the many applications of testing to measure current levels of skills and abilities. Applications of testing are enormous because so many of the HR programs involve learning.[19]

INTERVIEWS

One of the most useful data collection techniques is the interview. Because of their flexibility, interviews can be conducted by the HR staff, the participant's supervisor, or a third party. Interviews can secure data not available in performance records, or data difficult to obtain through written responses or observations. Also, interviews can uncover success stories that can be useful in a program's overall evaluation. Participants may be reluctant to fully describe the results of a program in a questionnaire but will volunteer information to a skillful interviewer who uses probing techniques. The interview process will help secure reactions, uncover changes in job-related behavior, and determine program results. In some programs, the interview process comprises the total evaluation, although it's not recommended.[20] A major disadvantage of the interview is that it is time-consuming. The interviewer must prepare to ensure that the process is reliable and is conducted in an effective manner.

Types of Interviews

Interviews usually fall into two basic types: structured and unstructured.[21] A structured interview is much like a questionnaire in that specific questions are asked with little room to deviate from the desired responses. The primary advantages of the structured interview over the questionnaire are that the interview process can ensure that all questions have been covered and the interviewer understands the responses supplied by the participant. When compared to the unstructured interview, the structured interview is more efficient and accurate for collecting factual information.

The unstructured interview allows for probing for more information and provides the most in-depth information for complex or elusive issues. This type of interview employs a few general questions that can lead to more detailed information as data are uncovered. The interviewer who conducts an unstructured interview should be skilled in the probing process and use typical probing questions such as these:

- Can you explain your response in more detail?
- Would you give me an example of what you are saying?
- Could you explain the difficulty that you say you encountered?
- What other factors influenced this?
- Can you explain this process in more detail?

By using probing questions, the interviewer can delve more deeply into the information needed from the participant and still follow no definite format. The interviewer may also acknowledge what has been said with a follow-up question for more information or can restate the previous comment and thus obligate the interviewee obligated to respond with more information.

Interview Design Issues

Although the same principles involved in designing questions for a questionnaire can also apply to interview questions, here are a few specific steps in the development of an interview that can lead to a more effective instrument:[22]

- **List basic questions to be asked.** After a decision has been made about the type of interview, itemize specific questions. Each question should be brief, precise, and designed for easy response.
- **Try out the questions.** Interview questions should be tested on several participants and their responses should be analyzed. If possible, the interviews should be conducted as part of the trial run of the HR program.

■ **Train the interviewers.** The interviewer should be trained to be effective with probing, collecting information, and summarizing it in a meaningful form.

■ **Provide clear instructions to the interviewee.** The person being interviewed should understand the purpose of the interview and know what will be done with the information. Expectations, conditions, and rules of the interview should be thoroughly discussed. Confidentiality considerations should be clearly communicated.

■ **Administer the interviews according to a plan.** As with the other evaluation instruments, interviews should be conducted according to a predetermined plan. The timing of the interview, the person to conduct the interview, and the place of the interview are all relevant issues in developing an interview plan. When there is a large number of participants, a sampling plan may be necessary to save time and reduce the cost of the evaluation.

Interview Applications

As with questionnaires, the interview represents another versatile data-collection technique. A few specific applications of the interview reveal the varied uses of this technique.

■ Many organizations conduct exit interviews with employees who are voluntarily leaving. These interviews provide important information for changing HR policies and practices to decrease employee turnover, improve efficiencies, etc.

■ A high tech firm uses telephone interviews to gather information from employment applicants who are not offered a job. The purpose is to ensure that they were treated in a professional way and that the correct procedures and policies were followed. Although these employees are not pleased with the outcome of the process, they will usually provide helpful information on the entire employment process.

■ Some organizations use field interviews to follow-up on supervisory training programs to ensure that supervisors used the program and achieved results. The interview uncovers specific actions taken and the successes achieved or the barriers to implementing the material.

■ An electric utility conducts random interviews with employees who recently used a new preferred provider organization (PPO). The interview is part of an evaluation of the effectiveness of the PPO. Interviewees relate their experiences with the new PPO and any problems encountered.

■ A large bank conducts interviews with a sample of employees to collect information on the effectiveness of the salary administration program.

Because the program involves several elements, from job descriptions to performance reviews, it is important for the bank to obtain information on how all of these elements are functioning. The information provides feedback to the program planners for possible changes in the program to increase its effectiveness. Often, the success of a salary administration program hinges on the users' perception of the program.

■ A multi-industry firm interviews a randomly selected group of participants from a productivity improvement effort. Employees are asked to detail their actions to improve productivity and the results they achieved from their efforts. If no results were achieved, participants are asked to explain what prevented improvements. Probing allows the interviewer to detail specifics.

This sample of applications illustrates the many ways in which interviews can be used to collect information to help evaluate the effectiveness of an HR program and demonstrates the program's impact on the organization.

FOCUS GROUPS

Focus groups are particularly useful when in-depth feedback is needed for HR program evaluation. For some HR professionals, the focus group process is becoming the evaluation instrument of choice.[23] The focus group is a small group discussion conducted by an experienced facilitator. It is designed to solicit qualitative judgments on a particular topic or issue following a planned agenda. Group members are required to provide their input and individual input builds on group input.

For years, the HR profession has largely ignored the focus group potential for evaluating HR programs. In other types of research—particularly marketing—the focus group has long been used to generate quality information on which to make decisions. Marketing researchers used the focus group to test new products, assess marketing campaigns, and evaluate advertising. The process is also used to secure input for changes in company policies, provide feedback on problems within an organization, and collect information for a program needs analyses. Now, HR professionals are using the focus group process to measure results from programs. With this process, individuals build on the ideas and comments of others to provide an in-depth view not attainable from questioning people individually. Unexpected comments and new perspectives can be easily explored.

The basic premise for using focus groups is that when quality judgments are subjective, several individual judgments are better than one. When compared with questionnaires, surveys, tests, or interviews, the focus group process has several advantages:[24]

■ A focus group is inexpensive and can be quickly planned and conducted.

■ The group process in which participants often motivate one another is an effective method for generating new ideas and hypotheses.

■ The format is flexible to allow for in-depth probing and confirmation.

■ Its flexibility makes it possible to explore an HR program's unexpected possible outcomes or applications.

In summary, the focus group is an inexpensive and quick way to determine the strengths and weaknesses of an HR program, particularly those that focus on management and supervisory topics. However, for complete evaluation, focus group information should be combined with data from other instruments.

Focus Group Design Issues

While there are no standards on how to use focus groups for measurement evaluation, the following guidelines should be helpful:[25]

■ **Plan topics, questions, and strategy carefully.** As with any evaluation instrument, planning is critical. The specific topics, discussion questions, and issues to be discussed must be carefully planned and sequenced. This enhances the reliability of the process as results are combined from one group to another. Also, it ensures that the group process is productive and stays on track.

■ **Secure management buy-in.** Because this is a relatively new process for HR evaluation, it might be unknown to some management groups. Managers should be informed about focus groups and their advantages in order to raise confidence levels for the information obtained from group sessions.

■ **Keep the group size small.** The group size should be appropriate to provide opportunity for one participant to build on another's comments. While there is no precise group size, a range of 6 to 12 seems to be appropriate for most focus group applications. A group has to be large enough to collect different points of view, but small enough to provide each participant a chance to discuss issues freely and exchange comments.

■ **Select an appropriate number of groups.** While there is no magic number of total groups, it is important that enough focus groups are assembled to provide the quality information that can be used to reach conclusions. While it is dangerous to suggest a percentage, a range of 5 to 20 percent of the target population may be appropriate for most focus group applications. This number depends on many factors such as the size of the target group, the

importance of having complete group representation of the target population, and the cost involved in conducting additional focus groups.

■ **Use a representative sample of the target population.** Groups should be
stratified appropriately so that participants represent the target population.
The group should be homogeneous in experience, job level, and influence in
the organization.

■ **Prepare facilitators.** Unlike some instruments, the success of a focus group
rests with the facilitator. The rapport that the facilitator builds with the group
can encourage participants to fully express their feelings. The facilitator
must be trained in the focus group process and have an opportunity to practice it before using it to collect evaluation data. Facilitators must understand
group dynamics, know how to filter opinions from vocal members of the
group, be able to moderate those who want to dominate the group, and be
able to create an environment in which participants feel comfortable in
offering comments. Because of these strict requirements, some organizations use external facilitators.

Focus Group Applications

The focus group is particularly helpful when information is needed about the
quality of an HR program or to assess behavior change resulting from the program. For example, the focus group process has been used in the following evaluation situations:

■ To evaluate an HR program design and implementation in a pilot test program.
■ To assess reactions to specific program elements, features, or components.
■ To judge the overall effectiveness of the program as perceived by the participants immediately following a program's implementation.
■ To determine the program's impact in a follow-up evaluation after the program has been completed or implemented.

Essentially, the process is helpful when evaluation information is needed that
cannot be collected adequately with other methods. Some specific applications of
the focus group are:

■ A large utility company undertook a program to change the culture of the
organization from bureaucratic and inefficient to creative and entrepreneur-
ial. As part of the evaluation for this program, groups of randomly selected
employees were assembled in focus groups to discuss the success of the program and note specific instances where the program was working.

■ A large bank was interested in the perception of the employee benefits package. A sample of employees was invited in focus groups to secure information about the perceived adequacy of the benefits package, problems with specific benefits, and specific concerns over the direction of employee benefit planning.

■ A government agency conducted a program on managing diversity. As part of the evaluation of a pilot program, all participants reported on changes in attitudes and perceptions in focus groups. Also, in addition to the evaluation information, participants outlined specific steps needed to continue with the implementation of the program.

■ An international service firm implemented a quality of work life program. In focus groups, evaluators determined reactions, successes, and failures of the program.

Essentially any application using the interview may be appropriate for the focus group. Its use is growing and the results are impressive.

OBSERVATIONS

Another useful evaluation data-collecting technique involves observing participants either before, during, or after an HR program to record changes in on-the-job behavior. This technique is appropriate for measuring the success of programs such as organizational change, safety, total quality, and training. The observer may be a member of the HR staff, the participant's supervisor, a member of a peer group, or an outside party. The most common observer, and probably the most practical, is a member of the HR staff. Observation is an excellent method of evaluating behavioral change because actual behavior is measured. Also, the participants' interactions with others, both verbal and nonverbal, can be evaluated.[26]

Observation Design Issues

The effectiveness of the observation process can be improved with the following guidelines for their design and development.

■ **Observers must be fully prepared.** Observers must fully understand what information is sought. They must be trained for the assignment and offered a chance to practice observation skills.

■ **The observations should be systematic.** The process must be planned so that the observation is executed effectively without surprises. In some cases, participants being observed may be informed in advance about the observation and the reasons they are being observed. The timing of observations should be planned. If an observer must observe a participant when times are not normal (that is, in a crisis), the data collected may be unreliable.

■ **The observers should know how to interpret and report what they see.** The observation process involves judgmental decisions. Observers must analyze behaviors as they are being displayed, including the range of actions taken by the participants. Observers should know how to summarize behavior and report results in a meaningful manner.

■ **The observer's influence should be minimized.** While it is impossible to completely isolate the effect of an observer, the presence of the observer and the significance of the activity should be minimized. Otherwise, participants being observed may display the behavior they think is appropriate, and they will usually be at their best. Observers should dress in a similar manner to the participant being observed and should stand at a discrete distance, if possible. Also, the longer the observation period, the less the disruptive effect of the observer.

Observation Methods

Five methods of observation are available: behavior checklist, coded behavior record, delayed report, audio monitoring, and video recording. The method should be selected according to the type of information needed.[27] A **behavior checklist** can be useful for recording the presence, absence, frequency, or duration of a participant's behavior as it occurs. To make observation more effective, only a small number of behaviors should be listed in the checklist and they should be listed in a logical sequence if they normally occur in sequence. Also, behaviors expected to be used more frequently should be placed first so they can be easily checked. A checklist has some disadvantages. It will not usually provide information on the quality, intensity, or possibly the circumstances surrounding the behavior observed. Measuring the duration of a behavior is difficult and may require a stopwatch and a section on the form to record the time interval.

A **coded behavior record** is more time-consuming than a checklist. Codes are entered to identify a specific behavior. This approach is useful when it is essential to document, as much as possible, what actually happened or when too many behaviors exist for a checklist. Also, coding can often be compiled on a computer. Disadvantages of this approach are that the data are difficult to summarize and interpret, and the observer must remember special codes or devise codes as the observation is taking place.

A third observation method is the **delayed report** in which the observer does not use any forms or written materials during the observation, but rather, information is either recorded after the observation is completed or at particular time intervals during an observation. The observer tries to reconstruct behavior during the observation period. An important advantage of this approach is that the observer is not as noticeable, because no forms are completed or notes taken during the observation. The observer can be a part of the situation and less distracting. A disadvantage is that the delayed information may not be as accurate and reliable as the information collected at the time the behavior occurred.

The fourth observation method is **audio monitoring of conversations of employees** who use the behavior learned from an HR program. While this approach may stir some controversy, it is an effective way to determine if skills are being applied consistently and effectively. For it to work smoothly, it must be fully explained and the rules clearly communicated.

A final, and possibly least useful, method is a **video recording of the behavior.** This technique records exactly what happened in every detail. Several disadvantages inhibit its use. It may be awkward and cumbersome to provide for video taping of the behavior. When compared to direct observation, the participants may be unnecessarily nervous or self-conscious when they are being video taped. If the camera is concealed, the privacy of the participant may be invaded.

Observation Applications

Although not as versatile as other data collection techniques, the observation process does have some important applications for measurement and evaluation of an HR function. Whenever a specific skill or the result of the application of a skill is to be verified, direct observation may be the most effective approach. Some specific examples of observations are as follows:

■ As part of a total quality management program in a telecommunications company, all customer contact employees are expected to respond to customer requests in a helpful and productive way, using a specific step-by-step procedure. To determine whether employees respond properly, supervisors monitor telephone conversations on a selected, and sometimes random, basis.

■ In a sales training program for a retail firm, new sales representatives learn a specific process to generate sales, using a series of steps. After the program is completed, the sales reps are observed by a "planted" potential customer. The use of specific skills is recorded through the delayed report method.

■ After the implementation of a corrective discipline program in a waste management company, a member of the HR staff attends randomly selected disciplinary performance discussions to see if the supervisor followed the specific steps for applying corrective discipline. The HR staff member uses the behavior checklist approach to determine if the supervisor followed the process, steps, and actions when discussing the disciplinary problem.

■ A claims processing center for an insurance company was experiencing a perceived tardiness problem. Although employees were not required to punch time cards, they could log in the times. Management was concerned that the times were not accurate. The company implemented a tardiness reduction program and stressed to employees that they must be on time and accurately record work hours. The number of employees arriving in the department late past the normal work period was observed and recorded prior to the program as well as after the program to measure the change. The delayed report method was used. Although this was not 100 percent accurate, it provided an adequate measure of the changes in tardiness.

These examples show the various applications of observation to HR measurement. It can be an important part of the data collection.

ORGANIZATIONAL PERFORMANCE DATA

Data are available in every organization to measure performance. Although it may appear awkward to refer to performance records as a data collecting technique or evaluation instrument, in the context of HR evaluation, records serve the same purpose as focus groups or attitude surveys. They enable management to measure performance in areas such as output, quality, costs, and time and are necessary for an accurate evaluation system. Table 5-5 lists common performance records or measurements for employees.

Existing data should be considered first in measuring and evaluating an HR program. In most organizations, this data will be available. If not, additional record-keeping systems will have to be developed for analysis and measurement. At this stage, as with many other stages in the process, the question of economics must be considered. Is it economical to develop the record-keeping system necessary to evaluate an HR program? If the costs are greater than the expected return for the entire program, then it is meaningless to develop them.

Using Existing Data

If existing records are available, specific guidelines are recommended to ensure that the measurement system is easily developed.[28]

■ Identify appropriate records. The performance records of the organization should be thoroughly researched to identify those that are related to the pro-

TABLE 5-5
EXAMPLES OF PERFORMANCE RECORDS

■ Absenteeism	■ Output
■ Accident Costs, Accident Rates	■ Overtime
■ Break-in Time for New Hires	■ Percent of Quota Achieved
■ Budget Variances	■ Production Schedules
■ Complaints, Employee and Customer	■ Productivity
■ Cost Reduction	■ Processing Time
■ Costs, Overhead	■ Project Schedule Variations
■ Costs, Unit	■ Rejects, Scrap
■ Cycle Time	■ Reports Completed
■ Design Time	■ Sales (Revenue)
■ Delivery Time	■ Sick Leave Costs
■ Downtime	■ Supervisor Bonuses
■ Efficiency	■ Tardiness
■ Employees Promoted	■ Terminations, Employee
■ Equipment Utilization	■ Time Card Corrections
■ Errors, Employee	■ Transactions Completed
■ Grievances	■ Turnover
■ Inventory Adjustments	■ Work Backlog
■ New Accounts	■ Work Stoppages
■ On-time Shipments	

posed objectives of the HR program. Frequently, an organization will have several performance measures related to the same item. For example, the efficiency of a production unit can be measured in a variety of ways:

■ The number of units produced per hour.
■ The number of on-schedule production units.
■ The percent utilization of the equipment.
■ The percent of equipment downtime.
■ The labor cost per unit of production.
■ The overtime required per unit of production.
■ Total unit cost.

Each of these, in its own way, measures the efficiency of the production of a work unit. All related records should be reviewed to identify those that are most relevant to the HR program.

■ **Determine if a sampling plan is necessary.** When a large number of participants are involved in a program or when total numbers are not available, a sampling of records may be adequate to supply the information needed. The sampling plan should be structured to provide an adequate sample size based on random selection. An example will illustrate this point:

An orientation program, coupled with new employee training, was planned for new machine operators in a large machining operation. The combination of orientation and entry-level training was expected to reduce waste and increase the output of new operators. Because the program began with new recruits, their output and scrap rates were collected and monitored. These items were compared to the records of a sample of other employees with approximately the same age and skill who began work with the company before the program was implemented. The performance over a three-month period was monitored through this approach. This method produced a realistic comparison of the performance of the two groups. Significant differences in performance could most likely be attributed to the new program. This approach was more appropriate than comparing the new group with the average of the entire work force of machine operators.

■ **Convert current records to usable ones.** Occasionally, existing performance records are integrated with other data and are difficult to isolate from unrelated data. In this situation, all existing related data records to be used in the measurement should be extracted and retabulated to be more appropriate for comparison in the evaluation. Conversion factors may be necessary. For example, the average number of new sales orders per month may be reported regularly in the performance measures for the sales department. In addition, another performance record may report the sales costs per sales representative. However, the average cost per new sale is needed for the evaluation of an HR program. The two existing performance records are combined to supply the data necessary for comparison.

■ **Develop a collection plan.** A data-collection plan defines when data are collected, who will collect it, how it will be collected, and where it will be collected. This plan should contain provisions for the evaluator to secure copies of performance records in a timely manner so that the items can be recorded and made available for analysis.

Developing New Data

In some cases, performance records are not available for the information needed to measure the effectiveness of an HR program. The HR staff must guide the development of these record-keeping systems, if they are economically feasible.

For example, one organization implemented a new employee orientation system on a company-wide basis. It planned to use several methods of evaluation, including comparisons in turnover in the first six months. This "early turnover" is the percentage of employees who leave the company in the first six months of their employment. An effective employee orientation program should influence this turnover figure. At the time of the program's inception, early turnover data were not available. The organization began collecting early turnover figures for comparison when it implemented the program, thus providing a basis for program evaluation.

When creating new records, several questions are relevant:

■ Which department will develop the record-keeping system?
■ Who will record and monitor the data?
■ Where will it be recorded?
■ Will forms be used?
■ Who will bear the costs?

These questions will usually involve other departments or a management decision extending beyond the scope of the HR department. Possibly the administration division, the finance department, or industrial engineering section will be instrumental in determining whether new records are needed and how they should be collected.

SUMMARY

Table 5-6 summarizes the features of evaluation instruments presented in this chapter. This table can serve as a quick reference to compare the various types of instruments used in evaluation. It is adapted in part from an aid developed by the U.S. Office of Personnel Management. It is important to remember that a variety of instruments is often appropriate in an evaluation effort. For example, Ames Department Stores uses three evaluation instruments for each of their training programs: direct observation, interviews, and performance records.[29] The instrument, or combination of instruments, used depends upon the particular situation.

TABLE 5-6
COMPARISON OF COMMON EVALUATION INSTRUMENTS

INSTRUMENTS	EVALUATION LEVELS PERCEIVED EFFECTIVENESS	PERFORMANCE	ROI	ADVANTAGES	LIMITATIONS

Questionnaire	*	*	*	Low cost
				Honesty increased
				Anonymity optional
				Respondent sets pace
				Variety of options
					May not collect
					  accurate information
					On-job responding
					  conditions uncontrolled
					Respondent sets pace
					Return rate rarely controllable

Attitude Survey	*	*		Standardization
				  possible
				Quickly processed
				Easy to administer
					Predetermined alternatives
					Response choices
					Reliance on norms may distort
					  individual performance
					May not reflect true feelings

Written Test		*		Low purchase cost
				Readily scored
				Quickly processed
				Easily administered
				Wide sampling
				  possible
					May be threatening to
					  participant
					Possible low relations to job
					  performance
					Reliance on norms may distort
					  individual performance
					Possible cultural bias

Performance Test		*		Reliability Simulation potential Objective based	Time consuming Simulation often difficult High development costs
Interview	*	*	*	Flexible Opportunity for clarification Depth possible Personal contact	High reactive effects High cost Face-to-face threat potential Labor-intensive Trained interviewers necessary

Focus Groups	*	*		Flexible
				Low cost
				Good qualitative
				  responses
				Personal contact
					Effectiveness rests with
					  facilitator
					Subjective
					Sometimes difficult to
					  summarize findings

Observation		*		Non-threatening to
				  participants
				Excellent way to
				  measure behavior
				  change
					Possibly disruptive
					Reactive effect
					Unreliable
					Trained observers necessary

Performance Records		*	*	Reliability
				Objectivity
				Job-based
				Ease of review
				Minimal reactive
				  effects
					Lack of knowledge of criteria
					  for keeping/discarding
					  records
					Information system
					  discrepancies
					Indirect nature of data
					Need for conversion to usable
					  forms
					Records prepared for other
					  purposes
					Sometimes expensive to collect

REFERENCES

1. Hronec, S. M. *Vital Signs.* New York: American Management Association, 1993.

2. Rosow, J. M. and Zager, R. "Teaching More for Less: IBM and Travenol Stretch Training Dollars," *The Human Resources Professional,* January–February 1989, p. 18.

3. Gatewood, R. D. and Field, H. S. *Human Resource Selection,* 2nd Edition. Dryden Press: Chicago, IL, 1990.

4. Smith, J. E. and Merchant, S. "Using Competency Exams for Evaluating Training," *Training and Development Journal,* August 1990, pp. 65–71.

5. Parry, S.B. "How to Validate an Assessment Tool," *Training,* April 1993, pp. 37–42.

6. Aiken, L. R. *Psychological Testing and Assessment,* 7th Edition. Boston: Allyn and Bacon, 1991.

7. Pedhazur, E. J. and Schmelkin, L. P. *Measurement, Design, and Analysis: An Integrated Approach.* Hillsdale: Lawrence Erlbaum Associates, 1991, pp. 207–252.

8. Neuman, W. L. *Social Research Methods.* Boston: Allyn and Bacon, 1991.

9. Rea, L. M. and Parker, R. A. *Designing and Conducting Survey Research: A Comprehensive Guide.* San Francisco: Jossey-Bass, 1992.

10. Wymer, W. E. and Carsten, J. M. "Alternative Ways to Gather Opinion," *HRMagazine,* April 1992, pp. 71–78.

11. Rosen, N. "Employee Attitude Surveys: What Managers Should Know," *Training and Development Journal,* November 1987, pp. 50–52.

12. Wilmot, R. E. and McClelland, V. "How to Run a Reality Check," *Training,* May 1990, pp. 66–72.

13. Rotondi, T. "The Assessment Factor in Questionnaire Surveys," *Personnel Journal,* February 1989, p. 92.

14. Ofsanko, F. J. and Napier, N. K. (Eds.). *Effective Human Resource Measurement Techniques: A Handbook for Practitioners.* Alexandria: Society for Human Resource Management, 1990.

15. "Testing Report," *Human Resource Executive,* May 1994, pp. 46–47.

16. Sharon, A. T. "Testing...1,2,3," *Training and Development Journal,* September 1989, pp. 30–33.

17. Heneman, H. G. and Heneman, R. L. *Staffing Organizations.* Middleton: Mendota House, 1994.

18. Martin, S. L. and Stora, K. B. "Employee Selection by Testing." *HR Magazine,* June 1991, pp. 68–70.

19. Solomon, C. M. "Testing Is Not at Odds with Diversity Efforts." *Personnel Journal,* March 1993, pp. 100–104.

20. Fetteroll, E. "Did the Training Work? Evaluation By Interview," *Training News,* pp. 10–11.

21. Noe, R. A., Hollenbeck, J. R., Gerhart, B., and Wright, P. M. *Human Resource Management: Gaining a Competitive Advantage.* Burr Ridge: Irwin, 1994.

22. Denzin, N. K. and Lincoln, Y. S. *Handbook of Qualitative Research.* Thousand Oaks: Sage Publications, 1994, pp. 361–372.

23. Greenbaum, T. L. "Focus Group Research: A Useful Tool," *HR Focus,* September 1994, p. 3.

24. Marrelli, A. F. "Ten Evaluation Instruments for Technical Training," *Technical & Skills Training,* July 1993, pp. 7–15.

25. Krueger, R. A. *Focus Groups: A Practical Guide for Applied Research.* Newbury Park: Sage Publications, 1988.

26. Emory, C. W. and Cooper, D. R. *Business Research Methods,* 4th Edition. Burr Ridge: Irwin, 1991.

27. Denzin, N. K. and Lincoln, Y. S. *Handbook of Qualitative Research.* Thousand Oaks: Sage Publications, 1994, Ch. 23, pp. 377–392.

28. Cortada, J. W., Ph.D. "Balancing Performance Measurements and Quality," *Quality Digest,* December 1994, pp. 48–54.

29. Myers, J. and Jones, E. "Training Triumphs at Ames Department Stores," *The Human Resources Professional,* Spring 1990, p. 32.

CHAPTER SIX

Evaluation Design and Implementation

The previous chapter focused on specific techniques for collecting data, such as surveys, questionnaires, and interviews. This chapter discusses the implementation of data collection techniques and includes the overall evaluation. The first part of the chapter focuses on evaluation design, which is sometimes ignored, but is important to the overall HR measurement and evaluation process. Evaluation design includes the timing of measurements and the minimization of factors that can threaten the validity of program evaluation results. In this chapter, the term measurement is the process of data collection and may involve implementing a test, conducting a survey, or monitoring performance data.

The second part of the chapter focuses on implementation issues including how and when data should be collected and from what audiences. While program participants are probably the best source of input, other people can also be helpful. This chapter presents specific methods to ensure that programs work effectively such as follow-ups, action planning, and performance contracting.

EVALUATION DESIGN ISSUES

In many HR program evaluations, the performance of participants involved in the program is monitored at different time frames and is compared to performance prior to the program. Group performance is sometimes compared with the performance of another group that is not involved in the same program or with the remainder of the population of potential participants. Various combinations of approaches are available for evaluation design.

Control Groups

Control groups and experimental groups are sometimes used in evaluation. A control group is a group of participants who are as similar as possible to those in the experimental group, but who are not involved in the HR program. Ideally, the only difference between the two groups is that one group participates in the program and the other does not. A performance comparison of the two groups should determine the success of the HR program. The procedures for selecting control groups and determining the appropriate sample size are important issues. The two groups should be equivalent in job settings, skills, abilities, and demographic characteristics. The true control group is formed by random assignment and, if possible, the identity of the control group should not be revealed because it could affect their performance. Because of these requirements, control groups may not be practical in many HR measurement and evaluation situations. However, for critical evaluations affecting a large number of participants, control groups are essential. For more information on control group selection, see other references.[1]

Timing of Measurements

Another important issue in evaluation is the timing of measurements. Measurements may be taken before the program is initiated and after the program is implemented or completed. Post-measurement should never be omitted because it directly measures the results of a program. Pre-program measurements are important for comparisons. When conducting pre-program measurements, three general guidelines should be followed:

- **Minimize the effect of pre-program measurements.** Ideally, a measurement should not alter the performance of participants. If there is evidence that the measurement had an impact on performance, it should either be omitted, modified, or conducted far enough in advance of the program to minimize the impact. If this is not possible, a control group then will be necessary to measure the impact of the measurement.
- **Pre- and Post-measurement techniques should be identical or equivalent.** When measurements are compared, they should have a common base for comparison. Identical measures may influence results when they are

taken the second time. Similar but equivalent measurements may be more appropriate.

■ **The measurements should be conducted under the same or similar conditions.** The length of time between measurements and conditions under which both measurements are taken should be approximately the same.

Measurements may be taken at different time intervals during and after a program. Time series measurements during the program measure participant progress toward the objectives. Time series measurements after a program show the long-term effects of the program.

Factors that Jeopardize Validity

From a practical standpoint, there are a variety of issues and events that can invalidate the results of a program evaluation. Program planners and developers should take precautions to ensure that no other factors enter into the process or program that would have an important impact on the results. If they do, steps must be taken to isolate the impact of those factors. From both a logical and research perspective, several problems can surface that can threaten the validity of the results of a particular program evaluation. Alternative designs can counteract or offset the effects of the threats or sometimes eliminate them all together. Four common threats are presented here. For additional information on other threats and more detail on how to counter those threats, see other references.[2]

■ **Time or History.** Time has a way of influencing program results. Performance can improve and attitudes can change over time—even without an HR program. When measuring the effects of an HR program, this question should always be asked: "Would the same or similar results have occurred without the program?"

■ **Effect of Testing.** As discussed earlier, it is possible that the actual experience of taking a measurement (administering an instrument, taking a test) can influence performance or attitude even if the individual does not participate in an HR program. This effect is more likely to appear when pre- and post-measurements are identical.

■ **Mortality.** Participants may drop out of HR programs for various reasons. If pre- and post-measures are used, the number in the group may change from one measurement to another. This change makes it difficult to compare the results of the two measurements, This problem is compounded by the fact that the lower-level performers are sometimes the ones who drop out of a program.

■ **Selection Bias.** The selection of the group to participate in an HR program can possibly have an effect on the outcome because some individuals will perform better than others. If mostly high achievers or underachievers are selected, program results will be distorted. The problem can usually be resolved by using random selection, when it is feasible.

While there are other internal threats to validity, the ones described here are the most common and should be of concern to HR professionals. The designs presented next will attempt to overcome these threats in varying degrees.

COMMON EVALUATION DESIGNS

Although selecting the appropriate evaluation design is a key component of the evaluation strategy, this is an area that receives little attention in organizations. In a comprehensive program of evaluation, this issue must be addressed, either implicitly or explicitly.[3] This section presents the common evaluation designs and a few advantages and disadvantages of each.

One-Shot Program Evaluation Design

One of the most common, and least valid, designs involves the "one-shot" program. As Figure 6-1 shows, this design evaluates a single group only once after an HR program is completed. No data are collected prior to the program's implementation. A measurement is taken after the program becomes fully operational. For education and training programs, the measurement is usually taken after the program is conducted.

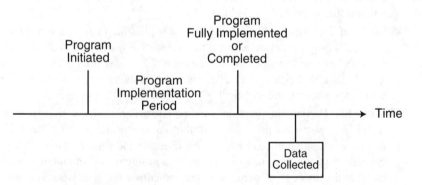

FIGURE 6-1. ONE-SHOT PROGRAM EVALUATION DESIGN.

Many uncontrolled factors might influence the measurement and invalidate conclusions based on results achieved through this design. However, the evaluation information obtained from this one-shot measurement is better than no evaluation at all. It is frequently used because of its simplicity and ease of application. This design may be useful for measuring the performance of a group when no means is available to measure performance before the program is implemented or possibly when no basis of a previous comparison is available. As an example, consider the implementation of an employee assistance program. One measure of success is the degree of participation in this program, but no previous measurement exists to compare it against because the program is new and employees did not have the opportunity to participate previously. A one-shot program design may be appropriate for the evaluation.

Single Group, Pre- and Post-Program Measurement Design

When comparisons are needed, the next logical design is the single group, pre- and post-program design as shown in Figure 6-2. This design is an improvement over the one-shot design because data is collected before and after the HR program is implemented. Data collected from a tracking system or from participants before the program is initiated is compared to data collected after the program is implemented to detect changes. This design can be illustrated by the health care cost containment program implemented by one company. The organization made several changes in medical benefits coverage to reduce medical costs. They compared the total medical costs before changes with the medical costs for six months after the changes. This pre- and post-comparison showed the impact of the newly implemented changes.

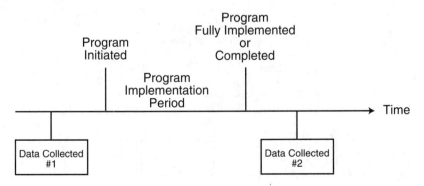

FIGURE 6-2. SINGLE GROUP, PRE- AND POST-EVALUATION DESIGN.

External factors can adversely affect this design. Changes in the organization, environment, work setting, or other factors may cause changes in the performance of participants. In the health care cost containment example, other factors could have an impact on the medical costs. The effect of a pre-program measurement is another disadvantage of this design. Because health care costs are being monitored (in a pre-program measurement), costs may decline.

Single Group, Time Series Design

A very popular design for evaluating an HR program involves a series of data collections, both before and after the program is implemented. In this design, referred to as a single group, time series design, the experimental group serves as its own control group. Collecting a series of data before implementing the program eliminates some of the problems incurred when a separate control group is not used. Repeated measurements after a program not only allow for comparison with the initial results, but enable measurement of the long-term effects of the program.

This design, as illustrated in Figure 6-3, may involve as many data collections as are practical for the setting. Consider for example the implementation of a total quality (TQM) program. To measure success, several quality, productivity, and process variables are monitored. Because many other factors may influence these factors over time, several measures should be taken prior to the implementation of TQM and at various intervals after implementing the program to provide a clearer picture of the success of the TQM effort. This design eliminates some of the threats to validity and is extremely useful when measurement data are readily available as part of the organization's performance reporting. With this design, the impact of HR programs can be compared with previous performance over a long time period.

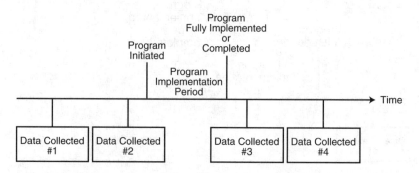

FIGURE 6-3. SINGLE GROUP, TIME SERIES PROGRAM EVALUATION.

Control Group Design

The next design compares two groups: an experimental group and a control group. Referred to as a control group design, the arrangement is illustrated in Figure 6-4. The experimental group participates in the HR program, while the control group does not. Data are gathered on both groups before and after the pro-

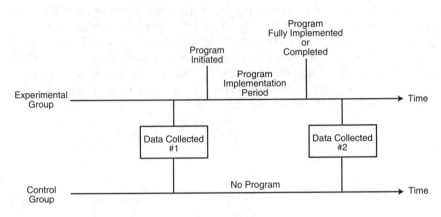

FIGURE 6-4. CONTROL GROUP EVALUATION DESIGN.

gram. The results of the experimental group when compared to the control group reflects the impact of the HR program. Although using a control group is akin to conducting a laboratory experiment, the process may not be difficult to achieve. In some situations, the control group does not have to be informed of their status and therefore are not necessarily aware that they are part of an experiment. For example, one organization implemented a gainsharing program on an experimental basis in two small crushed stone plants. Two other plants, with similar characteristics and production outlook, were selected as a control group. Productivity, costs, absenteeism, and turnover were monitored at both locations prior to the implementation of the plan. These same measures were monitored after the program had been operational to show comparisons and isolate the effects of the gainsharing program. The differences in the performance of the experimental group and the control group showed the amount of improvement attributed to the new program. The employees in the plants in the control group never knew they were part of an experiment.

This design is acceptable only when the two groups are similar in the appropriate selection criteria. Ideally, the participants in each group should be at the same job level, experience, ability, working conditions, and possibly even the geographic location. The best way to select control groups is on a random basis when it is feasible. The true control-group design is one of the most powerful evaluation tools available because all of the threats to validity, except the effects of measurements, are controlled. The next design eliminates all threats to validity.

Ideal Evaluation Design

Figure 6-5 shows an idealistic evaluation design. It involves the use of three groups, random selection of participants, and pre- and post-program data collections. Pre-program data is collected from experimental group A, which participates in the program and undergoes a post-program measurement. Data are also collected from the control group before and after the program, but the group does not participate in the program. Experimental group B has no pre-program data collection, but it participates in the program and has a post-program measurement.

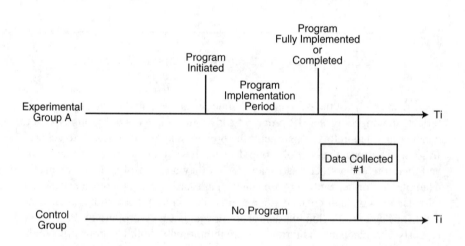

FIGURE 6-5. IDEAL EVALUATION DESIGN.

The control group eliminates the time and mortality factors that threaten the validity of the evaluation. If the data collected before and after the program are equal for the control group, then it follows that neither of these factors influenced the result. Random selection eliminates the selection bias threat. Experimental group B rules out the interaction of pre-program data collection (measurement, test) with the effects of the HR program. This was the weakness in the previous control group design. If the post-program data collected for groups A and B are identical, then the data collection apparently had no effect on performance.

This design is more difficult to put into practice in the work setting because it does involve three groups. However, programs with a significant investment in resources should be evaluated using an ideal design to completely isolate the various threats to validity. One organization, for example, implemented this design. It was considering significant changes in employee empowerment and participative decision making. Before embarking on the program organization-wide, the organization conducted an experiment involving the ideal evaluation design. Three groups were selected with two of them experimental. Pre-program attitude surveys were administered for experimental group A and the control group. The attitude survey was not administered to experimental group B. Post-program comparisons involved not only changes in attitudes, but also prescribed variables for work performance. The overall evaluation scheme eliminated threats to validity and gave the organization a true picture of the impact of the program, an assessment that was essential before making a decision to implement the program across the entire organization.

This design approaches the ultimate in experimental designs. From a practical standpoint, obtaining three randomly selected groups may be difficult or impossible. The time, expense, and administrative procedures required for this design may prohibit its use. However, other alternate designs such as the one presented next, can yield reliable results.

Post Measure Only, Control Group Design

A more practical and less expensive alternative to the previous design is called the post measure only, control group design as shown in Figure 6-6. A measurement is given to the randomly selected experimental group and the control group only after the program is implemented. The difference in the evaluation results of these two groups at the completion of the program shows the impact of the program. This design reduces the effects of the pre-program data measurement and reduces the time and expense of the previous evaluation design. In addition, this design isolates almost all of the threats to validity.

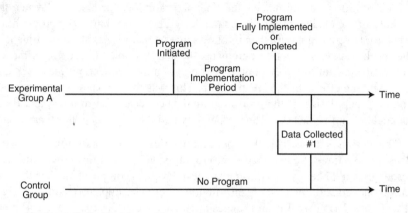

FIGURE 6-6. POST-MEASURE ONLY CONTROL GROUP DESIGN.

Which Design to Choose

Several possibilities exist for developing an evaluation system for an HR program, and many designs can be combined to form other alternate designs. The question of which design to use depends on several factors. The nature of the HR program and the practical considerations of the work environment may dictate the appropriate design. The more complex the design, the more costly the evaluation effort. The availability of control groups and the ease of randomization are other factors that enter into the decision. The effects of factors outside the immediate environment must also be considered. If a design is less than optimum, the HR staff should be prepared to defend its action in terms of trade-offs. Additional information on evaluation designs can be found in other references.[4]

PARTICIPANT FEEDBACK

Feedback from program participants is necessary for most HR programs. Collecting feedback has a wide variety of applications. Some examples include:

- In one company, a new employee orientation program was used to solicit reactions from new employees to the program at the end of the orientation sessions as well as in a three-month follow-up.

- In another situation, participants in an upward mobility program were asked to provide feedback about their perception of the program and its effectiveness.

■ A new team-based incentive program was implemented in another organization. The planners solicited feedback from team members to determine their level of satisfaction with the new system.

■ Store managers in one corporation were asked for their feedback on a new empowerment program that would make them entrepreneurs and independent operators.

■ Participants in an outplacement program, precipitated by an organizational restructuring, were asked to provide feedback on the effectiveness and efficiency of the program.

In addition to annual attitude surveys administered by many organizations, other participant feedback methods should be used in the evaluation of almost every type of HR program. When a program is changed or when routine feedback is needed, participants should be asked for their reaction. It is the most efficient way to measure customer satisfaction and explore ways in which satisfaction can be increased.

While participant feedback is popular, it is also subject to misuse. Sometimes referred to as a "happiness rating," it has come under fire from many HR professionals who consider it ineffective. The primary criticism concerns the subjectivity of the data. While there is no good substitute for hard data in evaluating programs, a carefully designed, properly administered participant feedback questionnaire during, or at the end of, an HR program might be sufficient for many HR departments with a modest budget. Feedback questionnaires have earned a place in HR program evaluation, and it would be difficult to implement a comprehensive evaluation without them.[5]

Areas of Feedback

The areas of feedback used on reaction forms depend to a large extent on the program and the purpose of the evaluation. Some reaction forms are very simple, while others are detailed and require a considerable amount of time to complete. The following areas represent the most common types of feedback solicited for HR programs:

■ Program content
■ Program materials
■ Program value
■ Communication medium
■ Program coordinator/facilitator
■ Relevance of program to job/work area

■ Overall evaluation
■ Planned improvements, if appropriate

Objective questions covering each of these areas provide feedback that can be extremely useful for making adjustments in a program and for judging program success. The coordinator/facilitator evaluation deserves additional attention. Because of the importance of an effective program leader, in some organizations the primary evaluation centers on the facilitator, and a separate form may be used. A facilitator evaluation process conducted at a telecommunications company illustrates this point. The process focused on five areas for evaluation:

■ General performance criteria referenced to company standards.
■ Knowledge of the subject matter including familiarity with content and depth of understanding.
■ Presentation skills that focused on clarity of the presentation, use of audio visual material, pacing of material, maintaining eye contact, and accessing participant understanding.
■ Communications that included the use of understandable language, real-life examples, and the promotion of discussion.
■ Receptivity that included responsiveness to participants, responding effectively to questions, and maintaining neutrality in responses to comments.

Appendix 3 provides a detailed participant feedback questionnaire that covers most of the previously listed areas.

Useful Guidelines

The design information on the questionnaires presented in Chapter 5 also applies to the design and construction of reaction or feedback questionnaires. In addition to those design principles, several useful tips can improve the quality of feedback.

■ **Consider an ongoing evaluation.** For lengthy programs, an end-of-the-program evaluation may leave the participants unable to provide accurate feedback on earlier parts of the program. To help improve the situation, an ongoing evaluation can be implemented. After certain program milestones, participants can be asked to evaluate the program using a feedback questionnaire. The information is timely and can be more useful to program evaluators.
■ **Try quantifying ratings.** Some organizations attempt to solicit feedback in terms of numerical ratings. Although subjective, these ratings can still be useful for program evaluations. When there are many participants or groups,

these ratings can be useful in making comparisons. In some cases, targets or norms can be established to compare ratings. When using a norm scale, a rating that is considered good may prove to be quite low when compared to norms on the factor being rated.

■ **Collect information related to improvement.** Many HR programs focus on improvement. Sometimes it is difficult to secure realistic input on a feedback form related to improvements such as cost savings or quality enhancement, but it is worth a try. The response may be surprising. For example, this simple question will sometimes cause participants to concentrate on improvement:

As a result of this program, please estimate the monetary benefit that will be realized (i.e., increased productivity, improved methods, reduced costs, etc.) over a period of one year. $_____ Please explain the basis of your estimate.

_____

_____

_____

Express as a percent the confidence you place on your estimate. (0%= no confidence, 100%= certainty) _____.

This statement encourages participants to focus on improvement. Asking participants to explain the basis of an estimate provides some insight into the specific techniques and strategies used to develop the improvement. It also helps initiate the specific actions necessary to make the program work. The input on the confidence level is helpful in the data analysis and makes participants feel more comfortable about providing subjective information. For example, if a participant is not very comfortable with an estimate, a low level of confidence may be indicated, such as 25%. If the participant is extremely comfortable with his/her estimate, a high level would be offered, such as 90%. To be conservative in data analysis, the confidence level is multiplied by the monetary benefit to develop an adjusted improvement amount. For example, a benefit estimated at $5,000, with a 50% confidence level, is reduced to $2,500, which is the figure used in reporting results from feedback questionnaires. Although this process is subjective, it has been used to estimate the ROI in an HR program.[6]

■ **Allow ample time for completing the form.** A time crunch may cause problems when participants are asked to complete a feedback form at the end of a meeting or program session. Consequently, the information may be abbreviated in an effort to leave the meeting. An alternative method is to allow ample time for evaluation at a scheduled time before the completion of the program. Another alternative is to allow participants to mail the evaluation later. With this approach, a reminder may be necessary to secure all of the forms.

■ **Put the information collected to use.** Sometimes participant feedback is solicited, tabulated, summarized, and then disregarded. The information is collected for one or more of the purposes of evaluation, otherwise the exercise is a waste of the participant's time. The last chapter on communicating program results presents several possibilities for disseminating this evaluation information.

Advantages/Disadvantages

Feedback questionnaires have several disadvantages. The data are subjective, based on the opinions and feelings of the participants at that time. Personal bias may exaggerate the ratings. Participants often are too polite with their feedback. At the end of a program, they may be pleased just to get it out of the way. Therefore, a positive rating may be given when participants actually feel differently. A good rating during, or at the end of a program, is no assurance that the program will be successful.

There are some advantages to feedback questionnaires. They obtain a quick reaction from the participants while information is still fresh on their minds. Participants usually have judgments on the usefulness of the program and its material. This quick reaction can be helpful for making adjustments or providing evidence of the program's effectiveness. Questionnaires are easy to administer, usually taking only a few minutes. Data can be easily analyzed, tabulated, and summarized. The information from questionnaires is easily understood.

There is a definite place for feedback questionnaires in HR program evaluation. They can provide a convenient method of data collection, but they should represent only a part of the total evaluation process.

FEEDBACK FROM OTHERS

Another useful source of feedback is that from other individuals closely identified with the participants in the program. Typically, these groups fall into four categories: (1) supervisors of the participants, (2) subordinates of the participants, (3) team members, and (4) members of the HR staff.

Supervisors

The most common group for feedback is the supervisors of those involved in HR programs. This feedback provides information on improvements or changes that have resulted from participation in the HR program. This "feedback from the boss" is usually obtained during a follow-up evaluation using an instrument such as a questionnaire or an interview. The questions on the instrument should be designed to solicit specific information that will reveal as much tangible change as possible. This method can develop reliable feedback data as was the case in the implementation of an employee involvement program in one organization. After the program was implemented, supervisors were asked to provide input on how well employees had accepted the program and to assess their individual behaviors related to program objectives. Supervisor input was critical in assessing the change in employees.

Subordinates

Probably the second most often tapped feedback group is the subordinates of the participants of an HR program. Their feedback is useful only in programs involving managers and supervisors who have employees reporting to them. In this type of data-collection method, employees are usually asked about changes or improvements in their supervisor's behavior or accomplishments since he or she participated in an HR program. The information will be subjective and may be biased or opinionated, depending on the employee's attitude toward the participant (supervisor). This information may not be as reliable as that obtained from the participant's supervisor, but can nevertheless be valuable in the evaluation process.

Subordinate input is particularly useful in supervisory training and leadership programs where skill building is an important part of the effort. In one organization, interpersonal skills were discussed as part of an extensive supervisory development program. To determine if their supervisors had changed their behavior, subordinates were asked to judge the effectiveness of their supervisors' interpersonal skills after the program had been implemented. This information provided reliable input on supervisor behavior change.

Team Members

Probably the least used feedback group is the team members or peer group. Their feedback is used to determine how participants accept and use an HR program. This data source is not frequently used because it is highly subjective and may be unreliable because of the informal relationship between the source and the participant. The data collection techniques for this type of feedback are questionnaires or interviews. This approach was used in one organization that wanted to assess the effectiveness of a team building program. Three months into the team building initiative, members were asked to judge the cooperativeness and helpfulness of other team members. Team assessments became an important part of the overall success of the program.

A word of caution is in order when collecting information from these three groups. Information collected from one of these groups may tend to place the participant on trial. Members of the particular group may observe a participant too closely to see whether he/she performs in an expected manner or contributes in a particular way. While this close scrutiny, may be important to evaluation, it may not be appropriate for the acceptance or endorsement of the HR program.

HR Staff

Another group used for feedback is the HR staff. Their feedback can be informal, as in the situation where an HR program coordinator provides informal feedback on the program or program participants. This feedback can be formal as in the situation where staff members, properly trained in observation techniques, observe participants and/or conduct interviews, and provide feedback on their performance. Staff evaluation can be helpful and can usually represent professional and unbiased information.

PARTICIPANT FOLLOW-UP

Most new HR programs are implemented to improve the organization, meet a requirement, or satisfy a regulation. To ensure that the program meets its objectives and has a long-lasting effect, follow-up information is sometimes desired. With some programs, routine monitoring and tracking of data provides a sufficient follow-up to evaluate a program's success. In other programs, where soft data is an important part of the evaluation, a follow-up must be implemented. For example, during the implementation of a new program to improve productivity, the planners may announce employee incentives, set standards, and explain the program, so that employees learn the various ways in which they can improve productivity. After the implementation, the actual measures of productivity might suffice for most evaluations, and preclude the necessity for a follow-up. However, a follow-up may be necessary if senior management is interested in knowing the lasting effects of the program and the relationship between the employee efforts and productivity changes. In this situation, a follow-up may ask employees about their specific actions to improve productivity and the impact the program has had on their work unit. In addition, the follow-up could identify problem areas where adjustments need to be made.

In reality, many HR programs are designed to be long-term programs that may not reap benefits for several months or years. For example, consider the implementation of a self-directed work team for a midwest manufacturing plant of a Fortune 250 company.[7] Table 6-1 shows the implementation schedule with

TABLE 6-1
SELF-DIRECTED WORK TEAM IMPLEMENTATION MODEL

EVENT	APPROXIMATE TIMETABLE
■ Development of the team concept	Initial introduction to the work team
■ Defining the role of the individual in a team	First day of training
■ Development of a team mission and objectives	Second day of training
■ Establish a departmental business plan	First month of training
■ Teach problem solving techniques	Frist two months of training
■ Establish quality standards as a team	First six months
■ Develop closer under-standing of team members through Myers Briggs Profile and analysis	After six months of working together
■ Develop a skill-based pay system including a peer performance plan	After the first seven months of working together and only after the team is functioning as a team
■ Assess the team's indepen-dence and cut back time and support as needed	After all teaching modules have been finalized and tested
■ Define maturity level of the group and develop new training programs if needed	Determine and develop as needed

Source: Adapted in part from Dobbelaere, A. G. and Goeppinger, K. H. "The Right Way and the Wrong Way to Set Up a Self-Directed Work Team," The Human Resources Professional, Winter 1993, pp. 31–35.

selected events. There are many opportunities to measure reaction from partici-pants and the progress made with the program. This type of program requires a variety of follow-up approaches involving several of the data collection tech-niques presented in Chapter 5. The challenge is to select the appropriate data col-lection technique to fit into a follow-up schedule.

The primary purposes of a follow-up are:

■ To help measure the lasting results of the program.
■ To identify the areas that show the most improvement.

■ To compare the responses at follow-up time with those provided during or at the end of the program.

■ To determine problem areas or barriers to improvement.

The follow-up evaluation almost always is preceded by an end-of-the-program evaluation and sometimes the follow-up is an extension of the previous evaluation. A follow-up can use a feedback questionnaire, surveys, interviews, focus groups, or observations. The follow-up usually focuses on learning retention, on-the-job application, and organizational impact. In some situations, a follow-up is considered the most important phase of evaluation.[8] It usually occurs three to twelve months after the implementation of the program, with the most common time frame being six months. For a more comprehensive evaluation, a follow-up could occur at repeated intervals (i.e., at six months or one-year intervals). The use of this approach depends on the organization's emphasis on measuring long-term results.

As an example of a follow-up evaluation, consider the approach one organization used for the evaluation of a sexual harassment program. With increased public awareness of sexual harassment, the organization used the opportunity to update its sexual harassment policy, communicate it to all employees through the employee handbook and newsletter, and conduct workshops with managers covering the company's policy, various definitions, legal considerations, and the consequences of sexual harassment. Six months after the program, the company conducted a follow-up with a randomly selected sample of employees and with all of the workshop participants. Among other items, the follow-up determined the specific changes in behavior of employees, changes in perceptions of employees, and changes in the environment.

Guidelines for Development

Chapter 5 outlined the design principles for a follow-up evaluation as well as the appropriate data collection technique. In addition to those principles, a few helpful guidelines will enhance the effectiveness of this follow-up.

■ **Determine progress made since implementing and completing the program.** A follow-up evaluation determines what participants accomplished with the HR program. Ideally, additional data should reflect the success of the program. To provide the continuity for data comparison, the questions asked at the end of (or during) the program should be repeated on the follow-up, if appropriate.

■ **Solicit reasons for lack of results.** Not all follow-up evaluations will show positive results. Some will indicate no improvement or will contain negative comments. The follow-up should determine the reasons the program is not achieving results and should identify obstacles to program success such as a lack of support from superiors, restricting policies and procedures, or lack of interest from participants. Identifying these obstacles is as valuable as identifying the reasons for success, since the obstacles can possibly be eliminated in future programs.

■ **Plan the follow-up carefully.** Develop a plan for the follow-up evaluation that responds to typical administrative questions such as who, what, where, when, and how. The time period for the follow-up is critical. It should be long enough for the desired improvement to take place, yet short enough so that the program material will still be relatively fresh.

■ **Inform participants to expect the follow-up.** There should be no surprises at follow-up time. The plans to administer a follow-up instrument should be clearly communicated during the program. Also, participants should know what information will be expected from them in the follow-up.

■ **Share follow-up information with the participant's supervisor.** Ideally, the participant's immediate supervisor should be involved in the implementation of the HR program. At a very minimum, the supervisor should be aware of the progress made and should receive the information on the follow-up evaluation.

■ **Require participation in the follow-up.** The follow-up evaluation usually should not be optional. Participants should expect it, and the HR department must see that it is accomplished. This input is essential to determine the impact of the program. Adequate response from the follow-up evaluations is not difficult to achieve.

■ **Consider a follow-up assignment.** In some cases, follow-up assignments can enhance the evaluation process. In a typical assignment, participants are required to meet an objective, perform a task, try out a new skill, or complete a project by a predetermined date.

■ **If feasible, conduct a follow-up session.** An additional session, with a primary purpose of evaluation, can be helpful to determine how the program is working and to identify possible obstacles to program implementation. This is usually an add-on session conducted a few weeks or months after the program is completed.

Advantages/Disadvantages

There are several disadvantages of the follow-up evaluation. The information supplied by the participant may be subjective. The process usually needs the cooperation of the supervisor and participants may not have the opportunity to apply what they have learned. Also, intervening factors may affect the results.

The follow-up evaluation has several advantages. It is easy to administer and data are easy to tabulate. It provides a more accurate assessment of the impact of the program and it helps to measure the lasting results of the program. Participant follow-up is a common technique for HR program evaluation. Even with its shortcomings, it is an important part of evaluation.

ACTION PLANNING

An extension of the follow-up evaluation, action planning, requires HR program participants to develop detailed plans for accomplishing specific objectives related to the program. Usually prepared on the organization's customized form, an action plan shows what is to be done, by whom, and when. The action plan approach is a straightforward, easy-to-use method for determining ways in which participants can implement improvements. It is particularly useful for HR programs in which changes are implemented or improvement is monitored. Virtually every functional area of HR is a likely target for action planning. Consider two examples from Labor Relations and Fair Employment.

One organization implemented a labor management cooperation program in which supervision and management met regularly with union members and leaders. Participants developed action plans to suggest ways to improve the cooperation between management and the union. In some cases, teams submitted combined action plans. Typical teams included first level supervisors and union leaders in a work unit area. The committee used the progress reported on the action plans to identify specific accomplishments and, in some cases, the measurable changes that developed from these plans.

The other example involves the affirmative action (AA) efforts of a large hospital. The hospital began a comprehensive affirmative action program. It conducted a series of meetings and training sessions with supervisors and department heads to discuss the rationale for affirmative action and the importance of achieving affirmative action goals. Some sessions were designed to make managers aware of the issue and secure their cooperation in reaching affirmative action goals. Each participant was asked to develop realistic plans to support the organization's affirmative action plan. Participants specified targets they would meet for each underutilized group. Goals were set for recruiting and new job assignments. The organization reported the progress on the plans as a way to monitor the success of the program. This program proved to be more successful than previous ones in which managers were simply told about the affirmative action plan, but were not required to develop their own action plans and report their results as they were in the new program.

The action planning process produces data that answers these typical questions:

- What accomplishment occurred since implementing the HR program?
- How much of the improvement can be attributed to the program?
- What is the monetary value of the improvement?
- Did the program designers achieve the anticipated results?
- What factors may have prevented participants from accomplishing specific action items?
- What program changes are recommended?

HR professionals can use this information to decide whether a program should be modified, and managers can use the information to evaluate the program.

The Approach

The action plan approach can have a tremendous impact on the organization. One example of this approach is a productivity improvement program from the CIGNA Corporation. In this program, supervisors developed productivity measures and action plans and provided feedback to the employees. Action plans were actually developed in a program. The program involved more than 200 supervisors, and a sampling of two groups representing 20 participants revealed some significant results. Three participants reported a savings of $270,000. This return alone represented two-thirds of the cost of the program for the entire 200 supervisors.[9]

Many organizations use the action plan approach with excellent results. Probably the most comprehensive application of this approach occurred in the U.S. Government. The Office of Personnel Management developed an action plan method called the Participant Action Plan Approach (PAPA), which can be used independently of the entire evaluation process or in conjunction with other evaluation methods.

Developing the Action Plan

Developing of the action plan requires two tasks: (1) determining the area for action, and (2) writing the action items. Both tasks should be completed during the program. The area for action should be job related and developed from HR program objectives, materials, and issues. A list of potential areas for action can be developed individually or generated in a group discussion. The following questions should be asked when developing the areas for action:

■ Is this action directly related to the HR program?
■ How much time will this action take?
■ If this action is completed, will it result in a significant benefit to the organization?
■ Are the skills for accomplishing this action item available?
■ Who has the authority to implement the action plan?
■ Will this action have an effect on other individuals?
■ Are there any organizational constraints for accomplishing this action item?

Wording of specific action items is usually more difficult than identifying the action areas. An action item must be worded in such a way that everyone involved will know when the action occurs. Each statement should begin with an action item. Some examples of action items are listed below:

■ Review the effectiveness of the various recruiting sources and concentrate efforts on the most effective sources.
■ Communicate the sexual harassment policy to all employees.
■ Identify departmental quality measures to support the Division's TQM program.
■ Handle every piece of paper only once to improve personal time management.

If appropriate, each action item should have a date for completion and indicate the names of other individuals or resources required for completion. Planned behavior changes should be observable. Appendix 4 presents a typical action plan form.

Action plans, as used in this context, do not require the prior approval or input from the participant's supervisor, although it may be helpful. Participants do not have to have prior knowledge of the action plan requirement for the program. Frequently, an introduction to and a description of the process is an integral part of the program. Action plans should be reviewed before the end of the HR program to check for accuracy, feasibility, and completeness. At that time, it should be made clear to the participant that the plan will be audited or reviewed.

Measuring Results

To tabulate the results achieved from the action plans, a follow-up is conducted usually three to six months after the program is completed. This review should reveal and document progress toward the planned objectives and is usually accomplished through either a questionnaire or interview.

In the questionnaire approach, questionnaires are mailed to participants at the specified follow-up time. Much like an audit, the questionnaire is composed of detailed questions about the action plan and should be accompanied by a cover letter. The questionnaire should provide the participant with ample space to describe for each action item what action was accomplished, how it was accomplished, who was involved, and how often the action was attempted. The results are documented and if the items were not accomplished, participants are asked to explain why they were not accomplished. They should be asked to list the problems or obstacles they encountered.

The interview method of follow-up begins with a letter reminding participants about the follow-up. This letter directs attention to the action items before interviews take place. The participant is interviewed at his or her own convenience to minimize distractions on the job. The interview secures the same information that is obtained with the questionnaire. The difference is that the information is gathered face-to-face or over the telephone.

Other options for collecting the information that can be just as effective are:

■ Contacting only a sample of the participants for a follow-up.
■ Reconvening a group of participants to complete the follow-up.
■ Obtaining input from both the participant and his or her supervisor.
■ Meeting with both the participant and his or her supervisor.

Advantages/Disadvantages

There are at least three disadvantages to the action plan method. Because it relies on direct input from the participant, the information can be biased and unreliable. Also, there may be a problem with the type of data collected because it is usually subjective, in the soft data category. Finally, the process can be time-consuming for the participant and, if the participant's supervisor is not involved in the process, there may be a tendency for the participant not to complete the assignment.

The action plan approach, however, is flexible and has several inherent advantages. The approach is simple, easy to administer, and participants can easily understand the approach. Action plans are useful for a full range of HR programs that collect a variety of information for measuring program results. Finally, action plans can be used independently as the only method of evaluation or in conjunction with other evaluation methods.[10]

PERFORMANCE CONTRACTING

Performance contracting is another effective follow-up method that is essentially a slight variation of the action plan process. Based on the principle of mutual goal setting, it is a written agreement between an HR program participant and the participant's supervisor. The participant agrees to improve performance in an area of mutual concern related to the HR program. The agreement is in the form of a project to be completed or goal to be accomplished. The agreement spells out what is to be accomplished, at what time, and with what results. A detailed performance contract would usually contain the following items:

- subject area
- objective
- goals
- problems
- solutions
- resources

- activities
- time
- costs
- benefits
- commitment

The commitment section requires both parties to sign the agreement and commit themselves to making the improvements as outlined in the contract.

The Approach

Although the steps can vary according to the specific kind of contract and organization, a common sequence of events is as follows:

1. The program participant and supervisor mutually agree on a topic for improvement.
2. A specific, measurable goal(s) is set.
3. The participant shares in the discussion of the contract and helps set the goals of the contract.
4. The participant makes progress on the contract against a specific deadline.
5. The participant reports the results of the effort to his or her supervisor.
6. The supervisor and participant document the results and forward a copy to the HR department along with appropriate comments.

The individuals involved in this process mutually select the topic for improvement prior to their involvement in the HR program. The topic can cover one or more of the following areas:

- **Routine performance** includes specific improvements in performance measures such as improvement in production, quality, customer satisfaction, costs, and profits.
- **Change efforts** focuses on changes associated with major change programs such as reengineering, restructuring, and total quality processes.

■ **Problem solving** focuses on specific problems such as an unexpected increase in accidents, a decrease in efficiency, a loss of morale, or a service delivery problem.

■ **Innovative or creative applications** includes initiating changes or improvements in work practices, methods, procedures, techniques, and processes.

The topic selected should be stated as one or more objectives, and should state the action to be accomplished when the contract is complete. Objectives should be understandable (by all involved), challenging, achievable, and largely under the control of the participant. The detailed activities needed to accomplish the objectives should be developed using the guidelines discussed under action plans.

Measuring Progress

If the contract extends more than three months from initiation, participants can submit progress reports outlining accomplishments thus far. Upon completion of the contract, a summary report should be submitted to the participant's supervisor. The report outlines the initial objectives, the problems encountered and their solutions, specific activities, costs, and benefits, as well as a detailed statement of the results. In addition, the participant's supervisor should review the report and make appropriate comments noting his or her satisfaction with the progress. The progress report should then be forwarded to the HR department to be used as additional data for evaluating the program.

Several variations are possible on the follow-up of the performance contract. The methods outlined with the action plan may be helpful to ensure that the participants complete the contract and ultimately send it to the HR department.

The performance contract represents another powerful technique for obtaining impressive results with an HR program. A major electronics company used this technique in a program for senior managers. It set objectives with managers prior to the program. The two-year program required the participants to produce a business impact project that directly related to the company's business. Some of the projects included the design of a new lab and the development of a new distribution method for one of the company's products.

Comparison of Approaches

While there can be many variations of follow-up for an HR program, the three presented here are the most common: (1) follow-up interventions, (2) action planning, and (3) performance contracting. Table 6-2 shows the basic differences in

TABLE 6-2
A COMPARISON OF FOLLOW-UP METHODS

FEATURES		FOLLOW-UP INTERVENTIONS	ACTION PLANNING	PERFORMANCE CONTRACTING
Topic selection	Little flexibility	✓		
	Much flexibility		✓	✓
Supervisor participation	Required			✓
	Optional	✓	✓	
	Unnecessary			
Announcement prior to program	Yes			✓
	No	✓		
	Optional		✓	
Techniques discussed in program	Yes		✓	✓
	No			
	Optional	✓		
Specific format required	Yes		✓	✓
	No			
	Optional	✓		
Feedback of results	Required	✓	✓	✓
	Optional			

these methods. By combining and using variations of these methods, the HR professional can develop a custom-designed follow-up method that is appropriate for the organization and that also optimizes results from HR programs.

SUMMARY

This chapter presented basic information on evaluation design and ways to implement an evaluation process in a follow-up setting. It presented common evaluation designs that can be useful in developing a reliable and valid evaluation scheme. The challenge for HR managers is to select an evaluation design that fits into the practical and economic framework of the organization. Collecting participant feedback is important. While feedback from other groups is often subjective, it can provide a wealth of valuable input.

The chapter also discussed the follow-up process and presented three possible approaches: follow-up interventions using interviews, questionnaires, surveys, focus groups, and observations; the action planning process; and the performance contract. Collectively, these approaches provide an array of follow-up possibilities to collect data to ensure the program is on track and long-lasting. By combining the information in this chapter with the data collection techniques in Chapter 5, the HR professional has the tools necessary to develop a comprehensive evaluation strategy.

REFERENCES

1. Pedhazur, E. J. and Schmelkin, L. P. *Measurement, Design and Analysis,* Lea Publishers: Hillsdale, New Jersey, 1991.

2. Neuman, W. L. *Social Research Methods.* Boston: Allyn and Bacon, 1991.

3. Davidove, E. A. "Evaluating the Return on Investment of Training," *Performance and Instruction,* 32 (1), 1993.

4. Emory, C. W. and Cooper, D. R. *Business Research Methods,* 4th Edition. Burr Ridge: Irwin, 1991.

5. Krein, T. J. and Weldon, K. C. "Making a Play for Training Evaluation," *Training and Development,* 48 (4), 1994.

6. Noonan, J. V. "How to Escape Corporate America's Basement," *Training,* 30 (12), 1993.

7. Dobbelaere, A. G. and Goeppinger, K. H. "The Right Way and the Wrong Way to Set Up a Self-Directed Work Team," *The Human Resources Professional,* Winter 1993, pp. 31-35.

8. Moseley, J. L. and Larson, S. "A Qualitative Application of Kirkpatrick's Model for Evaluating Workshops and Conferences," *Performance and Instruction,* 33 (8), 1994.

9. Paquet, B. *et al.* "The Bottom Line," *Training and Development Journal,* May 1987.

10. Carnevale, A. P. and Schulz, E. R. "Return on Investment: Accounting for Training," *Training and Development Journal,* July 1990, p. S1-S32.

CHAPTER SEVEN

Measuring the Total Human Resources Effort

One of the most important aspects of measuring the HR contribution is to identify appropriate measures that accurately reflect overall HR performance. This chapter describes important measures that can be used to relate the output of the HR function to organizational effectiveness. These measures will help management understand and appreciate the ways in which the human side of an organization interacts with and affects the financial side. This chapter concludes with an important study by this author that demonstrates how to develop a Human Resources Effectiveness Index and relate it to a company's productivity and profitability.

MEASUREMENT ISSUES

Measurement is essential to determine success of performance. To achieve success in organizations, employees must excel in their jobs and their energies must be focused on the areas that will make a difference to the bottom line of the organization. Success also depends on the ability to measure performance and to use these measurements persuasively to obtain needed resources. The following principles of performance measurements apply:[1]

■ The effectiveness of any function can be measured by some combination of cost, time, quantity, quality, or behavioral indices.

■ A measurement system promotes productivity by focusing attention on the most important issues, tasks, and objectives of the organization.

■ The performance of white collar workers is best measured in groups.

■ Managers can be measured by the effectiveness and efficiency of the units they manage.

■ The ultimate measurement is effectiveness, not efficiency.

In short, measurement is a vital part of an effective HR system that links HR activities with organizational performance.

One problem in using measurements is the false assumption that measurements, reduced to numerical values, are always accurate indicators of quantity, quality, cost, time, or behavior. Unfortunately, few measures accurately describe the phenomenon they measure. Financial measures, often regarded as precise and accurate reflections of an organization's health, may be based on measures that are not precise and, in some cases, may be entirely misleading. For example, the income statement for a typical business may contain entries that are sometimes assigned values on the basis of arbitrary procedures, subjectivity, bias, or managerial manipulation. Allocated cost is one such entry. The portion of indirect costs allocated to a product, service, department, plant or function is often based on a subjective decision by the cost accounting department.

Sources of inaccuracies from numeric measurements are plentiful, ranging from the procedure for collecting data to errors in actual recording and interpretation of measures. Oftentimes measures are developed from different recording procedures and are subject to different interpretation. This leads to an important question: Are inaccurate or imprecise measures better than no measures? Although this is an important consideration, it appears that some measures are better than no measures. Even though the measurement may not be precise, the information and understandings that come from developing these measurements is invaluable. It is generally better to have a rough estimate based on a good understanding than to have a precise statistic that is conceptually flawed.

In a work environment, several variables can affect individual or group performance, including individual drives and motives, environment, supportive reinforcement from management, policies and practices, and a variety of external factors. Many of these factors are not directly under the control of the HR department. Human performance and organizational performance are too complex for a single criterion or ultimate measure of output. It is more reasonable to develop several measures that can be combined to produce a macro-level measure.

Costs must be considered in the development of measures. For example, suppose a new, inexpensive employee benefit is added to a company's benefits package to keep it competitive and improve job satisfaction. Attitude surveys and detailed interviews can determine the improved job satisfaction as a result of the new benefit. However, the expense of collecting and analyzing the data may be greater than the cost of the additional benefit. Thus the fundamental issue of economic feasibility should always be addressed.

Overall, these measurement issues may raise questions about the appropriateness of HR measures. These questions, as well as other limitations discussed in this chapter, inhibit the development of ideal measures. Nevertheless, a group of measures can be identified that are meaningful, useful, and understandable.

THE HR CONTRIBUTION MODEL

Figure 7-1 presents the HR contribution model that shows the relationship between the HR function and organizational effectiveness. This model summarizes the overall relationship between three major elements: human resources management, human resources performance measures, and organizational effectiveness measures. The first block in the model includes specific functions, subfunctions, programs, and activities that account for the major thrust of human

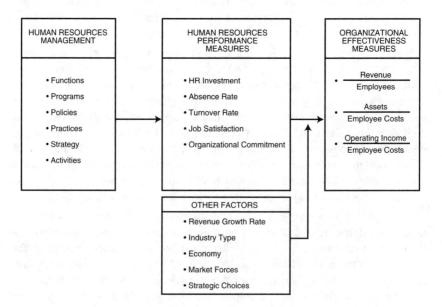

FIGURE 7-1. HR CONTRIBUTION MODEL.

resources management. It also includes HRM strategies, policies, and practices that exist in every organization and have an effect on organizational performance.

The success of HR efforts can be judged in part by the overall human resources performance measures such as HR investment, absence rate, turnover rate, job satisfaction, and organizational commitment. While these measures account for a major part of the measurable contribution of HR, other HR functions such as training, development, and compensation also affect organizational performance.

HR performance measures influence organizational effectiveness. Three measures of organizational effectiveness—revenue productivity, asset utilization, and operating income—are recommended to establish this relationship. HR performance measures are only one set of variables that impact organizational effectiveness. Other variables, such as revenue growth rate, industry type, economy, market forces, and strategic choices, also affect organizational effectiveness. The remainder of this chapter focuses on the rationale for selecting and applying these measures to a human resources effectiveness index.

HR PERFORMANCE MEASURES

There are literally dozens of ways to measure the contribution of the HR function. From a practical viewpoint, only a manageable number of measures should be used to assess the impact of the HR function on overall organizational effectiveness. To determine which measures to use, four rules should be considered:

1. Each measure should represent the impact of as many functions as possible within the HR department. This requirement eliminates measures that may have little impact on overall organizational effectiveness, such as employment cost per hire or the number of employee complaints.
2. Each measure should represent functions that are important across business and industry groupings. This requirement eliminates the measurement of a function such as safety and health. While accident frequency rates and injury costs could be related to organizational effectiveness, the safety function has its greatest impact in manufacturing and construction segments.
3. Each measure should represent data that is available and assessable. If measures are not readily available in a large number of organizations, comparisons will not be useful. This eliminates measures such as training impact or the number of counseling sessions conducted, since many firms do not measure these items.
4. Finally, all of the measures must collectively account for the large portion of the activities, programs, and services of the HR department. They should not be heavily skewed toward any one area or small group of activities.

Two factors should be considered when selecting measures to evaluate the impact of the HR function on organizational effectiveness: cost and investment. Actions or situations that represent significant or excessive cost can reduce the effectiveness of an organization. For example, excessive absenteeism and turnover create extra costs for recruitment and training. On the other hand, investments in additional funds for programs designed to improve productivity, efficiency, and the utilization of human resources should pay off in increased organizational effectiveness. An example of this is the approval of the overall budget for the HR function that shows the level of investment in HR in the organization. These two concepts, improvements in cost control and increases in HR investment, are used to select measures for overall HR evaluation.

HR Expenses

One of the most frustrating challenges the HR manager faces is the traditional view of the department as an expense center. While this may have been justified in decades past, it is no longer appropriate. A fully functioning, progressive HR department is a contributor to organizational productivity and profitability. Both directly and indirectly, the HR function enhances revenues and income. In a sense, it is a human asset investment management function. The greater the investment in HR, the greater the return on the investment.

Because HR department cost is relatively small when compared to other functions, some HR managers are puzzled about the pressure to continually reduce the cost of the function. The pertinent question therefore becomes, "What does management expect from the function?" If management believes that HR can and should make a difference, then it should provide an appropriate budget to make the contribution. Budget and staffing allocations will naturally follow what management tries to achieve. Many HR departments have learned how to break out of the expense mode and have little trouble obtaining the resources they need, when they need them. They demonstrate their contribution by developing a quantitative measurement system that proves they enhance the organization's bottom line.

Actual HR expenses vary considerably with the organization, not only because of its size and scope of operations, but in its overall philosophies, attitude, and strategies of the HR effort. Because of this, it is important to examine HR costs relative to other costs and factors. Then comparisons can be meaningful from one organization to another or from one industry to another. One possibility is to measure HR costs on a per employee basis. This simply involves developing HR costs and dividing by the number of full-time employees. Another potential measure is HR costs as a percent of payroll costs that shows the investment in the HR department relative to the total investment in human resources. Another potential measure, and one that is recommended, is HR costs divided by total operating expenses that shows HR costs relative to all operating costs that include compensation as well as other employee-related expenses. The SHRM/Saratoga Institute survey reports this measure.[2] It is possible to develop any of the above three measures from the SHRM/Saratoga data.

HR department expenses equal staff operating expenses including staff compensation and benefits, facilities, and equipment. They include the HR subfunctions of planning and research, staffing, compensation, benefits, employee and labor relations, and training and development. Safety and security are not included. Total operating expenses equal total costs and expenses as reported on the firm's income statement. Income taxes are excluded. Human resource department expense as a percent of total operating expense runs in the 2 percent to 4 percent range for most companies. Any number above 5 percent is most unusual. This is a very low cost when considering the range of valuable services that a progressive HR department provides.

Absence Rate

Few variables in an organization have received as much attention as absenteeism. Employers expect employees to be at work and when they are not, significant costs can mount. Several HR practices and policies are aimed at reducing or controlling absenteeism, and the costs related to absenteeism have been fully documented and calculated.

A major consequence of absenteeism is lost productivity. An employee's absence creates problems for the organization. Schedules have to be rearranged and substitutes must be found or the work goes undone. In either case, organizational effectiveness is reduced because substituting employees, rearranging work schedules, or missing deadlines will ultimately impact the productivity of the organization. And when organizations hire additional employees to cover for absenteeism, additional costs are accumulating. Even then, rearranging schedules and substituting employees will reduce organizational effectiveness because the skill level of the replacement employee is usually less than the job incumbent.

A few studies have investigated the impact of absenteeism on productivity. The findings suggest a negative relationship. The most important negative consequence of absenteeism is cost. A few studies suggest the magnitude of absenteeism cost varies significantly with an organization's policies toward absent workers.[3]

The absence rate is usually calculated by tabulating the days lost for the reporting period and dividing it by the product of the average number of employees during the period and the days available for work (workdays). The absence rate is usually meaningful for non-exempt employees only. Of all the variables associated with HR performance, this one will probably receive the most attention and can be easily discussed with management. For example, almost every manager will have an opinion as to what constitutes an acceptable absence rate. The negative consequences of absenteeism is enough reason to track this important variable. In addition, since absenteeism is related to organizational commitment and job satisfaction (discussed later), it is a reflection of how an organization uses its human resources.

Turnover Rate

Employee turnover is another variable that has received much attention in recent years. An excessive turnover rate clearly has a tremendous negative impact on an organization's costs, and HR programs designed to reduce turnover can result in a tremendous bottom-line improvement.

Under normal conditions, voluntary turnover is greater than involuntary, and voluntary is more often studied by management due to the desire to reduce or contain it at an acceptable level. The reasons for turnover must be identified to help prevent it in the future. Several causes of turnover can be traced to inadequate HR programs and policies. A recent meta-analysis of turnover studies confirmed some of the above findings as well as additional relationships.[4] Table 7-1 shows the variables that have a moderate to strong impact on turnover, all of which have important ramifications for the HR function. Although turnover can be viewed as having both negative and positive consequences, it is generally viewed as negatively related to organizational effectiveness.

The impact of turnover becomes significant when its costs are calculated. Although detailed dollar amounts are difficult to calculate, estimates, at least in major categories, can be obtained with little difficulty. The timing of the turnover significantly affects turnover costs. For example, if a new employee leaves after only one week on the job, the total costs may not be excessive, depending on the costs involved in recruiting, orientation, and the initial week of training or education. On the other end of the spectrum, an employee who remains on the job for over five years has probably made a contribution that offsets the cost of recruiting, training, and other adjustment activities. The greatest turnover cost probably occurs when a new employee leaves the organization soon after reaching full productivity. This time period varies considerably among organizations and may range from one week to two years, depending on the individual organization, specific job, and initial training.

Probably the most significant component of turnover costs are the costs connected with the various phases of HR programs designed to recruit and train replacement employees. Total administrative costs can be quite significant. They are partially offset by the employee's contributions on the job, although these

TABLE 7-1
RELATIONSHIP OF TURNOVER TO SELECTED VARIABLES BASED ON THE
RESULTS OF A META-ANALYSIS (MODERATE TO STRONG
RELATIONSHIP)

EXTERNAL	
Employment Perceptions	Positive
Unemployment Rate	Negative
Union Presence	Negative

WORK RELATED	
Pay	Negative
Performance	Negative
Role Clarity	Negative
Overall Satisfaction	Negative
Pay Satisfaction	Negative
Satisfaction With Work Itself	Negative
Satisfaction with Supervision	Negative
Satisfaction With Coworkers	Negative
Satisfaction With Promotion	Negative
Organizational Commitment	Negative

PERSONAL	
Age	Negative
Tenure	Negative
Gender	Women positive
Education	Positive
Number of Dependents	Negative
Behavior Intentions	Positive
Met Expectations	Negative

contributions are very difficult to quantify. In situations where new recruits produce soon after employment, this offset can be significant. These costs are usually in the range of 1 to 2 times annual salary.[5]

The most common turnover rate takes into consideration both voluntary and involuntary turnover. It is calculated by dividing the average total of employees by the number of employees terminated for any reason during that time period. The turnover rate is calculated for all job levels (exempt and nonexempt) based on the assumption that turnover is equally disruptive for higher level jobs as it is at lower levels.

Job Satisfaction

Probably the most important overall HR performance measure to examine, monitor, and analyze is job satisfaction. Organizations always aim for employee satisfaction with their pay, work, coworkers, environment, management, and promotional opportunities. More than anything else, HR practices and policies determine the extent to which employees are satisfied or dissatisfied. Yet no single function within the HR area impacts job satisfaction. It is related to virtually every program of the HR department.

Why the concern for job satisfaction? Its popularity stems from research that focuses on the happy/productive worker concept. For years, management attempted to keep employees both happy and productive. Although there have been mixed results, some research efforts link job satisfaction with productivity.[6] This potential relationship led practitioners and researchers to focus on job satisfaction as a measure of HR contribution. As job satisfaction changed over the years, organizations adjusted HR strategies to meet the challenges of these changing attitudes. Job satisfaction has been found to be related to absenteeism, turnover, and organizational commitment.

Job satisfaction can be measured in several ways. One of the most popular is the Job Description Index (JDI), which describes five dimensions of job satisfaction: work, supervision, pay, promotions, and coworkers.[7] The data are collected by means of a questionnaire. Five sets of questions are used to collect data about the five dimensions of job satisfaction. Means and standard deviations are available for male and female employees pooled across companies.

Organizational Commitment

Another important HR performance measure is organizational commitment. Employers want loyal employees who are committed to the organization's goals, philosophies, and mission. If this is not the case, overall organizational effectiveness is reduced.

Organizational commitment can be defined as the relative strength of an individual's involvement in a particular organization. Conceptually, high levels of commitment can be characterized by at least three factors: (1) a strong belief in and acceptance of the organization's goals and values, (2) a willingness to exert considerable effort on behalf of the organization, and (3) a strong desire to maintain membership in the organization. Organizational commitment of this type represents something beyond mere passive loyalty to an organization. It involves an active relationship with the organization that encourages individuals to give something of themselves in order to contribute to the organization's well-being.

Many HR practices and policies affect the degree to which employees are committed to the workforce. Currently a significant movement from a management-controlled workforce to an employee-committed workplace is developing. A variety of practices are responsible for this move. Among these are:

- Job redesign with emphasis on the whole task and combining doing and thinking.
- Frequent use of work teams as basic accountable units.
- Flat organizational structures, with mutual influence systems.
- Coordination and control based on shared goals, values, and traditions.
- Minimal status differentials to de-emphasize inherent hierarchy.
- Individual pay linked to skills and knowledge.
- Assurances that participation will not result in loss of job.
- Widespread use of employee voice mechanisms.
- Mutual cooperation in labor relations.

In almost every case, the above practices are initiated and/or coordinated by the HR function.

The impact of organizational commitment has been noted in many research efforts. There are at least five measurable outcomes related to organizational commitment: job performance, absenteeism, tenure, tardiness, and turnover. The weakest relationship is with job performance and the strongest is with turnover.[8]

Several measures of organization commitment are available. A popular measure is the organizational commitment questionnaire (OCQ).[9] In this instrument, commitment is defined as the relative strength of an individual's identification with and involvement in a particular organization. Data are collected on a self-administered questionnaire of 15 items. A seven-point Likert scale is used for all items.

ORGANIZATIONAL EFFECTIVENESS MEASURES

One of the most difficult tasks in evaluating the HR function is to determine the appropriate organizational effectiveness measures. As depicted in Figure 7-1, organizational effectiveness measures represent output directly related to human resources. The difficulty with these measures stems not only from the problems surrounding a particular measure, but also from the lack of generally accepted measures of effectiveness for organizations. Even the use of financial measures is questionable because no real consensus on proper financial performance measures has been established. Attempts to relate the impact of the HR function to organizational effectiveness create unique problems. Another problem surfaces when HR specialists attempt to conduct research on the impact of HR practices on organizational effectiveness but are hampered by the lack of data available on both HR practices and appropriate measures of organizational effectiveness.

Financial Performance Measures

One important financial performance measure is return on equity (ROE), which is typically income before extraordinary expenses and discontinued operations divided by common equity. Some researchers argue that four measures of financial performance are important in studies involving organizational effectiveness: return on equity (ROE), return on total capital employed (ROCE), sales growth rate (SGR), and earnings per share growth rate (EPSGR). Many studies have used these measures. Two of these measures (SGR and EPSGR) tap the firm's growth, while the other two (ROCE and ROE) reflect the productivity of capital employed.

Using profitability as a measure of financial performance can be criticized because indicators can be manipulated and they do not always reflect a firm's true underlying value or performance. Depreciation policies, inventory procedures, use of short-term noncapitalized leases to obtain production equipment, and window dressing techniques, such as holding borrowed money as cash until the end of the year, are all potential problems when interpreting accounting data.

Despite its widespread use in practice, the return on investment (ROI) has been criticized for not being an adequate reflection of the rate of return. ROI does not properly relate a stream of profits to the investment that produced it. The earnings portion of the ROI is a result of an investment decision made in the past; however, the assets are influenced not only by past and current earnings, but they also influence future earnings. Because ROI provides an inaccurate mapping, critics have said it is so seriously flawed it bears little, if any, resemblance to the underlying concept of internal or economic rate of return.

Any measure of financial performance should be moderated by the variable that produced the performance: employee costs. Measurements that relate the cost of the investment in human resources to the return provide a better indicator of a company's productive use of its human resources. When relating HR practices to organizational effectiveness, the recommended financial measure is to divide pretax earnings by employee costs.

Productivity Measures

When developing organizational effectiveness measures to link with HR practices, it is essential to include some type of productivity measure. While productivity is an important operational performance measure, measuring of productivity creates extraordinary problems because of the uniqueness of performance in many organizations and the peculiarities of their measurement systems. Monitoring, analyzing, and forecasting the number of employees in an organization is important because changes in this statistic sometimes are a reflection of HR policies and overall management philosophy toward the use of human resources. Too many organizations hamper their profitability and, in some cases, even create their own demise by having an excessive number of employees. Often this situation is a result of company-union negotiations and HR policies that create job security and work rule practices that hamper the organization's ability to maintain a lean and productive workforce. In other cases, lack of automation, bureaucratic style of management, or a less than adequate work ethic lead to excessive employee staffing.

Drucker suggests that it is useful to measure overall productivity as a ratio of the number of units of output, such as automobiles made or patient bed days utilized in the hospital, divided by the number of people on the payroll.[10] This is a gross measure of productivity and measures a company's or an industry's competitive standing. However, differences in organizational philosophy, structure, strategies, and other unique characteristics make this measure unreliable, even when comparing one organization with another in the same industry. What might be more meaningful is to compare overall output in terms of sales value, income, or assets related to the number of employees in the organization. This comparison provides some measure of the utilization of those employees to produce the revenue, generate income, or utilize the assets.

Given the current concern for productivity and profitability, the relationship of the number of employees to revenues, operating expenses, and pretax income are vital. The HR function must help management apply employee skills to positively affect these basic financial indices. For example, the HR function should implement more training programs to improve skills that can lead to better performance which, in turn, should increase revenues and decrease expenses.

Revenue per employee is the most common measure of the gross productivity of the organization. The use of the term "employee" here generally means a full-time equivalent rather than head count. Revenue is a common measure of output, and output per employee is one of four basic labor productivity measures recommended by the American Productivity Center and is also one of the measures used by *Business Week* to develop its list of the most competitive companies. The Revenue Factor, as it is sometimes called, varies widely by industry. The chief value of this measure can be realized by comparing one organization with another in the same position within industry. By tracking this factor through time, productivity changes can be monitored as well as changes to an organization's position within the industry. The Revenue Factor is a measure of output that can be related to HR performance measures.

Recommended Measures

The following points should be considered when reviewing potential measures:

- Select a balance of productivity and profitability measures.
- Select measures that logically relate to the human side of the organization by emphasizing measures that relate to the number of employees or to the amount of employee costs.
- Select measures that relate to the output of the organizations involved.

Based on these criteria, three measures of organizational effectiveness are recommended. The first measure is productivity calculated as total revenue divided by the total number of full-time employees. This gross measure of productivity reflects the efforts of employees to produce sales and service income for the organization. The second measure is productivity calculated as total assets divided by employee cost. This measure recognizes the fact that employees are charged with the responsibility for securing and managing assets. The third, a profitability measure, uses operating income that excludes interest income and taxes. Operating income is used because it relates closely to employee efforts. Interest income and taxes may represent items completely out of the control of employees, at least in the short term. Operating income is divided by employee costs, which represents operating profitability relative to the number of employees needed to generate the profit. Together, these three measures should provide a framework for adequately measuring the overall effectiveness of the organization and the HR function.

DEVELOPING THE HUMAN RESOURCES EFFECTIVENESS INDEX

Chapter 2 discussed more than a dozen approaches to measurement and evaluation of the HR function's effectiveness. Most of these approaches are based on perceptions, adherence to policies, and performance measured against departmental goals. Although it is important to analyze the soundness of policies, to respond to feedback from constituencies, and to meet departmental standards, these approaches may fall short of a comprehensive evaluation. To deal with the new business environment, HR professionals must use objective data related to the organization's goals and overall effectiveness. HR departments can monitor objective performance data, particularly since they now enjoy the benefits of computerized data on employee performance and costs. They can use this information in creative ways to improve management's understanding of the impact of the HR function and they can focus their efforts on those areas that produce the greatest contribution to success. One important way to accomplish this is to transform objective data into standardized measures and/or indices that can be used as management tools. The following study conducted by this author develops one such index. Before this study, standardized measures or indices with criterion-related validity were not available.

Objectives and Phases

The following study is based on three fundamental, interrelated objectives:

- To develop a Human Resources Effectiveness Index (HREI) composed of a selected group of measurement formulas that reflect the extent to which an organization effectively and efficiently uses its human resources.

- To determine the relationships between HR performance measures and measures of organizational effectiveness.

- To determine the relationships between one or more proposed indices and measures of organizational effectiveness in order to identify an index or group of measures that can be used to predict organizational performance.

The study to develop the HREI involved four phases of research. The first phase was an extensive literature search. This author thoroughly reviewed and analyzed existing literature and research efforts to take advantage of previous attempts to measure and evaluate HR performance and link it to organizational effectiveness.

The second phase involved selecting HR measures and organizational effectiveness measures. Appropriate measures from previous efforts were reviewed and a small group of HR practitioners provided input to help select measures of HR performance and measures of organizational effectiveness.

Phase three involved gathering information from practitioners participating in the Society for Human Resources Management (SHRM) Saratoga Institute Measurement Project. (This project is described later.) HR managers from participating organizations were asked to provide their input on the proposed measures, index weights, and potential uses of the index.

The fourth and final phase of research examined the validity of the index with data from the same group of organizations. The results from this effort provided evidence of significant correlations between HR measures (and/or index values) and criterion measures of organizational effectiveness.

Why an Index?

As described in Chapter 2, several studies have verified the relationship of individual HR variables, formulas, or factors with organizational success. However, few research attempts explored the relationship between a group of measures and organizational effectiveness. While it is important to understand how individual factors relate to organizational effectiveness, it is sometimes more important to understand the total impact of several interacting factors. Certainly, HR performance is reflected by many variables, and therefore, a statistical combination of such variables would best indicate the underlying relationship between HR performance and organizational effectiveness. An index is composed of individual measures that, when combined, reflect the success of the overall HR function. Weighing the different measures in an index allows for different levels of emphasis on each measure. Thus, an index of HR performance linked with organizational effectiveness should be a valuable addition to the HR field.

In addition, an index reflecting the effective use of human resources should be an important management tool for organizations. The index has four potential uses. First, an index would allow for comparisons with previous performance. Organizations could monitor the index and/or individual index measures over time, comparing current performance with last month's, last quarter's, or last year's. This comparison allows the organization to observe trends, identify problems, and take corrective action when necessary. Abrupt changes in measures could reveal potential problem areas that need immediate action.

Second, the index can be useful in HR goal setting. Most organizations use some type of management by objectives (MBO) process in which goals or objectives are established for each function of the organization. The HR function is no exception. Annual goals reflect the efforts of the HR staff to fully utilize human resources. An index provides a quantitative measure and greatly simplifies this goal-setting process. Targets can be established for the overall index as well as individual index measures.

Third, if an index becomes widely used, norms could be developed to reflect average values for each measure. This would allow an organization to compare itself with others in the same industry. At best, only industry norms can be useful because many of the measures vary significantly from one industry to another and are dependent on the products manufactured or services delivered.

Fourth, the index could be used in comparisons with other specific organizations. Many organizations pride themselves on how well they stack up with certain other organizations. An index reflecting HR utilization would allow an organization to compare itself with another organization, even in a different industry. From a practical viewpoint, this type of comparison might be meaningless, yet, it could be a source of motivation and pride for an organization to compare itself with companies such as Motorola, Federal Express, or 3M.

Database

To overcome some of the above concerns and meet specified objectives, the study used HR performance data collected by the Saratoga Institute in its measurement project with SHRM. SHRM is the HR field's largest professional society. The Saratoga Institute is a private consulting and service firm specializing in HR measurement and evaluation. The SHRM/Saratoga Institute project involves collecting standardized HR performance data that allows companies to compare their performance with others. The project contains data on 62 factors covering overall HR performance, compensation expenses, benefits expenses, staffing rates and costs, absence and turnover rates, and training rates and costs.[11]

Seventy-one companies from eight industries participated in the study. The database for the sample included organizations in health care, electrical, insurance, banking, chemicals, drugs, heavy manufacturing, and miscellaneous manufacturing. Table 7-2 shows this group represents 521,466 employees scattered over a cross section of geographic regions. The electrical segment was combined with the manufacturing groups in the analysis. Combining groups may limit the comparability within the grouping, but would nevertheless provide a larger sample from which to draw conclusions. The total sample represented 59 percent of the participants in the SHRM/Saratoga survey for that year. With few exceptions, the organizations in the sample are classified as medium growth firms.

TABLE 7-2
STUDY SAMPLE BY INDUSTRY TYPE

	NUMBER OF COMPANIES	PERCENT OF SAMPLE	TOTAL NUMBER OF EMPLOYEES IN SAMPLE
Health Care	18	25.4%	48,450
Electrical	9	12.7%	124,106
Insurance	11	15.5%	30,448
Banking	10	14.1%	35,697
Chemicals	6	8.4%	30,178
Drugs	7	9.9%	96,683
Miscellaneous Manufacturing	5	7.0%	9,210
Heavy Manufacturing	5	7.0%	146,694
Total	71	100.0%	521,466

Theoretical Framework and Hypotheses

Figure 7-2 presents a modified version of the general HR contribution model (Figure 7-1), that specifies variables available in this study. Job satisfaction and organizational commitment measures were not available in the study sample.

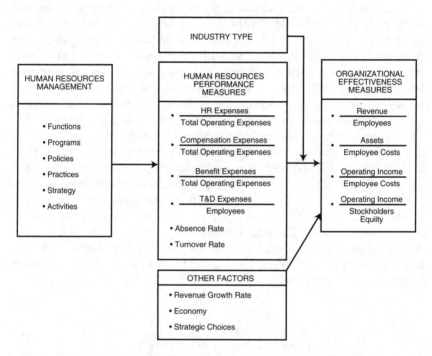

FIGURE 7-2. HR CONTRIBUTION MODEL FOR STUDY.

Three additional measures were included that represent investment data. Because employee compensation represents a significant expense in the organization and its proper utilization can spell success or disaster, it is included in the study. Employee Compensation is divided by operating expenses to allow for comparison of one organization within an industry to another. Using the same logic, employee benefits expense was included and is divided by the operating expense. Finally, training and development expenses were included under the assumption that additional investment of training and development should improve productivity and profitability of the organization. These expenses are divided by the number of employees to allow comparisons with other firms. The success of HR efforts is judged in part by six measures: HR expenses, compensation expenses, benefits expenses, training and development expenses, absence rate, and turnover rate. They are all important outputs of human resource management in an organization and account for a major part of the measurable contribution of HR.

Four measures of organizational effectiveness were selected for the study: revenue productivity, asset utilization, operating income, and operating return on equity (ROE). The ROE measure was added because of its popularity and availability. HR performance measures are only one set of variables that impact these measures of organizational effectiveness. Other variables such as industry type, revenue growth rate, economy, and the strategic choices of the organization also affect organizational effectiveness.

The literature review provided an indication of the relationships between HR performance measures and organizational effectiveness measures. The impact of absenteeism and turnover on organizational effectiveness is well documented. However, because of the lack of research on HR performance, empirical evidence on some of the other relationships was not extensive. Based on what evidence is available and on logical conclusions extracted from the literature and HR practitioners, the expected relationships between the variables are depicted in Figure 7-3.

It is important to consider the two basic approaches used in this study to relate HR performance to organizational effectiveness: costs and investment. HR ele-

MEASURES OF
ORGANIZATIONAL EFFECTIVENESS

HR PERFORMANCE MEASURES	Revenue Employees	Assets Employee Cost	Operating Income Employment Cost	Operating Income Stockholder's Equity
HR Expenses/Total Operating Expenses	+	+	+	+
Compensation Expenses/Total Operating Expenses	-	-	-	-
Benefits Expenses/Total Operating Expenses	-	-	-	-
Training and Development Expenses/Employees	+	+	+	+
Absence Rate	-	-	-	-
Turnover Rate	-	-	-	-

+ = Positive Correlation
- = Negative (Inverse) Correlation

FIGURE 7-3. EXPECTED RELATIONSHIPS.

ments that represent excessive costs (high compensation expenses, an excess number of employees, excessive absenteeism, etc.) serve to reduce organizational effectiveness by increasing costs and/or decreasing output. Using the investment approach, additional funds allocated to the HR function represent an investment in human resources that pays off with increased output and/or reductions in costs. One important assumption is that these additional funds will be used wisely and efficiently. These two approaches form the basis for the specific relationships outlined in the following paragraphs.

Compensation expenses increase in direct proportion to the number of employees and the level of employee costs, because employee costs are defined as total salaries and benefits. This statement assumes that average levels of compensation are competitive. Therefore, as the number of employees increases, compensation costs and employee costs increase proportionately. Efforts to reduce the number of employees will directly affect compensation and employee costs.

Benefits expenses vary directly with the number of employees and the level of employee costs. As with compensation, this statement assumes that the benefits package is competitive so that the principal variable in total benefits expenses will be the number of employees. Therefore, as the number of employees increases, so do employee costs and benefits expenses.

Increases in the investment in human resources through additional HR staff and programs will result in a corresponding increase in output (production, services delivered, sales, profits, etc.). This relationship assumes that the staff is used efficiently and that programs are effective. Also, an increased HR investment will result in a reduction in employee costs through cost savings, more efficiency, improved productivity, etc.

Increases in training and development expenses will have a corresponding increase in the output of employees through increased sales, production, profits, etc., as well as a corresponding reduction in total employee costs through improved employee utilization, increased efficiencies, and additional cost savings. This relationship assumes that training programs meet legitimate needs and are implemented properly.

Increases in the absence rate will decrease output in terms of sales, production, and profitability. Also, increases in this rate will increase employee costs through inefficiencies, delays, and excessive staffing required to confront absenteeism. As with absenteeism, increases in the turnover rate will decrease output in terms of sales, production, and profitability, while increasing employee costs.

Constructing and Weighting the Index

The HR measures used for the index were developed from the literature and with input from a small pilot group of HR practitioners. The rationale for selecting these measures and their importance was discussed earlier in this chapter. The index represents the combinations of all six measures: HR expenses, compensation expenses, benefits expenses, training and development expenses, absence rate, and turnover rate. Each measure was divided by the standard deviation of its industry segment to yield standardized values. Also, each measure was weighted based on the relative importance of the measure as determined by the pilot group. Their recommended weights were rounded and were included on the questionnaire to sample participants. These weights changed in the final analysis based on the input from the study sample.

Questionnaire Results: A Reaction to the Index

The results from the questionnaire administered to participating organizations showed signs of endorsement of the concept of an index. After follow-up requests, 39 organizations returned questionnaires, representing 55 percent of the 71 organizations mailed questionnaires, a response rate higher than most mailed surveys. The respondents represented all industry segments contained in the sample. Because little variation is apparent in responses from one segment to another and because of the small number of responses in some segments, the results are presented as a total group.

The potential use of the index scored high marks. Table 7-3 shows the average value of responses to four potential uses. The respondents to the questionnaire indicated that the greatest potential use of the index is to compare HR perfor-

TABLE 7-3
UTILIZATION OF THE INDEX

POTENTIAL USE OF THE INDEX	AVERAGE VALUE
1. Compare present with past human resources performance within the organization.	4.52
2. Compare your human resources performance with industry norms.	4.76
3. Compare your human resources performance with that of other specific organizations.	4.00
4. Establish goals and objectives for your human resources performance.	4.33

Note. Scale: 5 = Very likely, 4 = More likely than not, 3 = Neutral
         2 = Less likely than not, 1 = Very unlikely

mance with industry norms. This is surprising because industry norms are not established at this point. Not surprisingly, the second most likely potential use is to compare present with past HR performance. The next likely use is to establish goals and objectives for HR performance, while the least likely use is to compare HR performance with that of other specific organizations. No other potential uses of the index were suggested.

Managerial perceptions of the index were positive. Table 7-4 shows the respondents gave the highest favorable responses to top management's ability to under-

TABLE 7-4

MANAGERIAL PERCEPTIONS OF THE INDEX

TOP MANAGEMENT PERCEPTION	AVERAGE VALUE
1. Top management in my organization recognizes the need for this index.	3.38
2. Top management would understand this index.	3.71
3. Top management will use this index in judging human resources performance.	3.57
4. Top management will view this index as the primary measure of human resources performance.	2.86

Note. Scale: 5 = Strongly agree, 4 = Agree, 3 = Neutral
2 = Disagree, and 1 = Strongly disagree

stand the index and the lowest marks to the possibility that top management would view the index as a primary measure of HR performance. The word "primary" was a concern to several respondents who conceded that it would be viewed as an important measure but not necessarily the primary one. There was moderate agreement on the statement that management would use the index to judge HR performance. Finally, management's recognition for the need of the index received slightly favorable results.

The appropriateness of each measure in the index received favorable responses. HR expenses and benefits expenses obtained the highest ratings, followed closely by compensation expenses and training and development expenses. Absence rate and turnover rate achieved the lowest ratings. While absenteeism and turnover are easily measured, comments from respondents indicated some concern about their relationship to organizational effectiveness. The respondents also indicated that HR expenses and training and development expenses were expected to become more important as a measure in the future. Because data on training and development expenses was lacking, it appears that many organizations do not keep track of their training and development costs.

The usefulness of each HR measure also received favorable responses. HR expenses, compensation expenses, and benefits expenses received the highest ratings, while training and development expenses, absence rate, and turnover rate received lower responses. The reaction to the measures was considered sufficiently favorable to use them in the analysis. The appropriateness and usefulness of the index is summarized in Table 7-5.

TABLE 7-5
APPROPRIATENESS AND USEFULNESS OF EACH MEASURE IN THE INDEX

MEASURE	APPROPRIATENESS AVERAGE VALUE	USEFULNESS
1. HR Expenses	4.19	4.24
2. Compensation Expenses	4.14	4.28
3. Benefits Expenses	4.19	4.33
4. Training and Development Expenses	3.95	3.67
5. Absence Rate	3.81	3.81
6. Turnover Rate	3.71	3.95

Note. Scale for Appropriateness: 5 = Definitely appropriate, 4 = More appropriate than inappropriate, 3 = Neutral, 2 = More inappropriate than appropriate, and 1 = Definitely inappropriate.

The respondents provided recommendations for changing the weighting of the HR measures. Table 7-6 shows the adjusted weights. These adjustments bring the recommended weighting closer to equal values than those presented in the questionnaire. The recommended weights were used in index calculations.

Participants were asked whether other measures should be used in the index. In only two isolated cases were other measures suggested, and they involved employment and recruiting. This appears to confirm that the selected measures are appropriate, useful, and comprehensive for measuring total HR performance.

Finally, respondents were asked to provide a ranking of the proposed organizational effectiveness measures. Table 7-7 shows, operating income divided by employee cost received the highest ranking, followed closely by revenue divided by the number of employees. Assets divided by total employee cost and operating income divided by stockholder's equity received the lowest rankings. Only two other alternative measures were recommended, suggesting that there is some agreement that the selected measures are appropriate to gauge organizational effectiveness.

TABLE 7-6
WEIGHTING OF MEASURES AND ADJUSTMENTS

MEASURE	INITIAL ASSIGNED WEIGHT	AVERAGE RESPONDENT WEIGHT FROM PILOT GROUP	RECOMMENDED WEIGHTS FROM STUDY SAMPLE
HR Expenses	16.67	15.7	18.7
Compensation Expenses	16.67	17.6	19.0
Benefit Expenses	16.67	13.9	16.7
Training and Development Expenses	16.67	12.4	12.6
Absence Rate	16.67	20.1	16.3
Turnover Rate	16.67	20.3	16.7
Total	100.02	100.0	100.0

TABLE 7-7
RANKING OF ORGANIZATIONAL EFFECTIVENESS MEASURES

MEASURE	AVERAGE VALUE	RANK
1. Revenue Divided by Number of Employees	2.28	2
2. Assets Divided by Total Employee Costs	2.91	3
3. Operating Income Divided by Employee Costs	1.67	1
4. Operating Income Divided by Stockholder's Equity	3.05	4

Note. Scale: 1 = Most valid, . . . , 4 = Least valid. No ties allowed.

Relationship Between Human Resource Performance and Organizational Effectiveness

Table 7-8 shows significant correlations exist between the measures of human resource performance and measures of organizational effectiveness. The data in this table are for the all industry group. Specific detail on correlations of other segments in this study can be obtained directly from the author. Revenue divided by the number of employees correlates with the investment in human resources as measured by the total HR investment divided by operating expenses (HRMEX). Also, revenue has a significant, negative correlation with compensation expenses (COMPEX) and benefits expenses (BENEX). There is a significant, positive correlation between revenue and training and development expenses (T&DEX), and a significant negative correlation between turnover and revenue. No significant correlations were developed with assets divided by employee cost with any of the HR performance measures. This is apparently the

TABLE 7-8
SUMMARY OF SIGNIFICANT CORRELATIONS BY INDUSTRY SEGMENTS
MEASURES OF ORGANIZATIONAL EFFECTIVENESS

	REVENUE	ASSETS	INCOME	O.R.O.E.
HRMEX	Electrical, All Data	Electrical, Manufacturing Combined	Electrical, Insurance, Health Care, Manufacturing Combined, Banking and Insurance, All Data	Banking, Banking, and Insurance, All Data
COMPEX	Health Care, Banking, Banking and Insurance, All Data		Health Care Heavy Manufacturing, All Data	Electrical
BENEX	Electrical, Banking, All Data		Electrical, Manufacturing Combined, All Data	
T&DEX	Insurance			Banking Banking and Insurance, All Data
Absence	Electrical		Electrical, Health Care (Positive), Manufacturing Combined, All Data	All Data
Turnover	Electrical, All Data		Electrical, All Data	All Data

Note. P<.01, one tailed.

result of missing data for that category. Income divided by employee cost correlates significantly with HRMEX, COMPEX, BENEX, absence, and turnover. The operating return on equity correlates significantly with HRMEX, T&DEX, absence, and turnover with the expected sign on the relationship.

In this group of all industry data, all of the correlations were in the expected direction. Table 7-9 shows a summary of significant correlations by industry segments. Significant correlations were developed in every segment. As the table shows, the two organizational effectiveness measures with the most significant correlations are revenue divided by the number of employees and income divided by employee cost. Also, the HR performance measures showing the most correlations are HRMEX, COMPEX, and BENEX.

Overall, these correlations show some support for the expected relationships outlined for this study. The strongest evidence suggests that an investment in human resource expense increases organizational effectiveness and that decreases in compensation expense and benefit expense correlates with increases in organizational effectiveness. Little correlation exists in the study between training and development expenses and measures of organizational effectiveness. This is pri-

TABLE 7-9
CORRELATIONS BETWEEN VARIABLES WITH NUMBER OF CASES IDENTIFIED—
ALL INDUSTRY DATA

	REVENUE	ASSETS	INCOME	O.R.O.E.	HRMEX	COMPEX	BENEX	T&DEX	ABSENCE	TURNOVER
Revenue	1.000	30	68	19	68	71	71	23	48	55
Assets	.457	1.000	29	19	29	30	30	13	22	22
Income	.629*	.384	1.000	19	67	70	70	23	47	54
O.R.O.E.	.545*	.200	.654*	1.000	18	19	19	10	14	13
HRMEX	.374*	.202	.656*	.741*	1.000	68	68	20	45	53
COMPEX	-.619*	-.359	-.714*	-.259	-.422*	1.000	71	23	48	55
BENEX	-.527*	-.390	-.559*	-.228	-.433*	-.757*	1.000	23	48	55
T&DEX	.564*	.006	.465	.819*	.569*	-.323	-.435	1.000	19	22
Absence	-.217	-.102	-.367*	-.750*	-.333	.232	.160	-.391	1.000	43
Turnover	-.489*	-.078	-.635*	-.713*	-.376*	.505*	.372*	-.543*	.390*	1.000

Note. Number of cases shown upper, right area of table.
$p<.01$, one tailed.

marily due to the lack of data in this particular variable. And, finally, there is some relationship between absence and turnover and organizational effectiveness, although this relationship did not appear as strong as others. However, many other studies have supported the assumption of a negative relationship between absence and turnover and various measures of organizational effectiveness. Significant correlations were developed at the .01 level of significance. A .05 level of significance would have generated additional correlations, but a more conservative approach was used.

Index Values

The data for the six independent variables were standardized by industry segment and weighted based on the weighting scheme recommended by survey participants. The data were transformed to all positive values, because four of the six variables were expected to have a negative relationship with organizational effectiveness. Also, the data values were added to develop the index.

One problem with this analysis is that index values were only calculated when data values were present for all six independent variables. Doing this produced a total of 16 cases for all of the data. Because of this situation, the initial analysis was inconclusive. The variable with the most missing data, T&DEX, was dropped as an index component in an effort to increase the number of complete data sets. (T&DEX is the variable receiving the lowest weight from the survey participants.) Weights were adjusted to fit the five variables and a new index was developed. Correlation coefficients were computed between index values and measures of organizational effectiveness. Table 7-10 shows the results. In the all

TABLE 7-10
CORRELATIONS WITH INDEX VALUES

INDEX VALUES FOR:	REVENUE	ASSETS	INCOME	R.O.S.	O.R.O.E.
All Industry Data	.633* (41)	.523 (19)	.873* (40)	.418* (40)	.663* (12)
Health Care	.497 (10)	—	.795* (10)	−.133 (10)	—
Chemicals and Drugs	.940 (4)	—	.986* (4)	.925 (4)	—
Banking and Insurance	.868* (12)	.675 (11)	.854* (11)	.564 (11)	.312 (6)
Combined Manufacturing	.444 (15)	.030 (4)	.912* (15)	.568 (15)	.947 (4)

Note. Number of cases shown in parentheses.
*p. < .01, one tailed

industry data group, significant correlations appear between index values and revenue, income, and OROE. An additional organizational effectiveness measure was used in the correlation analysis with index values. This measure, return on sales (ROS), is income divided by the revenue. As expected, this measure has a significant, positive correlation with the index value.

The only individual segment with a significant correlation was the health care segment where income has a significant, positive correlation with the index. In the combined chemicals and drugs segment and the combined manufacturing segment, income had a significant, positive correlation with the index value. Also, in the banking and insurance combined segment, a significant, positive correlation existed between the index value and both revenue and income. Although these results are encouraging, the conclusions were somewhat hampered by the small sample size and missing data items.

Results Compared to Framework

Figures 7-1 and 7-2 presented the HR contribution model for the proposed relationship between HRM practices, HR performance, and organizational effectiveness. Overall, there appears to be general support for the model based on the limited amount of data used in this study. By design, this study did not examine the impact of other factors such as strategy, growth, or the economy. However, because most of the participants involved in this study were classified as medium growth, the growth variable should not significantly alter the results. Also, because all of the data were collected in the same time frame under generally good economic conditions, it appears that the impact of the economy variable is minimized. The greatest concern, not accounted for, is the relationship between the strategic alternatives selected by the firms and measures of organizational effectiveness. This examination is left to other research efforts.

Conclusions

Four major conclusions can be drawn from this study. First, the concept of a human resources effectiveness index and the variables contained in this study received favorable reaction from HR executives. Second, significant correlations emerged between HR performance and organizational effectiveness. The strongest relationships were found to exist between organizational effectiveness and HRM expenses, compensation expenses, and benefits expenses. Third, this is the first major study to show empirical support for the relationship between the investment in the HR function and organizational effectiveness. Fourth, support exists for a relationship between index values, which represent the combination of the HR performance measures, and organizational effectiveness.

Overall, these four conclusions make this study important to the field of human resources management and should result in important implications for practitioners and researchers.

Implications for HR Managers and Specialists

HR managers have always been eager to learn more about the relationship between HR performance and organizational effectiveness. The notion of an index composed of HR measures is an attractive concept. The study identified five measures that, when combined, have a significant correlation with measures of organizational effectiveness. While organizations should, and do, focus their attention on these measures, future research should identify other variables to be included in the index. For maximum effectiveness, the concept of an index should be communicated to potential users to stimulate interest, adoption, and use.

HR managers should feel some comfort with the conclusions regarding the relationship between variables. The conclusions confirmed many of the expectations derived from the literature and identified important HR variables that affect organizational performance. For years, HR managers have said that larger investments in HR departments should result in improved organizational performance. And recently, because of the problems of over-staffing and rising compensation costs, executives have suggested that a lean organization is one that trims its payroll costs. The same logic has been applied to benefits. As organizations try to reduce benefits expenses to get the most out of their benefit dollar, bottom-line results should improve. This study supports these relationships.

Overall, HR managers should find this study useful and encouraging as they try to gain a better understanding of the complex relationship between what they do and the output of the organization.

REFERENCES

1. Fitz-enz, J. *How to Measure Human Resource Management*. New York: McGraw-Hill, 1984.

2. Fitz-enz, J. *SHRM/Saratoga Institute Human Resource Effectiveness Survey: 1994 Annual Report*. Saratoga, CA: Saratoga Institute, 1995.

3. Cummings, L. L. and Staw, B. M. *Evaluation and Employment in Organizations*. Greenwich: JAI Press, Inc., 1990.

4. Cotton, J. L. and Tuttle, J. M. "Employee Turnover: A Meta-Analysis and Review with Implications for Research," *Academy of Management Review,* 11(1), 55-70, January 1986.

5. Taylor, T., CPM. "The True Cost of Turnover and How to Prevent It," *Journal of Property Management,* November/December 1993, pp. 20–22.

6. Cranny, C. J., Smith, P. C., and Stone, E. F. *Job Satisfaction*. New York: Lexington Books, 1992, pp. 165–194.

7. Smith, P. C., Kendall, L. M., and Hulin, C. L. *The Measurement of Satisfaction in Work and Retirement*. New York: Wiley, 1969.

8. Cranny, C. J., Smith, P. C., and Stone, E. F. *Job Satisfaction*. New York: Lexington Books, 1992.

9. Mowday, R. T., Porter, L. W., and Steers, R. M. *Employee-Organization Linkages: The Psychology of Commitment, Absenteeism, and Turnover.* New York: Academic Press, 1982.

10. Drucker, P. F. "How to Measure White-Collar Productivity," *The Wall Street Journal,* November 26, 1985, p. 34.

11. Fitz-enz, J. *SHRM/Saratoga Institute Human Resource Effectiveness Survey: 1994 Annual Report*. Saratoga, CA: Saratoga Institute, 1995.

CHAPTER EIGHT

Measuring Specific Human Resources Functions

The previous chapter covered specific measures for the overall human resources function. While important to the HR contribution, these measures should be supplemented with specific measures related to the success of a program or function within the human resources department. Together, overall and specific measures provide a comprehensive measurement and evaluation system.

Fortunately, dozens of measures are available to cover every type of function and program within the human resources department. Because of the wide range of possibilities, selecting appropriate measures is sometimes difficult. The HR staff should select measures that reflect their concerns and needs based on the availability of data or the ease of collecting new data. More importantly, the objectives of the particular program should be reviewed to ensure that measures are selected that reflect or support those objectives, either directly or indirectly.

This chapter presents measures in the five general categories described earlier: productivity, quality, costs, time, and soft data. This distinction encourages the HR staff to focus on potential measures in each of these categories. In some cases, measures in one category may overlap with measures of another category. Quality measures, for example, measures are often contained in soft data items.

No attempt is made to make a judgment on which measures are best. That decision will depend on the needs and values of the HR staff. Unfortunately, standard measures do not exist, although some are more common than others. Because there are no standard measures, the HR professional should exercise caution when comparing measures. As an example, the measure of cost per hire, as defined in this chapter, uses all recruiting and employment costs. Cost per hire measures from other reports may use different costs in the total cost figure. Therefore, it is important to fully understand what goes into the measure being considered for comparison.

Some measures focus on both process and performance. This is particularly true for measures in the time and cost categories. The process measures focus on the efficiency—faster with lower costs. Performance measures focus on improving program or function output.

The discussion that follows briefly describes each major function in HR. No attempt is made to detail all of the specific duties and functions of each department. Many other references are available that provide complete information on each area.

RECRUITMENT AND SELECTION

Recruiting

The recruiting function, the beginning of the HR process, represents one of the important elements of a successful human resources effort. Effective recruiting practices can have a significant positive impact on the organization; whereas, poorly designed and executed recruiting strategies will have both short-term and long-term negative impacts. Recruiting involves all of the various activities aimed at attracting candidates to the organization such as recruitment planning, internal recruitment sources, external recruitment sources, special inducements, and special recruiting projects.

Two important issues involved in recruiting are the cost of the various recruiting sources and the relative effectiveness of the sources in terms of attracting top quality candidates in appropriate numbers. The quality of the individuals recruited is a difficult issue to measure and is usually based on long-term measures that are sometimes unreliable. Consequently, the measurement focus is on cost and productivity in the short term and quality in the long term.

Measures of **productivity** focus on the number of applicants generated by a specific recruitment source. The measure can be in absolute terms or expressed as a productivity ratio. Specific measures include:

- applications per recruiting source
- applicants interviewed per recruiting source
- applicants selected per recruiting source
- applicants selected per recruiter

Quality recruiting focuses on the performance and tenure of the individuals recruited through a particular source. For example, a recruiting source that generates new employees with longer tenure than employees recruited from another recruiting source may be considered to be more effective. Also, if the employees recruited through one source are higher performers when compared to employees recruited from another source, the first source is considered more effective. Therefore, quality of recruiting will focus on employee performance and tenure related to a recruiting source. Because of the complexity of this issue, measures should be taken on a sampling basis to evaluate a recruiting source or else all recruiting sources should be reviewed at the same time. Specific measures include:

- employee performance ratings by recruiting source
- early turnover (first six months) by recruiting source
- tenure by recruiting source
- applications per candidates hired for a recruiting source

Costs are an important concern in the recruiting process because the number of recruiting channels increases along with the cost per channel. Fortunately, the cost of recruiting candidates from one source to another is easy to compare. The specific measure is cost per applicant per recruiting source. The costs include all cost items involved with recruiting and processing needed to move the applicant to the point of job application. These include cost of advertising, agency and search firm fees, employees referral bonuses, applicant and staff travel, and recruiter pay and benefits.

Time is important in many recruiting situations, particularly for critically needed occupations or when recruiting in tight labor markets. The response time for recruiting is an important measure because some recruiting sources have quick responses while others take much longer. Also, it is important to compare response times from one time period to another to determine whether recruiting efficiency has improved and whether the specific measure being used is response time per recruiting source. Response time is measured from the time that the recruiting action is initiated until the individual applies for employment.

Soft data is used to measure candidate satisfaction with the recruiting process. Candidates are often attracted to an organization because of information obtained from recruiting materials. Specific measures include:

- satisfaction with a specific recruiting source
- the reasons for applying to the organization
- the quality of the service delivered by the HR staff involved in the recruiting process
- satisfaction of internal clients who requested the new recruits

These measures are usually obtained from a multiple item attitude survey. In addition to these measures, soft data items may include information on areas such as recruiting candidates with special skills, meeting affirmative action requirements, or building a diverse workforce. No specific measures are recommended for these items except the number of candidates recruited with special skills or backgrounds.

Selection

Closely related to recruiting, the selection process involves processing applicants to the point where a selection decision is made and the applicant is employed. While an effective recruiting process will bring an adequate supply of top quality prospects, an effective selection system will select the best candidates from a pool of applicants. The selection process involves a systematic chain of events and activities that leads to a selection decision. Selection involves screening methods, tests, interviews, simulations, job previews, decision making, and employment processing.

As with recruiting, the primary focus of selection is on efficiency and cost. Quality of the selection process is difficult to determine in the short term, but it can influence long-term performance and tenure. The speed with which applicants proceed through the selection process and the cost of the steps are two important efficiency variables.

The **productivity** of the selection process focuses on the number of applicants who are selected and employed from the process. The specific measure is the number of candidates moved through the process in a given time frame such as a day, week, or month. This number reflects the volume of the employment process.

Quality of the selection process is reflected in the number of candidates who successfully make it through the process, the performance of the new employee on the job, the length of time the selected employee remains with the organization, and the degree to which the process is nondiscriminatory in the selection decision. The measures can be based on the total employment process or a particular selection method. Specific measures include:

- The ratio of the candidates hired divided by the number of applicants through the process (selection ratio)
- The performance of new employees after a specific time period as compared to the expected performance or to the performance of a comparison group. (Performance is measured by performance ratings or objective measures of performance such as sales or production.)
- Voluntary terminations divided by total employees. (This early turnover is a measure of the number of employees leaving in the first six months of employment.)
- Selection ratio of a minority group divided by the selection ratio of a majority group. (This is adverse impact of a selection process.)
- The degree to which the selection process accurately predicts future performance.

The last measure is derived in the validation process and is measured by a correlation coefficient that expresses a mathematical relationship between the performance on the selection device and later on-the-job performance. The higher the correlation coefficient, the greater the match between the two processes. Ideally, a correlation coefficient should be statistically significant at the appropriate confidence level. For more information on this approach see other references.[1]

Costs are easily tabulated and represent an important way to compare the efficiency of the various components of selection. The specific measures include:

- The employment costs per new employee hired. (This is a common cost per hire measure.)
- The cost per hire for a particular selection process such as the assessment center or a specific step such as interviewing.
- The cost per hire grouped by different employee classifications such as exempt and nonexempt, professional and nonprofessional, managerial and nonmanagerial, etc.

The total costs includes recruiting costs, the salaries and benefits of the employment staff, applicant and staff travel, relocation, and all the direct expenses connected with administering the employment function.

The **time** to process applicants through the system is an important measure to monitor. Clients served by the employment process usually want applicants recruited and selected as quickly as possible. Often the ability to respond rapidly and process applicants efficiently makes the difference in success for work units and departments. Specific measures include:

- Time in calendar days to recruit, process, and select applicants and have an offer accepted. This is the time to fill a job and represents the time interval from the date of receiving the approval to recruit to the date the applicant accepts the offer.
- Time in calendar days to recruit, process, and select applicants and have them at work. This interval represents the time from the date of receiving the approval to recruit to the date the new employee is on the job.
- The time in calendar days necessary to process an applicant from the preliminary screening interview, the first step in the process, until the employment decision is made. This is a basic measure of employment processing efficiency and usually includes factors under the control of the HR department.

Several **soft data** measures are possible:

- The candidates' reaction to, and satisfaction with, the employment
- Suggestions for improving the process
- The quality of service of the HR employment staff
- Satisfaction from clients, who requested the new employee.

In addition to the above measures, it may be appropriate in certain circumstances to measure success in areas such as selecting candidates with special skills, meeting affirmative action requirements, or building a diverse workforce. No specific soft measures are recommended for these items except the number of candidates recruited with special skills or background requirements.

Orientation

The orientation process may have other labels such as indoctrination or socialization, and includes all activities necessary to bring the new employee into the job and prepare him or her for the initial job assignment. Orientation activities span a period ranging from one day to one month depending on the nature of the job and the organization's emphasis on orientation. The effectiveness of orientation can be measured by the new employee's adaptation to the job, which should increase productivity and efficiency.

Productivity measures of orientation focus on the productivity of the new employee on the job and use measures specific to the job such as units produced, items shipped, or products sold. An effective orientation process should improve productivity, and measures can be taken at predetermined time intervals and compared to expected performance. Productivity measurements can also be used to compare a new and improved orientation process to the previous orientation process. Finally, productivity measurements taken in the early stages of employment can be used to measure the effect of orientation as compared to the orientation programs of other divisions or even other organizations.

Orientation **quality** measures focus on the quality of the work performed by those who participate in the orientation process. Quality measures such as late shipments, error rates, scrap, rejects, and mistakes are typical measures of quality. These measures can be used for comparisons in the same ways as productivity measures. For example, the levels of quality before and after the implementation of a revised orientation program show the impact of the program.

Cost is an important factor and represents all of the costs of planning, organizing, and conducting the orientation process. Salaries and benefits of new employees should be included to provide an accurate assessment of the total costs. The specific measure is the cost per new employee participating in orientation.

Time is another important consideration in the measurement of orientation effectiveness. A process measure includes the length of time necessary for an employee to complete the orientation process. A performance measure is the time necessary for the employee to reach a certain minimum level of performance or competency. This variable is difficult to pinpoint and is specific to the job and organization. Because of the low costs of orientation, it is unusual to track this variable unless a major expenditure has been made to revise the orientation program. In this case, a pilot test should be used to determine the length of time necessary for an employee to meet a certain level of performance as compared to previous levels.

An important **soft data** measure involves reactions to the orientation program. Often the program focuses on building enthusiasm and shaping the attitudes of employees. During orientation, employee motivation may be at its highest peak, and therefore, it is important to capture that enthusiasm quickly and turn it into positive energy. Therefore, the orientation program should be realistic, efficient, and positive. Soft data measures include:

■ The new employee's reaction to the program and the usefulness of the material

■ The new employee's supervisor's satisfaction with the outcome of the orientation process

■ The new employee's image of the organization. (Possibly before and after measures would be an appropriate comparison.)

HUMAN RESOURCES DEVELOPMENT

Training

Training is an important HR function that can contribute directly to an organization's productivity and profitability. The scope of training programs vary and include technical, operator, customer service, sales, supervisor and management training. The training staff is involved in needs assessment, program design, program development, program acquisition, program delivery, and program evaluation.

With training budgets growing, companies expect programs to show results. Training programs are now measured at five levels.[2] The first level is the participant's reaction, which is taken during or at the end of training. The second level measures learning and determines the skills and knowledge gained during the program. The third level measures the extent to which employees apply what they have learned to the work setting. This measure is usually behavior oriented. The fourth level measures the actual business results obtained from the program such as improved productivity and quality. The fifth level, return on investment, compares the monetary value of the benefits to the cost of the program. Figure 8-1

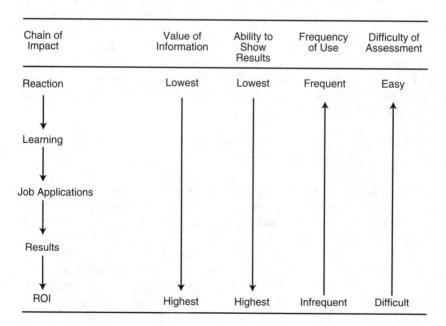

Chain of Impact	Value of Information	Ability to Show Results	Frequency of Use	Difficulty of Assessment
Reaction	Lowest	Lowest	Frequent	Easy
Learning				
Job Applications				
Results				
ROI	Highest	Highest	Infrequent	Difficult

FIGURE 8-1. EVALUATION LEVELS

shows this framework for measurements. The focus here is on measures at levels 3, 4, and 5, which relate to productivity, quality, cost, time, and soft data.

One of the difficulties in measuring training program results is the absence of standardized techniques. Another problem is that while measurements musr be specific to the individual program they often involve the performance of employees at the work site using records maintained at other locations. For example, a training program designed to teach effective sales techniques may result in increased sales at the job. Therefore, the most important and useful training measures are contained in the departments where the participants actually work.[3]

Productivity performance measures are related directly to participant output in work units including total units produced (or services provided), units produced per time period, and units produced per employee. In this situation, the training program teaches employees to improve productivity, and a wide range of appropriate measurements are available. Process measures include the total number of employees trained, the percentage of employees receiving a particular type of training, and the total hours of training per employee.

In terms of **quality,** the training program teaches participants to improve quality in the work unit, and improvement is measured by a variety of quality measures, including reject rate, scrap rate, rework, error rates, defects, and downtime.

Cost measures are in two categories. As a performance measure, cost reductions are often achieved when training program participants develop more efficient methods and apply cost control techniques learned in the program. Actual costs saved is a measure of training program output. A process measure is the cost of training. In this situation, all costs related to initiating, developing, delivering, and evaluating training are included. The cost components include salaries and benefits of participants, travel, facilities, supplies, materials, and other related items. Specific measures include:

- Training cost per participant per program
- Annual training cost per employee

For more information on training costs, see other references.[4]

Time measures include both performance and process measures. Some training programs bring about improvements in time, and thus, time is a performance measure. For example, a program may enable employees to work more efficiently and thus reduce their own time necessary to complete a job or project. Collectively, participants then have additional time to be more productive, work less overtime, or work on other projects. Sometimes training program participants develop ways to save time, avoid penalties for being late, or receive discounts for being ahead of schedule. The performance measure of time savings for most programs will be the actual hours saved per participant and can easily be converted to monetary values.

A process measure is the time needed for training. For example, a training program may be redesigned and the time needed to train an employee is reduced, resulting in a significant savings of participant time.

All training programs should attempt to measure **soft data.** Participants are usually asked for their input and their reactions to the effectiveness of program content, facilitator, audio visual materials, handout materials, class activities, exercises, cases, learning environment, and training support services. Measurements are often taken on the job through one or more types of follow-up instruments to determine the extent to which training participants use the new skills they learned. Typical measures include skill application, skill frequency, and the level of success obtained with each skill. Training measures often include a variety of soft data items.

Career Development

Many organizations are interested in the careers of their employees and want to match employee interests with present and future needs of the organization. Career development programs enhance this matchmaking process and enable employees to remain with an organization for an extended period of time. Consequently, several payoffs of career development programs include increasing employee satisfaction, reducing turnover, meeting staffing needs in the future, and developing needed critical employee skills. Unfortunately, it is difficult to establish a direct connection between career development programs and these payoffs. They have long-term consequences and their impact is difficult to measure. The short-term focus is on process measures such as the number of participants in the program. This focus is acceptable because in many cases, participation in a career development effort is on a volunteer basis, and the extent to which individuals are involved is a measure of the attractiveness and usefulness of the program as perceived by the target group.

Measures of **productivity** include the number of participants in the programs or the percentage of employees involved in career development activities. Also, for programs aimed at preparing individuals for specific jobs, the number of individuals determined to be qualified for those jobs in a given time frame is a measure of productivity of the career development effort.

Measures of **quality** focus on the relative success of the program in terms of participants completing the program, the level of preparedness, and the match of needs of the organization with the availability of candidates for the program. Ultimately, the quality of the career development program should be measured in terms of reduced turnover and enhanced performance resulting from improved job satisfaction or skills acquisitions. This connection is difficult to obtain, however, and therefore is not very reliable.

Career development **cost** measures focus on the actual cost of conducting the programs. As with other programs, all of the related costs that can be isolated should be included in the total. Specific measures include cost per participant and annual cost per employee.

Time measures of career development focus on the average length of time participants are involved with the program. Also, it may be important to measure the average time to complete the program when this measure is under the control of the participant, program developers, and/or administrators.

Soft data measures are important in career development. In these situations it is helpful to measure:

- participant's reaction to the program and the degree of satisfaction
- participant's perceived value of the program
- employee's perceived value of the program (all employees, including non-participants)
- client satisfaction with the program
- participant job satisfaction of participants

Career development programs also generate related skills. For example, a career development program may develop job seeking and interviewing skills.

Organizational Change and Development

Few functions within HR have grown in importance and significance as much as organization development (OD) and change. Although they may not use the actual term OD, many organizations engage in OD activities such as transforming, rebuilding, revitalizing, restructuring, or reengineering to improve productivity, quality and customer service, or increase growth, stop decline, or control cost.

A return on investment in organization development programs is not usually generated for years, sometimes as long as three to ten years. For example, at Litton Industries, an OD program evolved, developed, and was implemented over a ten-year time frame and resulted in a return on investment of 650 percent.[5] Because the output of an OD effort will be long-term and in part subjective, it is difficult to relate it directly to the OD effort. In the short term, the focus is on efficiencies: managing the process to deliver programs with the least cost and greatest efficiency. Also, customer or client satisfaction is critical in the early stages of the process in order for everyone involved in the process to see the need for it, understand its purpose, and support it fully.

Organization development efforts produce all types of improvement variables for **productivity.** Typical measures include items produced per time or per employee, absolute volume (or services provided) such as sales, units produced, and units serviced and delivered. These measures are obtained in a follow-up process that monitors the variables after the program has been implemented. A key step in measuring the improvement is to isolate the effect of the program from other variables that could influence the results. Additional strategies for accomplishing this step are presented in another chapter.

Quality improvement is another important target for OD programs with measures such as scrap rate, reject rates, error rates, mistakes, and losses. Programs focus on any data that is related to improving the quality of products, services, or transactions with internal or external customers. As with productivity improvements, a follow-up intervention taken months or even years after the program is implemented is necessary to measure long-term changes. Measures are compared to levels prior to the program to determine the extent of improvement.

Cost measures include both performance and process variables. On the performance side, many OD programs focus on cost reductions, and consequently, cost data are monitored after the program is implemented. On the process side, the costs of the program are monitored, including those associated with designing, developing, and delivering the program. A typical measure is the cost per participant to implement the program. Because it is often an organization-wide program, the annual cost per employee may be a more appropriate measure.

Time is another important variable that can involve performance and process. As a performance measure, some OD programs aim at reducing the time needed to perform tasks or complete projects such as the time necessary to introduce a product or develop a procedure. In these cases, time improvement measures are treated the same way as productivity, quality, and cost measures. As a process measure, the time necessary to develop the program and to reach certain milestones is monitored. If not carefully managed, the OD effort can take much longer than it should. An effective program should use objectives with established time frames to change participants from one "state" to another.

Soft data measures are important to the success of the OD effort. All individuals involved in an OD program should have a positive reaction because an OD program is often a subjective and intangible process. Some specific measures include:

■ participant's reaction to the usefulness of the project or program
■ participant's plans to use program material
■ client perception of the program

An OD effort will usually generate many types of **soft skills** similar to those described in the training section.

Performance Appraisal

Performance appraisal (PA) is an important process in every organization. In some organizations, performance appraisal is more formally structured and is staffed as a separate department. In others, it is less formal and is coordinated by other departments such as compensation, employee relations, or human resource development. Regardless of its structure and format, it is a process that can either generate significant improvement or create problems depending on its design and implementation.

In recent years, the performance appraisal process has changed significantly. At one time, it was a subjective function controlled primarily with input from the employees' immediate supervisor. It is now more objective and uses specific, established measurable targets that are often based on a variety of inputs. The purpose of performance appraisals vary significantly and usually involve one or more of the following:

■ improve employee performance
■ serve as a means for providing salary increases
■ serve as a developmental process
■ document employee performance
■ defend the organization against legal challenges

Several concerns continue to surround the performance appraisal process, although there has been much improvement in recent years.[6] In many organizations, all the parties involved in the traditional performance appraisal (the appraisee, the supervisor of the appraisee, and the program administrator) are still uncomfortable with the process. Also, the problem of subjectivity still exists. Measures often include a rating of skills that are subjective in nature and leave some individuals feeling uncomfortable with the outcome. Another issue is the input for the appraisal process that creates some measurement problems. In recent years, employees and team members have been given more freedom to provide input into their appraisal process.

Productivity measures from the appraisal process come in a variety of formats. Several process measures are available such as the percentage of employees with completed appraisals on time or the number of appraisals completed during the quarter. Because some supervisors and managers will not meet this responsibility, HR must ensure that the appraisal process is completed properly. Performance measure can be used to identify trends as well as to compare one department, division, or plant with another. Probably the most important performance measures are the actual changes in productivity of the employees as a result of the appraisal process. For example, an organization may implement a revised performance appraisal system that combines measurable goals with effective coaching. The improvement in performance of individuals is an important measure of success.

Quality measures are similar to productivity measures and include process improvements as well as performance improvement of individuals. Process measurements indicate how well the performance appraisal system has been managed. Specific measures include:

■ the percent of appraisals completed
■ the number of appraisals completed on time
■ the accuracy of the appraisal process to judge individual performance

The performance appraisal process should result in individual improvements in quality, which is indicated by changes in errors, reject rates, scrap rates, losses, etc.

Costs measures for the appraisal process include both process and performance measurements. A process measure is the cost involved in conducting and administering the performance appraisal process and may be reported as the cost per employee appraised. Staff time, direct supervisor and employee time devoted to the process, supplies, record keeping, and other administrative expenses are included in the costs. Performance measures include improvement in cost control and cost reduction is sometimes a result of the performance appraisal process. These cost items related directly to improvement are measured in a follow-up intervention similar to the one used to measure productivity and quality.

Time measures in performance appraisal are similar to cost measures. Process measures include average length of time necessary for the appraisal to be completed. On the performance side, individuals often respond with time-based improvements such as reduced response times, delivery times, and cycle times. Improvements are measured after the program is implemented, following the same procedures used with productivity, quality, and cost improvements.

Soft data measures include reactions from those employees who are involved in the process as well as those people who support the appraisal process such as top management. With these groups, it is important to measure the following:

■ satisfaction with the process
■ degree to which the process changes and improves the organization
■ degree to which the process meets its objectives
■ specific improvements that have been documented from the process

The performance appraisal process also yields soft skills measures such as the acquisition of new skills, specific behavior changes, and improvements in the frequency and success of skill use.

COMPENSATION

Direct Compensation

Direct employee compensation represents a powerful tool for improving organizations. If used properly, employee pay systems can enhance job satisfaction and create high levels of motivation that translate into productivity improvement. Direct pay includes the traditional practices of base salary and merit increases as well as nontraditional pay plans involving a variety of bonus arrangements and incentive plans. Collectively, they provide a full array of possibilities for tremendous performance improvement.[7]

Several important issues surround direct compensation and influence the measurement and evaluation process. As always, there is an issue of maintaining a competitive compensation package that will enable the organization to attract, retain, and motivate a capable staff. Another issue involves internal equity, which means all employees should be compensated properly for their efforts, contributions, and responsibilities, regardless of background and demographic characteristics. More recently, issues linking pay directly to performance have taken on new dimensions. A variety of nontraditional pay plans have been introduced with much success. These include plans such as gain sharing, team based compensation, skill-based pay, and profit sharing. Total compensation has taken on new dimensions as companies become more concerned with efficiency. Organizations attempt to keep labor costs low and payrolls at minimal levels while ensuring that employee pay is competitive with industry averages.[8] This balance requires organizations to carefully monitor compensation costs to ensure that they are in line with appropriate benchmarks or targets.

Productivity measures from direct compensation involve several important issues. One group is the performance measures linked to the output of the pay plans. One measure of the effectiveness of a pay-for-performance plan is the change in output attributed to the plan. Measures, usually obtained in a follow-up evaluation, are analyzed and compared to the same measures before the program was implemented. These measures are very specific to the organization and situation and include outputs of production and services measured in absolute values or on a per employee or per unit of time basis. Productivity in compensation is sometimes measured relative to where the organization expects pay to be positioned:

- average salary of employee by job group
- average salary increase
- average of current salaries divided by an industry average
- compensation as a percent of operating expenses

- compensation as a percent of revenues
- percent of employees involved in pay-for-performance programs or nontraditional pay plans. (The greater the number of employees involved in pay-for-performance programs, the greater the likelihood of significant performance improvement in the organization.)

Quality measures are used when pay plans focus on quality improvement objectives. For example, if a plan pays off for quality improvement, then the degree to which the pay plan is successful is determined by the change in the quality variable. Another measure of the quality is the flexibility of the pay plan to adjust to changes with the organization and with client needs.

Because compensation represents **costs,** appropriate measures for cost are included in the productivity category. An additional measure is the administrative costs for implementing, coordinating, and monitoring compensation expressed as a percent of compensation, department budget, or total compensation. **Time** is an appropriate performance measure when a pay plan is linked with time improvements such as cycle times, delivery times, schedules, and completion time, just as a process measure is appropriate when tracking processing time for salary changes and plan payouts.

Soft data is important because of the importance of pay satisfaction with employees. It is often necessary to determine the degree to which employees are pleased with pay practices and how effective they perceive them to be. Most attitude surveys include items related to satisfaction with pay and include reactions to:

- actual pay
- internal equity
- external competitiveness
- pay policies
- administration of policies
- effectiveness of pay to improve productivity

Employee Benefits

Employee benefits have become a major component of the employment package with the cost of benefits averaging about 39 percent of payroll in the USA.[9] This adds to an already costly total unit labor cost. Benefits are linked closely with job satisfaction and often influence an employee's decision to join or remain with an organization. Therefore, the consequences of an uncompetitive employee benefits package is extremely important, while costs are significant to its profitability.

Because benefits have grown considerably, there is a trend to shift some of the cost to employees. Also, while there have been previous efforts to match individual needs and interests with programs, there is some evidence that the variety and scope of benefits have been curtailed.[10] Regardless of the level and status, benefits represent a tremendous expenditure and are of critical importance to employees.

The **productivity** of employee benefits is measured in several ways. In a sense, the number of benefits offered is a measure of the quantity of the total benefits package. The level of competitiveness of the plan features and design is another measure. Because it is important to have a high participation rate in some benefits plans, this figure is sometimes a measure of plan productivity. For example, in a wellness program offered at no charge to employees, a high participation rate is desired because of the subsequent positive consequences the plan can have on employee health costs. Specific measures include:

- number of benefit plans
- plan features
- percent of employees covered
- percent of employees participating in voluntary plans

Several **quality** measures are involved in benefits. The degree to which a plan matches needs and the degree to which employees use the plan appropriately is an indication of quality. Specific measures include:

- benefits provided compared to industry and geographic averages
- percent of employees who abuse a specific plan
- percent of employees who use a plan

Employee benefit **costs** are probably the most important areas to measure and monitor. Specific measures include:

- benefit costs as a percent of operating expenses
- benefit costs as a percent of revenue
- cost of a specific benefit plan as a percent of the total benefits cost
- administrative costs of benefits as a percent of the total benefits cost
- benefit costs per employee
- health care costs per employee (or other plan cost per employee)
- plan cost compared to perceived value
- number of cost containment features and how well they work

Time measurements are often tracked in two ways. The processing time for specific claims or requests for services is an important measure. Excessive delays, for example, in the time to process a medical claim or the time to receive a reimbursement for a flexible benefit plan can be very irritating to employees. The other time factor is the response time for a particular request or inquiry concerning benefits.

Soft data measures are extremely important because of the nature of employee benefits. The primary rationale for having a benefits package is to increase job satisfaction to help attract and retain employees. Specific measures include:

- the perceived value of the benefits plan
- the appropriateness of the plan to meet individual needs
- the flexibility of the plans to adjust to changing situations
- the degree of competitiveness of the plan
- the fairness of the plan relative to cost sharing arrangements

With soft data, it is important to build an understanding and awareness of benefits so that they are used properly.

FAIR EMPLOYMENT PRACTICES

No portion of the HR system has grown more rapidly than that responsible for coordinating fair employment practices. Virtually nonexistent in the early 1960s, fair employment or equal employment opportunity departments are now fully staffed and are clearly a mainstream function within HR. The staff has increased in response to a variety of legislative initiatives at the local, state, and federal level as well as executive orders from the federal government.

One of the biggest challenges is that these departments must cope effectively with an increasing number of laws and regulations affecting the employment and employment discrimination. A staff is often required to monitor and stay abreast of regulations and interpret what they mean to the organization. Most organizations take preventive measures, such as affirmative action, to head off potential problems before they occur. The concept of affirmative action creates a dilemma. The organization must continue to make progress on affirmative action efforts by making possible the upward mobility of minorities and other protected groups, yet at the same time, it must create a perception of fair and equal treatment of all employees.

The cost of compliance can be divided into three parts. The first cost involves direct compliance with regulation to ensure that the forms, policies, and procedures are in place. The second cost area is the cost for the programs needed to change attitudes and the culture of organization to head off future problems or to ensure compliance with current regulations. A third cost component is the cost of non-compliance that involves defending the organization against charges and complaints and losing court cases and settlements.

Productivity measurements of fair employment practices involve several areas. Specific measures include:

- progress made toward the goals and timetables in the affirmative action plans
- number of special programs to promote fair employment
- number of participants enrolled in special programs aimed at upward mobility and workforce diversification
- number of employees who participate in special awareness training programs on nondiscrimination, diversity training, etc., (particularly those who attend on a volunteer basis)

Quality measurements in fair employment efforts involve challenges to the system and complaints from employees. Specific measures include:

- number of informal complaints in the organization
- number of informal complaints per employee
- number of charges filed with external groups
- percent of complaints resolved before they become external charges
- actual settlements made and cases lost (the hard measures of the quality)

Cost is monitored in terms of the cost of compliance and the cost related to administering the program. Specific measures include:

- fair employment costs as a percent of the overall HR budget
- fair employment costs per employee
- cost of adverse action by employees and groups
- cost of specific programs as a percent of budget
- total costs associated with the compliance and affirmative action efforts

Time measures focus on specific programs and the responses to programs. Specific measures include:

- average time to achieve target levels with affirmative action plans
- average time needed to fully prepare the appropriate number of individuals for jobs
- average time needed to respond to questions, charges, and complaints. (This is an indication of how quickly the organization is willing to investigate and react to concerns.)

Soft data are important because all groups must view the organization as proactive, successful, and effective with fair employment efforts. The degree to which protected groups of employees feel that the organization is fair and aggressive in their efforts is an important measure. The reaction to specific programs, progress made, and the actual policies are critical. Soft data items involve attitudes changed and culture shifts within the organization that are measured by surveys and questionnaires.

EMPLOYEE AND LABOR RELATIONS

Labor Relations

The labor relations (LR) function has undergone change in recent years primarily because of declining unionization and the changing nature of the union-management relationship. Unionization, expressed as a percent of the nonfarm workforce has steadily declined since the 1950s, reaching a level below the 16 percent range.[11] Although the numbers have declined, the union's influence is still evident, not only for the employees they represent, but for potential targets of unions where employers attempt to prevent unionization. The labor relations function coordinates activities relative to the labor-management contract. For the system to work smoothly, there has to be some mutual understanding and trust between all of the groups.

There is much evidence of a more cooperative environment in which all management and unions are working together to save an organization or to make it more profitable and efficient. Programs come in a variety of formats and structures, and produce mixed results. The tremendous changes taking place in the workplace often supplant the need for unions, sometimes by design. These programs, involving concepts such as self-directed teams, employee involvement, and employee empowerment often are aimed at improving the relationship between management and employees and at making employees assume more responsibility in the organization. This approach appears to minimize the need for unions, which cause them to change their role dramatically.

While it is difficult to measure the **productivity** of the labor relations function, some specific measures are available:

- number of grievances processed per labor relations staff member (internal staff productivity)
- number of changes in the collective bargaining agreement achieved that were desired by the management

■ number of labor-management cooperative efforts
■ number of participants in those efforts

In the long term, cooperative labor relations efforts should result in improvements in organizational productivity measurements such as total volume of goods and services per employee.

Quality measures are meaningful in the labor relations process. Specific measures include:

■ number of grievances (although this is a measure of quality of the labor relations function, the number can be influenced by other factors)
■ number of grievances resolved prior to arbitration (a measure of the quality of LR staff skills)
■ number of arbitrations won
■ number and magnitude of work stoppages (compared to what was "given up" to prevent the work stoppage)

All of the quality measures must be viewed in the content of the environment and in conjunction with other measures.

Costs are important and include internal costs of managing and administering the LR function. Specific measures include:

■ total LR cost as a percent of the HR budget
■ cost per grievance
■ cost of arbitration
■ cost of settlements
■ cost associated with a work stoppage
■ cost of collective bargaining agreement changes (when improvements are made or when reductions are negotiated)

Time involves several measures, including:

■ time to respond to employee issues
■ average time necessary for a grievance to move through the steps to arbitration
■ duration of work stoppage

Soft data measures in the form of attitudes can be obtained from those who must work with the process. Often employee dissatisfaction with the process causes grievances. An important source of input to measure satisfaction/dissatisfaction is the first level supervisor who often works with modified agreement. Supervisors should perceive the labor relations process as being a productive and helpful ingredient in the workforce setting.

Employee Relations

Employee relations is often a collection of miscellaneous programs and activities aimed at improving employee satisfaction. When based on legitimate needs and administered properly, these programs can contribute to the organization's bottom line as well as improve job satisfaction.

Because of changing demographics and workplace issues, new programs are needed. Programs such as job sharing, part-time employment, flexible working hours, and child care arrangements meet important needs of employees. Another example of new programs meeting employee needs is the increasing use of the HR function to help employees cope with situations such as drug, alcohol, marital, financial, or legal problems. The helpful, nurturing role of HR is still in existence and is a part of many HR functions.

All employee relations programs are designed to help meet specific needs of employees or address societal problems. Although the payoff is sometimes difficult to determine, the cost can be staggering. For example, the cost of an employee assistance program can be tremendous, while the payoff is long-term and difficult to quantify.

Because employee relations involve such a diverse group of programs, it is difficult to associate measures with the entire function. It is best to focus on the objectives of specific programs. **Productivity** measures focus on the number and activity levels of programs. Specific process measures include:

- number of programs
- number of events in program (the number of counseling sessions)
- number of participants in a program (e.g., the employee assistance program)
- participation rates (e.g., child care program)
- Application rates for program (e.g., scholarship program for dependent children)

Ultimately, performance measures should improve as a result of employee relations programs. For example, an employee assistance program (EAP) should have a long-term financial impact in order to prevent a problem in the future.

Quality measures focus on how well a specific program meets needs of employees. **Cost** measures focus on the cost of a particular program, expressed as cost per participant or a cost per employee. For example, an EAP program could be monitored on total cost, the cost per employee served, or the cost per employee. **Time** measures include the time necessary for those involved in programs to complete parts or all of the program. Response times are important when responding to requests for information.

Soft data measures are possibly the most important measure for employee relations, because most of the employee relations efforts are undertaken to improve job satisfaction. Specific measures from surveys can be very helpful. Employees are usually asked directly about their perception of a program, how they used it, and whether they view it as an important part of the culture, climate, or employee relations atmosphere.

SAFETY AND HEALTH

In today's climate, most organizations allocate a significant amount of time and money to the safety and health of their employees. Some of these programs are implemented because they are needed and others because they are required by legislation. Still other programs are implemented to prevent costs or consequences of an unacceptable safety and health record.

Employee safety is regulated by local, state, and federal governments, although many employers go beyond regulatory requirements and embrace the process with enthusiasm. The continued spiraling cost of workers compensation coverage and the resulting cost of accidents and injuries has an impact on many organizations. Although safety records have improved, there is still the tremendous cost for medical care, insurance premiums, and legal costs associated with the process.[12]

Productivity measures focus on number and frequency of programs and activities. Specific measures include:

- number of safety and health programs
- number of safety meetings
- number of internal safety inspections
- number of safety committees
- number and hours of safety training programs
- job redesigns for safety and health considerations
- safety incentive awards

Quality is probably the most important area to measure in a safety and health function. Virtually all of the accidents, injuries, and illnesses are a reflection of the quality of the program. Specific measures include:

- number of accidents
- accident frequency rate

■ accident severity rate
■ OSHA incident rate
■ number of lost-time accidents
■ number of deaths
■ number of near misses
■ number of violations found in safety inspection
■ total citations from OSHA
■ liability accidents
■ property damage accidents
■ industrial hygiene monitoring results
■ industrial hygiene compliance results

All of these are important measures that can be reported by department, plant, or company.

Next to quality in safety and health areas are **costs,** which are significant and measured in a variety of ways. Specific measures include:

■ average cost per accident
■ total lost time costs
■ workers compensation costs
■ accident costs per hour of work
■ cost of OSHA fines
■ liability costs
■ property loss costs
■ cost of safety and health as a percent of HR budget
■ cost of safety and health per employee
■ cost to comply with a new regulation

These costs can become quite significant and force many organizations to focus considerable attention on them.

Time measures are also important in safety and health. Specific measures include:

■ the average number of lost-time days
■ average time to correct a citation
■ average rehabilitation time

A process measure is the time necessary to implement a new safety practice, comply with a new regulation, respond to a particular issue, or to process a claim.

Soft data measures the skills of employees as they learn new behavior and safety practices from safety training programs and safety meetings. Both the frequency and application of the skills are monitored. Also, soft data measures the attitudes of employees toward the safety and health environment of the organization, safety and health practices, and specific policies and procedures.

HUMAN RESOURCE INFORMATION SYSTEMS

With the explosive development and use of the computer, the human resource information systems (HRIS) function within the HR department has mushroomed in its scope and capabilities. The HRIS includes elaborate networks, hardware, and software to tackle a variety of HR issues, tasks, and problems. Originally developed to process employee records, the systems are now used to make decisions by bringing together large amounts of data. The next generation of HRIS will link HR systems with organizational output and, in this context, as changes are made in HR programs, systems, and practices, the output on the organization can be monitored.[13]

Implementing the human resource information systems involves several key issues. The first, and most important issue, is selecting the appropriate system from a wide range of hardware and software options. The second major issue is deciding what types of data will be processed by the system and the manner in which it will be used to develop effective measures to meet the particular needs of the organization. The third issue is keeping the cost of the system reasonable. While the implementation of HRIS should save in the costs of managing the data, in actual practice, project costs can get out of control and exceed planned budgets and expenditures. The fourth and probably most critical issue is ways to integrate the HRIS into important decision-making routines—how to move the system from a record keeping, employee data base to an effective HR decision-making tool.

As computer technology continues to improve and software applications increase, tremendous opportunities exist for organizations to use computers in innovative and creative ways to help with HR solutions. In the concept of HR measurement and evaluation, HRIS actually serves as a tool to measure and monitor other programs. However, the system must be subjected to its own accountability. The system itself must be evaluated along with other HR functions.

The **productivity** of HRIS is often measured in terms of the number of reports it generates, or is capable of generating, whether weekly, monthly, manually, or on-line. The vast array of reports can become somewhat cumbersome and often excessive. A second productivity measure is the range of data available from the system. Some systems can integrate data in creative and innovative ways to create a variety of data options. A third productivity measure is the number of inquiries the system experiences in its regular use, based on the assumption that a more productive system is one which is fully utilized.

Quality measures are also very important and usually involve the accuracy and completeness of the data in the system. Improved system quality should improve the quality of decisions made by managers and executives. Having more accurate data in a faster time frame should allow an organization to improve its decision-making possibilities. Data accuracy can be determined through random sampling of files and output reports and is measured by error rates.

Cost represents a significant part of the HRIS implementation and should be closely monitored. Total system costs, which may be allocated on a per employee basis, is one measure. Another is the routine operating cost, which is measured as cost per report, cost per inquiry, or cost per employee. Finally, system cost as a percent of overall HR budget is another appropriate measure of efficiency.

Time savings includes process measures such as the time necessary to generate a report, response time for inquiries, and the timeliness of the data. Also, the time necessary to implement new HRIS data projects is another measure. On the performance side, the system should generate a time savings when decisions are made quicker because of faster processing with the HRIS.

It is also important to measure **soft data** with the system. Users are often surveyed to determine their understanding of the system, how well they know how to use it, their frequency of use, and their satisfaction with the output. Another soft data measure is the degree to which

- users are equipped to work effectively with the system
- the system represents the latest technology
- the system represents the most effective approach to automating HR decision making

Conclusion

This chapter presented a variety of potential measures for each of the major functions of the human resources department. Measures are presented in categories of productivity, quality, costs, time, and soft data. There is no attempt to judge which measures are best, but rather, the chapter offered a wide range of possibilities. Each HR department should select the measures appropriate for evaluating the efficiency and effectiveness of the function. When combined with the overall measurements presented in Chapter 7, a comprehensive measurement and evaluation system can be developed and implemented.

REFERENCES

1. Noe, R. A., Hollenbeck, J. R., Gerhart, B., and Wright, P. M. *Human Resource Management.* Burr Ridge: Irwin, 1994.

2. Phillips, J. J. "Return on Investment—Beyond the Four Levels," In E. Holton (Ed.) *Academy of HRD 1995 Conference Proceedings,* 1995.

3. Pulley, M. L. "Navigating the Evaluation Rapids," *Training & Development,* September 1994, pp. 19–24.

4. Phillips, J. J. *Handbook of Training Evaluation and Measurement Methods,* 2nd Edition. Houston: Gulf Publishing, 1991.

5. Phillips, J. J. (Ed.) *Measuring Return on Investment.* Alexandria: American Society for Training and Development, 1994.

6. Wilson, T. B. *Innovative Reward Systems for the Changing Workplace.* New York: McGraw-Hill, Inc., 1995.

7. Berlet, K. R. and Cravens, D. M. *Performance Pay as a Competitive Weapon: A Compensation Policy Model for the 1990s.* New York: John Wiley & Sons, Inc., 1991.

8. Schuster, J. R. and Zingheim, P. K. *The New Pay: Linking Employee and Organizational Performance.* New York: Lexington Books, 1992.

9. Thompson, R. "Benefit Costs Surge Again," *Nation's Business,* February 1993, p. 38–39.

10. Ivancevich, J. M. *Human Resource Management.* Chicago: Irwin, 1995.

11. Ettorre, B. "Will Unions Survive." Management Review, August 1993, pp. 9–15.

12. Miner, J. B. and Crane, D. P. *Human Resource Management: The Strategic Perspective.* New York: HarperCollins College Publishers, 1995.

13. Forrer, S. E. and Leibowitz, Z. B. *Using Computers in Human Resources: How to Select and Make the Best Use of Automated HR Systems.* San Francisco: Jossey-Bass, 1991.

CHAPTER NINE

Using Benchmarking to Measure HR Effectiveness

Benchmarking has experienced phenomenal growth in the last decade. Virtually every function of an organization has been involved in some type of benchmarking to evaluate activities, practices, structure, and results. Because of the popularity and effectiveness, this chapter focuses exclusively on benchmarking as a tool to measure HR effectiveness. Although the process may not show the HR contribution, it is an effective way to set standards and improve processes. In many cases, the benchmarking process develops standards of excellence from organizations that are considered to have best practices.

The emphasis in this chapter is on how to develop and implement a benchmarking project because few, if any, appropriate national benchmarking efforts are available. With the proper focus and effort, an organization can develop its own benchmarking study and the results can be very rewarding. Benchmarking should be undertaken as an integral part of a comprehensive evaluation process.

A STRATEGIC EVALUATION TOOL

Originally designed to focus on improving quality in organizations, benchmarking quickly spread to other functions and has become an indispensable management tool for continuous improvement. Benchmarking is a continuous process of collecting information from other organizations that is considered to represent best practices, and using the information to improve the current organization. Benchmarking is a process of learning from others, but is not a process of duplicating what others have done. It represents a pragmatic search for ideas. The process is usually time-consuming, and requires much discipline to make it effective and successful. It is not a quick fix, but a continuous, ongoing process.

Benchmarking satisfies a variety of needs and is used for several purposes. It is extremely helpful in the strategic planning of the HR function. The information and measures derived from the process can enable HR managers to help their organization meet its strategic objectives. It is also useful in identifying trends and critical issues of the HR function. Measures from benchmarking can become the standards of excellence for an activity, function, system, practice, program, or specific results. In this sense, it has become an important evaluation tool. Benchmarking also allows the organization to compare certain product features such as the features of the employee benefits package. For these and other reasons, the benchmarking process is an important tool for the HR function.

PHASES OF THE BENCHMARKING PROCESS

Benchmarking is a logical process involving systematic steps or phases. When implemented successfully, the benchmarking process should become an integral part of the organization. Figure 9-1 presents seven phases that represent a modification of the phases reported in other works.[1] Although several approaches are available, these phases appear to address the HR department's needs. Each phase is outlined below.

Phase One: Determining What to Benchmark

The first step is to identify precisely what type of information is needed from benchmarking. This step deserves much attention because of the tendency to explore more areas than are feasible or to delve into issues because "it would be nice to know." Because of the time involved in securing the information, the problem of availability of information, and the difficulty in finding suitable partners, benchmarking initiative must stay within prescribed boundaries of needed information. Attempts to collect information that is generally unavailable or difficult to obtain will be unsuccessful. Also, a lengthy request may be too overwhelming, making it difficult to obtain the information from a benchmarking partner. The potential target areas of HR benchmarking information include:

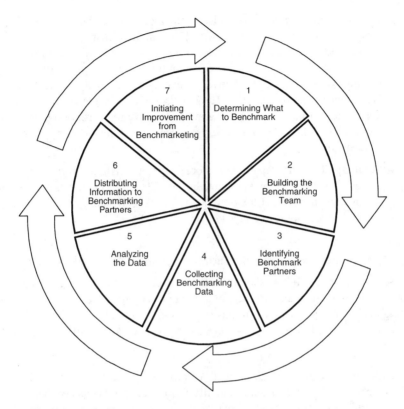

FIGURE 9-1. THE SEVEN-PHASE BENCHMARKING PROCESS.

- **Product or service features.** It is sometimes helpful to compare product features. For example, the various design features of an employee suggestion system can be compared to determine similarities and differences. Also, the features of an employee assistance program could be explored.
- **Work processes.** To improve efficiencies, it may be necessary to determine how a particular service is delivered or an internal process is executed. For example, it might be helpful to know the processing times and the procedures used to process medical claims. The time necessary to recruit and select a new professional employee may be an item for comparison.
- **HR function.** Some organizations want to know the features, costs, outputs, etc., for a particular function of HR. For example, the percent of payroll spent on the employee benefits package is useful information that is often collected. The amount spent on HRD is another useful item.

■ **HR performance measures.** Key indicators closely related to HR programs are important for the survey. These include costs, output indicators, quality indicators, and time factors of various services and functions within HR. For example, the sales per employee is an output variable representing gross productivity. The HR expenses as a percent of operating costs is another important variable. Turnover could be considered a quality variable, and the time to implement a major improvement program is an important time variable. Key indicators represent one of the most important areas to measure.

■ **Strategy.** The HR department should compare its current and long-term goals with those of other organizations. This information helps develop trends and ensures that the organization is at the leading edge of improvements and technology changes.

These areas provide an excellent array of opportunities for HR benchmarking.

Several important points should be emphasized at this phase. There is a temptation to take on too much in a benchmarking project by collecting data on everything available. The challenge in this phase is to select only those items that represent critical success factors—measures that make a difference in the organization.

These factors can be identified by three different processes. First, the HR staff should be consulted and asked to identify those areas they consider to be important or critical to their overall effectiveness. This input can be derived in focus group meetings or from surveys. Next, top management should be asked to identify the items that are most important to them and what items they see as critical to the effective use of human resources in the organization. Either a brief meeting or short questionnaire should suffice for this input. Finally, the customers (i.e., the users of the HR services and programs) are another source of input on critical success factors. Sometimes they will express what they would like to see improved in the organization. For example, if managers complain about the length of time to recruit a new employee, recruitment may be an area to identify as a critical success factor for the employment function.

The items planned for the survey should be easily identified, monitored, and measured in other organizations. (Apples must be compared to apples.) Otherwise, the measures are distorted, comparisons are difficult, and the interpretation will be vague. Because benchmarking is a long-term, continuous process for improvement, performance measures that are critical to short-term success should be avoided. An organization, attempting to use benchmarking for a quick fix worthless. The factors selected should be those that can be improved over the long term.

Although it is risky to show what should be included in a list of data collected from a benchmarking survey, Table 9-1 shows the type of data collected in one study, labeled the best practices in HR and developed by the Saratoga Institute.[2] This table shows a variety of measures covering most of the HR functions. However, the list will probably differ from a benchmarking project in a specific organization.

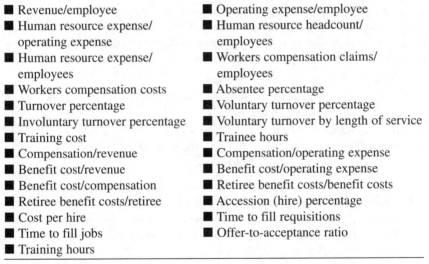

TABLE 9-1
SHRM/SARATOGA INSTITUTE
NATIONAL STANDARD HUMAN RESOURCE MEASURES

■ Revenue/employee	■ Operating expense/employee
■ Human resource expense/ operating expense	■ Human resource headcount/ employees
■ Human resource expense/ employees	■ Workers compensation claims/ employees
■ Workers compensation costs	■ Absentee percentage
■ Turnover percentage	■ Voluntary turnover percentage
■ Involuntary turnover percentage	■ Voluntary turnover by length of service
■ Training cost	■ Trainee hours
■ Compensation/revenue	■ Compensation/operating expense
■ Benefit cost/revenue	■ Benefit cost/operating expense
■ Benefit cost/compensation	■ Retiree benefit costs/benefit costs
■ Retiree benefit costs/retiree	■ Accession (hire) percentage
■ Cost per hire	■ Time to fill requisitions
■ Time to fill jobs	■ Offer-to-acceptance ratio
■ Training hours	

Phase Two: Building the Benchmarking Team

The appropriate team makes a difference, and this phase is designed to ensure that an effective team is in place. When this issue is not taken seriously, the results can be disastrous. Although an individual could actually perform the tasks in a benchmarking project, a team approach is better and is recommended. Based on the volume of work alone, it may be necessary to use a team to ensure that the proper time is devoted to each step of the process. Also, using a team increases the ownership of the process. It enhances the credibility of the final product and helps to ensure that benchmarking results are applied within the organization. The team should be carefully selected and prepared to achieve the desired purpose.

Types of Teams. Three types of teams can be developed. The most common arrangement is composed of individuals representing different functional areas of HR who bring unique expertise, viewpoints, and perspectives to the process. Another team structure, which is highly recommended, is a cross-functional team composed of HR specialists and generalists along with a group of line managers who are the principle customers and users of HR services. This is a helpful collaborative effort that builds partnerships with line management. Unfortunately, in many organizations, it is difficult to entice line management to devote the time needed to assist in this type of project. A third possible team arrangement is a voluntary group of individuals who have a strong interest in the benchmarking process and are willing to put forth the effort to help make it work. These individuals may come from marketing, quality assurance, engineering, or manufacturing. Their desire to participate may compensate for their lack of HR knowledge and may overcome the voids that might exist because some key areas are not represented. Because this is a new process, eagerness to participate is an important consideration that some groups use as a basis for selecting team members.

Role of the Team Leader. Every team needs a leader, and it is important for an internal champion of benchmarking to serve as leader or project manager. Usually the team leader is the HR officer, a senior manager, or specialist in the HR department. The project leader ensures that the process is implemented properly. The leader performs three major functions:

- **Organize the team and define duties.** Ideally, the team leader should participate in selecting other team members, but this is not always possible. Beyond that, the team leader must develop the team, assign tasks, and define duties and responsibilities for team members.

- **Train and facilitate.** The leader is usually the expert in the benchmarking process and will teach other team members the process and will outline steps that must be followed to make it successful. The team leader serves as a facilitator for group discussions as participants tackle various issues, problems, and concerns. A team leader who does not possess benchmarking expertise will usually coordinate the use of external benchmarking specialists who will train, teach, facilitate, and otherwise provide guidance.

- **Provide leadership.** The most critical aspect of the team leader's role is to provide leadership to ensure that the team works cohesively, stays on target, and focuses on the goal to produce a product acceptable to the sponsors. This is an essential skill and is often used as the key selection criterion for team leader.

Because the role is so critical, the team leader should be an individual who has a strong desire to make benchmarking work and who can visualize the potential for improvement with the benchmarking process. The team leader "begins with the end in mind." Also, he or she must have the credibility and reputation in an organization to make the process work and be willing to open the HR function and practices to the scrutiny of others.

Team Characteristics. Ideally, when selecting a team, each member should meet certain minimum requirements:

■ **Specific functional expertise.** A team member should have expertise in an area needed in the benchmarking process. A variety of knowledge and experience is necessary for the team to function effectively. In the best case situation, team expertise should expand outside the organization to include a general knowledge of the industry.
■ **Interest in benchmarking.** Because benchmarking may be new to the organization, success often rests with the enthusiasm and spirit of the individuals involved in the process. Their willingness to venture into unknown territory and work long hours to produce a final product is an important ingredient for team success.
■ **Reputation in the organization.** Team members must have an excellent reputation in the organization. They must have a proven work record with above average performance. Benchmarking should not be considered a developmental experience nor a place to assign individuals who do not have anything else to do. It is an assignment for those who have the credibility to enhance the team's final product and are willing to work hard.
■ **Level of interpersonal skills.** Team members need to have excellent interpersonal skills because of the number and variety of relationships that must be managed in the process. Team members must be able to communicate effectively—orally and in writing—and work with diverse groups, internally as well as externally.

Demanding these characteristics in team selection can help ensure that the team is capable of finishing the project and providing the credibility necessary to apply the results.

Team Support. The team must have effective support throughout the organization. Five support groups are usually involved in the process. The first, administrative support, provides clerical assistance for benchmarking. A tremendous amount of data must be processed, analyzed, and reported to a variety of individuals and groups. Because of this, it may be necessary to employ temporary help to take care of the workload, if it cannot be handled properly with existing HR staff. The second group, technical support, may be necessary to assist with data tabulation and analysis. Appropriate statistical processes must be followed, data must be converted properly, and survey instruments must be designed for efficient data collection and analysis. Technical specialists are often needed to provide guidance on these issues. In conjunction with technical analysis, a third group, computer support, may be necessary. Most of the computer support can be provided with an existing PC network and software usually available within the HR department. If this is not the case, the data processing or MIS department may be available for assistance. A fourth group from the marketing department can be helpful. Benchmarking involves collecting information that will often be used by the customers of the HR function. Having assistance from individuals with a marketing orientation can be very useful, particularly for packaging and presenting data for various user groups. Finally, there must be top quality support from the management team, the fifth support group. Although management provided the initial approval for the project, their continuous support will be necessary as the process consumes valuable time and resources. Collectively, these support groups must be organized in this phase of the process as the benchmarking team is formed.

Phase Three: Identifying Benchmark Partners

Identifying specific partners for a benchmarking project is another critical part of the process. Data can only be useful if it is collected from organizations that represent best practices. The first step of this phase is to consider the scope of benchmarking and potential target organizations. Several possibilities emerge:

- **Internal units.** For large organizations, internal benchmarking may be appropriate, at least as an initial benchmarking activity. With this approach, a plant, a region, division, or company (owned by a holding company) may compare HR practices and plan improvements. This process is recommended because it can provide useful information for comparative purposes. The data is easily collected and will usually be compiled in the same format from one unit to another. However, the comparisons will not necessarily represent best practices and may only show which unit is best among a captive group.
- **Competitors.** One of the most popular comparisons is to contact organizations considered to be direct competitors. These firms are in the same business and compete for market share with products and services. Many HR managers want to know more about the HR performance measures of competitors in order to make some comparisons. However, in a competitive market, it may be difficult to obtain the data because of the fear of divulging information that might alter competitive advantage.

■ **Noncompetitors in the same industry.** In some situations it may be appropriate to select organizations in the same industry who do not compete directly in the marketplace. It may be easier to secure information from this type of company, and still make the same comparisons as direct competitors because of similar processes, products, services, and distribution mechanisms. A regional firm may appropriately use this approach to survey a firm in another region that produces the same service or product but is not in direct competition.

■ **Organizations in the same geographic location.** Some benchmarking projects are undertaken to identify organizations within a geographic location. This approach may limit the number of available firms that represent best practices. An advantage to this type of benchmarking is that it allows comparisons in the same local or regional environment, which may be an important issue. For example, the recruiting strategies and results for a firm in Los Angeles may be vastly different from recruiting strategies and results of a firm based in Boston. Employee benefit issues often vary from one region to another. For these reasons, geographic comparison may be helpful.

■ **Other organizations in the U.S.** This approach crosses industry lines and examines other organizations within the confines of the United States. This approach broadens the range of available firms that represent best practices. For example, Prudential Insurance may want to compare HRD strategies with Apple Computer. This approach does have limitations. Because the organizations are considerably different, some data items may be inappropriate for direct comparison.

■ **International organizations.** One of the fastest growing areas of benchmarking is global comparisons in which firms strive to develop "world class" practices. The challenge of this approach is to find benchmarking partners who represent best practices throughout the world, whether in the same industry or outside the industry. A disadvantage to this approach is that data is difficult to compare because of differences in culture, local practices, and government regulations. This approach is usually used by large multinational companies with operations in several countries who have no need to compare local measures.

These are all potential strategies to define targets for benchmarking. After a particular strategy or combination of strategies is determined, the next steps are to define best practices and locate the organizations.

Defining Best Practices. The concept of best practice is an elusive term. A best practice is not always the least expensive approach or process with the shortest time frame or shortest duration. The fastest recruiting method may not be a best practice if it is too expensive. A best practice is not always the lowest or highest number for a measure. For example, in a turnover comparison, the best practice may not be the organization with the lowest turnover. Some organizations with low turnover, such as telecommunications companies, face the most difficult problems and are restructuring and streamlining to remain profitable. A low turnover may mean that organizations keep employees by offering above average salaries and benefits—not because of innovative employee relations programs. A higher turnover would be welcomed. The appropriate answer to the best practice question is that "it depends." It depends on what is accomplished in the situation, within the framework, environment, and economic conditions. Often the benchmarking team can define best practice when it examines the factors that represent outstanding performance on a particular data item. Some insight into this value may be obtained from previous studies in the literature or other published data. An organization's published report on what it considers a best practice may provide some insight into what the best value should be. It is important to reach a conclusion on what is a best practice early in the process because this definition drives the selection of the organization.

Finding the organization. This step in phase three is both simple and complex. It is simple because the benchmarking team can usually identify several organizations they want for partners, a "wish list" for comparison. It is complicated because the target group should represent organizations that actually offer best practices. It is helpful to identify as many organizations as possible to cover the benchmarking scope of possibilities—competitive, same industry, international, etc. Then, the process becomes a matter of trimming the list to the appropriate size.

TABLE 9-2
SELECTED SOURCES OF INFORMATION TO IDENTIFY POTENTIAL BENCHMARKING PARTNERS

■ Previous Award Winners	■ Federal Government
■ State Governments	■ Business School Faculty
■ Academic Resources and Databases	■ Professional Societies
■ Consultants	■ Trade Associations
■ Business Information Services	■ Internal Sources
■ Business Newspapers and Magazines	■ Directories and References
■ Technical Journals	■ Customers
■ Vendors	

Table 9-2 shows the sources of information for identifying potential partners are plentiful. Several sources need further explanation. One approach is to identify firms that have been recognized in some way as having best practices. For example, organizations that have been presented with the Malcolm Baldrige National Quality award are excellent targets for a benchmark survey because much of the criteria for the award focuses on HR issues.[3] Business school faculty are usually resourceful and are eager to help. They should be unbiased and objective. Professors keep track of organizations through their research and consulting and can sometimes identify those with best practices. Input from several HR professors is recommended.

Professional societies, such as the Society for Human Resource Management, Human Resource Planning Society, International Personnel Management Association, American Compensation Association, and American Society for Training and Development are important resources for identifying organizations with best practices. In some cases these organizations attempt to conduct benchmarking projects to develop best practices. For example, the American Society for Training and Development initiated a comprehensive benchmarking project to define the best practices in training and development. Initially, 19 companies formed the benchmarking project called the Benchmarking Forum and represent such firms as American Express, Motorola, Xerox, Dow Chemical, Amoco, and Chase Manhattan. Later, 19 additional companies joined the group including Abbott Laboratories, Ford, Hallmark Cards, and 3M. Other firms are now joining the forum, and collectively, they represent some of the world's largest and most prestigious organizations. The forum provides a way for participants to measure and benchmark practices on human resource development. The first report has been released and other data will be released periodically.[4] The Society for Human Resource Management attempted to develop standards through their Human Resource Effectiveness Report conducted by the Saratoga Institute.[5] This project began in the early 1980s and has grown to include data from thousands of firms across many industries. Participation in this project is available to any organization, and collectively, it provides a way in which the average of all participants can be presented as benchmarks. Thirty-two factors are reported on such items as the HR department expense as a percent of the company operating expense, benefits costs as a percent of company operating expense, exempt termination, exempt cost per hire, and training cost.

Consultants represent another important source because they work within organizations and often know about the quality of internal practices. They usually will identify what they consider to be best practices, if divulging this information does not violate confidentiality agreements. Trade associations in the industry is another important source. Often industry groups attempt to develop benchmarking projects for the human resources area. For example, the American Bankers Association has an HR Benchmarking project and similar projects are underway in other industry groups.

Another important source is internal resources. Almost any staff member has some perception of what represents a best practice in the field. These opinions should be the starting points for identifying organizations to partner with. The vendors of HR products and services are also important sources. They implement programs, products, and services in a variety of organizations and often know about their internal results and effectiveness.

Collectively, these sources can provide a rich database from which to identify target organizations. The team's challenge is to narrow the initial list down to a desired list of participants and prepare to contact the selected organizations.

Contacting the organization. It is frustrating for the team to identify an organization for participation only to have involvement in the project declined. Even more disappointment occurs when so little data is shared by a partner that they become, in essence, an invalid source of information. Potential partners should be contacted early to determine whether they will participate in the benchmarking project. This step often creates difficulty for some HR staffs, because they assume certain organizations will not participate because of their reputations or competitive relationship. However, benchmarking experts report that many organizations first preceived as uncooperative usually become involved in benchmarking projects.[6] Several strategies are recommended to convince them to be involved.

- One approach is to use a professional affiliation for contact. If the organization is a member of a national professional society or trade association, that affiliation might provide the incentive for the organization to participate in the benchmarking project, particularly if the project is initiated or supported by the association.
- Some organizations will participate if there is a large database from which to share information. Participation in several benchmarking projects provides the potential partner the opportunity to tap information from different surveys. By supplying data, they have an opportunity to compare their situation and measures with many other organizations. In these cases, specific data identifying an organization is usually kept confidential.
- Another approach is to consider the competitive advantage of the data. Most organizations are curious about how their practices compare with others, and they are willing to provide information to make this comparison. This is particularly true for those organizations striving to "maintain" best practices. These organizations want more evidence that they are leaders in the field and that their practices are the "best." The most efficient way to obtain this information is to participate in a variety of benchmarking projects.

■ Professional responsibility is another reason organizations participate. An often overlooked strategy is to ask the organization to participate as a matter of professional courtesy. It is surprising the number of firms that will provide data because someone asked for it in a very professional way. HR managers often have a sense of duty and responsibility to help other organizations, particularly if they are considered leaders in the field.

■ Finally, some organizations will initially be receptive because a friend of a key manager asked them to participate. Every networking opportunity should be used to reach the desired participants.

One or more of these strategies should help the organization identify and secure the appropriate partners. Using these strategies helps ensure that benchmarking participants are the leaders in the field.

Phase Four: Collecting Benchmarking Data

The next important phase in the benchmarking process is to actually collect data from the benchmarking partners. Data collection arrangements may have been negotiated previously because of specific requests from organizations agreeing to participate. The very first step of this phase is to collect internal data. The data collection process, including the use of the instrument, should be thoroughly tested within the organization to gain additional insight in the process. This process provides a way to check the flow of the data, the quality of data collected, data interpretation, and the potential areas where problems may occur. This is an ideal situation for a trial run. If there are problems with providing the information internally, other organizations will have greater problems in providing information.

Data Collection Methods. The types of data collection techniques mirror the methods mentioned elsewhere in this book. Benchmarking projects usually involve four methods:

■ **Telephone interviews.** A common technique is a telephone interview with the benchmarking partner to gather as much information as possible. The telephone interview is flexible and economical. The telephone interview should be preplanned to allow the respondent time to collect the material prior to the interview. This interview is a follow-up to a preliminary agreement to participate in benchmarking. Partners should have an opportunity to review the questions ahead of time.

■ **Personal meeting at a site visit.** Although more costly and time-consuming than the telephone interview, a site visit represents an excellent opportunity to provide the best information possible. With this approach, the benchmarking team member meets with one or more individuals at the benchmarking partner's premises to collect as much information as possible. As with the telephone interview, this visit is preplanned, and an advance list of questions and data needed is provided. Face-to-face interviews offer several advantages over the telephone interview. The quality of information is improved and there is an opportunity to probe to clarify information.

■ **Questionnaires.** Another important data collection technique is the questionnaire. In this approach, benchmarking partners are sent a detailed questionnaire which they fill out and return to the sponsoring organization. This approach has limitations because it is difficult to clarify information when there is confusion. Also, there is no assurance that the survey will be accurate or complete. Respondents are tempted to shortcut the process or provide incomplete information. There is no guarantee of a certain response rate or participation by all planned partners. The questionnaire has an advantage of being inexpensive, and consequently, it is a common approach.

■ **Public documents.** A final method is to examine documents such as trade publications, press releases, industry reports, annual reports, and other public records of participating organizations. With this approach, the organization does not have to give permission to participate because the information is public. While the data in the documents may be accurate and reliable, usually not enough data is published for an HR benchmarking project.

A combination of approaches is recommended. For example, a detailed questionnaire can be sent and the telephone can be used as a follow-up to clarify specific information. Also, a combination of telephone and personal visits may be appropriate. The important point is to collect reliable information as economically as possible. In selecting the method, four issues must be considered: quality of information, cost of data collection methods, the time considerations of the survey respondent, and the intended use of the information.[7]

Phase Five: Analyzing the Data

After the information is collected, it must be tabulated, organized, analyzed, and interpreted to be meaningful. Data is typically organized within a spreadsheet program that lists the organizations on the left side and the various headings representing the data items across the top.[8] Table 9-3 provides an example of this type of spreadsheet. The spreadsheet analysis is appropriate for tabulating raw

TABLE 9-3
BENCHMARKING INFORMATION MATRIX

| | RECRUITING AND SELECTION DATA—EXEMPT EMPLOYEES | | | |
	RECRUITING COST PER HIRE	EMPLOYEE COST PER HIRE	SELECTION RATIO	AVERAGE DAYS TO HIRE
Partner #1	6500	7500	.31	55
Partner #2	6900	8000	.25	67
Partner #3	5500	5850	.29	48
Partner #4	6000	6900	.40	39
Partner #5	5400	7900	.28	51

data that is converted into a format for presentation at a later date. In some cases, data has to be converted into usable quantities or values that are important in the organization. For instance, a total cost might be reported and a cost per unit may need to be calculated for comparison. Data that seems to be inaccurate or out of line should be checked to determine whether items are incorrect, misinterpreted, or transferred improperly from the original data collection sheets. If the data is extreme but appears to have no mistakes, then some consideration must be given to eliminating the data for use. If good reason exists to suspect the data contains an erroneous item, then it would be appropriate to omit it from analysis.

During the initial stage of analysis, the statistical processes and procedures outlined in another chapter may be appropriate for calculating averages, percentages, and in some cases, standard deviations. Surveys should be checked for particular patterns of the data or trends that may be appropriate. In order to draw conclusions, it is important to consider the context in which the numbers are reported. Some information may be contrary to what's expected or it may confuse the analysis. Conclusions should be reached with input and consideration for the entire benchmarking team. The data analysis phase, although sometimes confusing, complex, and frightening for some HR practitioners, is a critical part of the process. Incomplete data analysis will lead to incomplete information on which inaccurate decisions are made later, either by sponsoring organizations or other benchmarking partners.

Phase Six: Distributing Information to Benchmarking Partners

A phase that can easily be slighted is developing and distributing a report for all the benchmarking partners. There is a tendency to shortcut this effort because it is not perceived as adding value within the sponsoring organization. However, for other benchmark partners, this is the most important part of the process. If this is a continuous, long-term partnership relationship, then this phase must be handled with the utmost care. Benchmarking partners must have a report that provides useful information they can use internally to improve their own processes. At a minimum, the report for the partners should contain the following:

- An executive summary, which presents a brief conclusion from the survey data and provides a brief description of the overall process
- A statement of the purposes of the benchmarking project with details on the objectives
- A listing of all participants. (Specific data is not linked to the benchmarking participant)
- Summary of benchmarked items
- A description of the methods for collecting and analyzing the data
- An outline of the overall results and conclusions that shows what the data may mean to the organization
- A description of the strengths within the group that attempts to determine best practices for each of the items benchmarked
- A request for this procedure to be a continuous process with potential future plans. This often overlooked step is critical to keep the benchmarking partners intact as a data collection team.

The confidentiality of this report is extremely important. Most organizations do not want their names tied to specific data items, and steps must be taken to ensure that this is handled properly. Also, any plans to disclose the information, even in a general way with average numbers, should be fully discussed in advance and approved by all partners. Reports should be delivered on-time as planned. The packaging of the report should be professional and easy to use. It should also be useful for future comparisons.[9]

Phase Seven: Initiating Improvement from Benchmarking

The final, and probably most critical, phase involves the actual improvements that must be implemented as a result of the benchmarking process. This involves three important issues: performance gaps, action plans, and an internal report.

Performance Gap. A first step of this phase is to calculate performance gaps, that is, deviations between the current level of a particular measure and the desired or ultimate level represented as the best practice. The difference in the two levels becomes a deficiency or performance gap that represents an opportunity for improvement. For example, in one organization, the cost per hire for exempt employees was almost twice that of the average of the partners in the benchmarking study. This became an area for improvement because it clearly identified a gap between best practices and the organization's own experience. The vehicle to accomplish this improvement is the action plan, described next. Each data item from the survey should be examined for a potential performance gap. Team leaders should make a tentative decision to determine whether a significant performance deficiency exists. If one does, it should be considered an item for improvement.

Action Plans. The use of action plans represents one of the most effective ways to overcome performance gaps. An action plan is a detailed series of steps to be taken over a predetermined time period to improve a current situation. Appendix 4 presents a copy of an action plan used in the follow-up evaluation of an HR program. As with any planned change, it is important that all the parties involved understand the process, take steps to overcome the resistance to change, gain acceptance with all those involved, and implement the change. Each performance gap should be addressed with an action plan(s). More information on the action planning process is contained in Chapter 6.

Application Report. A final part of the process is to develop a report for the internal customers in the organization, the individuals for whom the process has been initiated. It contains the following elements:

- Executive summary
- Purpose of the project
- Benchmarking participants
- Internal customers
- Project team
- Timetable

- Items benchmarked
- Methodology
- Data analysis
- Performance gaps
- Action plans
- Planned follow-up

This report provides management and internal customers of benchmarking the data necessary to understand the process, see the need for change, know how improvements will be implemented, and build confidence that the organization is moving toward best practices.

PARTICIPATING IN EXISTING BENCHMARKING PROJECTS

It is sometimes helpful to join or become a part of existing benchmarking projects. These initiatives are often available within a professional human resources society. For example, the American Society for Training and Development, as described earlier, conducts a significant benchmarking forum to identify the best practices in human resource development. Also, the Society for Human Resource Management, in conjunction with the Saratoga Institute, conducts an ongoing project to benchmark practices in the human resources area. Other professional societies within human resources are pursuing similar projects. Also, the human resource section of participating organizations within some business or industry trade groups develops benchmarking projects for their members. In either case, these represent excellent opportunities to tie into an existing network and secure valuable information.

Benchmarking with an existing project has several advantages. First, it is usually inexpensive. The cost of the entire project is shared by participating members who usually represent a large database. In some cases, the trade group or professional society underwrites part of the cost of the project.

A second advantage is that this process is less time-consuming because data collection instruments are already designed and the process has been streamlined to allow for efficient input. Most of the work has been done by others.

A third advantage is that most of the projects represent a large database, thus making the data more significant and meaningful for comparative purposes. For example, the Saratoga Institute data represents over 1,000 firms, and it is still growing.

A fourth advantage is the exposure that often comes from participating in this effort. Most organizations are drawn to these projects seeking the best practices and are sometimes labeled as having best practices themselves whether the label is accurate or not. It sometimes represents "good company" to be associated with one of these benchmarking groups.

There are several disadvantages of participating in this type of project. First, the participants may not represent those with the best practices. Often there is no screening process for new participants. Any organization with a predetermined size and willingness to pay the fee can participate. Participant lists are typically dominated by large, well-known organizations, which are preceived to have the best practices. While this may be the case, there is certainly no guarantee of this as witnessed by the situation with IBM. A few years back, everyone wanted to include IBM on their lists of organizations with which to benchmark. If IBM participated, other organizations were drawn as if to a magnet. Recently, however, few firms want to compare their practices to IBM because of the problems IBM experienced and the difficulties of their struggling organization. It is easy to get lulled into assuming that a large organization will always have the best practices.

The second disadvantage is that an existing group may not be made up of similar organizations. For example, a financial institution may want to compare its successes with a large database of other financial institutions, but this may not be possible with the existing database. A trade group database usually alleviates this concern.

A third disadvantage is that by joining an existing project, there is no way to influence what measures are taken and the ways in which the process actually works. These decisions have been made by others, and consequently, the data may not be the items desired by the organization.

The fourth disadvantage is related to the third. Because the data is not necessarily the exact items sought by the organization, it is difficult to provide a basis for change. At the heart of the benchmarking process is the need to take action to improve areas where performance gaps are clearly identified. An existing database is unlikely to provide information in all of the areas desired so that gaps can be identified.

The process, described in this chapter, shows a proactive approach to benchmarking that allows organizations to develop their own benchmarking project. It shows ways to analyze critical areas for improvement and to collect data from organization that have been identified as having best practices in those areas. This ultimately leads to action necessary to make improvements to move toward using the best practices. Simply by participating in a current benchmarking project, an organization will not achieve this goal. A comprehensive approach is needed that ties into existing benchmark projects, while at the same time develops a custom designed benchmarking effort for the organization. The two approaches bring together the best of both worlds, while not adding much to the cost and the time involved in the process. This approach will, however, provide a variety of sources of information on key variables that may need to be improved.

CONCLUSION: MAKING THE PROCESS WORK

To ensure that the process works effectively, it is helpful to review two important benchmarking myths and success factors. Table 9-4 shows that a number of myths about this process exists, even though it is a relatively new activity in organizations.[10] These misunderstandings keep some organizations from attempting to use benchmarking as an important improvement tool for the human resources function.

The success indicators, shown in Table 9-5, represent conditions and factors that should be present for the process to produce meaningful data to improve the organization. Without an adequate level of each of these indicators, the process will be doomed and consequently will not be a viable process to measure and evaluate HR and improve the effectiveness of the human resource function in the organization.

TABLE 9-4
BENCHMARKING MYTHS

- There is only one way to benchmark, against direct product competitors.
- Benchmarks are only quantitative, financially based statistics.
- Benchmarking investigations are focused solely on operations showing a performance gap.
- Benchmarking is something that needs to be done occasionally and can be accomplished quickly.
- There is a single company, somewhere, most like my firm, only much better, that is "the benchmark."
- Staff organizations cannot be benchmarked.
- Benchmarking is a target-setting stretch exercise.
- Benchmarking can most effectively be accomplished through third party consultants.
- It is not obvious what should be benchmarked for each business unit.
- Processes don't need to be benchmarked.
- Internal benchmarking between departments and divisions has only minimal benefits.
- There is no benefit in qualitative benchmarking.
- Benchmarking is comparing an organization to the dominant industry firm and emulating the firm six months later.

Source: Adapted from Camp, R. C. Benchmarking: The Search for Industry Best Practices that Lead to Superior Performance. *Milwaukee: ASQC Quality Press, 1989.*

TABLE 9-5
SUCCESS FACTORS FOR THE BENCHMARKING PROCESS

- A strong commitment to benchmarking from management
- A clear HR understanding of present practices as a basis for comparison to best practices
- A willingness to change HR practices based on benchmark findings
- A realization that competition is constantly changing and there is a need to plan ahead on the trend line
- A willingness to share information with benchmark partners
- The concentration of organizations that are recognized leaders in HR
- Adherence to the benchmarking process
- A continuous benchmarking effort

REFERENCES

1. Spendolini, M. J. *The Benchmarking Book.* New York: AMACOM, 1992.

2. Fitz-enz, J. *SHRM/Saratoga Institute Human Resource Effectiveness Survey: 1994 Annul Report.* Saratoga, CA: Saratoga Institute, 1995.

3. Blackburn, R. and Rosen, B. "Total Quality and Human Resources Management: Lessons Learned from Baldrige Award-Winning Companies," *Academy of Management Executive,* 1993 Vol. 7, No. 3.

4. Ford, D. J. "Benchmarking HRD," *Training and Development,* June 1993, pp. 36–41.

5. Fitz-enz, J. "How to Make Benchmarking Work for You," *HRMagazine,* December 1993, pp. 40–47.

6. Hequet, M. "The Limits of Benchmarking," *Training,* February 1993, pp. 36–41.

7. Scovel, K. "Learning from the Masters," *Human Resource Executive,* May 1991, pp. 1, 28–29.

8. Karlof, B. & Ostblom, S. *Benchmarking: A Signpost to Excellence in Quality and Productivity.* New York: John Wiley and Sons, Inc., 1993.

9. Ogilvie, T. J. "Lost in Space: Typical Benchmarking Problems," *Management Review,* September 1993, pp. 20–22.

10. Camp, R. C. *Benchmarking: The Search for Industry Best Practices that Lead to Superior Performance.* Milwaukee: ASQC Quality Press, 1989.

CHAPTER TEN

Human Resources Costs

Top management often asks important cost and investment questions. How much does the employee assistance program cost our organization? Are we spending more on benefits than our competitors? Are our payroll costs as a percent of operating expense higher than others in the industry? How much has our new employee empowerment program cost us in the past two years? Finding answers to these questions may not be easy in many organizations. Cost monitoring and cost tracking have not always been a top priority among human resources, and consequently, cost data has not always been available or accurate.

The cost of maintaining an organization's human resources is increasing. As top executives stretch resources to fund HR programs, it is imperative that they know where the money is spent and for what purposes. This chapter explores the rationale for identifying, monitoring, and managing costs as well as specific methods and techniques for classifying, allocating, and reporting those costs. Although the methods must be tailored to the organization, several general principles and guidelines can be useful for any organization.

DEVELOPING COSTS

Three broad categories of HR costs must be developed, monitored, and managed in the organization. The first group involves the direct cost of maintaining employees, and the largest component of this goes to direct salaries and benefits of employees. Unless these staffing costs are monitored and managed closely, the organization can become bloated, inefficient, and uncompetitive. Another important cost is the cost of maintaining the HR function in the organization. This includes the direct cost for all the HR programs as well as HR department expense. HR department staffs have increased, and consequently, the costs of HR programs have increased. The use of outside services has grown dramatically, resulting in increased cost. Finally, the third category is the cost savings that result from the implementation of many HR programs. These impact costs are the costs that are usually not tracked or monitored by HR, but often can represent the most important data to track.

Figure 10-1 shows the relationship of these cost items. The HR department costs are those costs that are associated with the programs and are applied to all employees. The employees represent the largest cost item in most organizations.

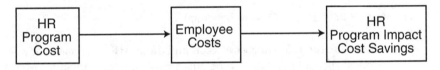

FIGURE 10-1. DYNAMICS OF HR COSTS.

The implementation of HR programs should realize a cost savings, usually called an impact cost. For example, the HR department may initiate a program on absenteeism prevention. The expenditures associated with the program are HR department costs which must be tracked and monitored. The program would have an impact on the overall employee cost because lower absenteeism would lower the payroll costs. Some organizations hire additional employees to cover excessive absenteeism. The amount of cost saved is calculated and reported as an impact cost, the cost of the reduced absenteeism. These three cost categories are covered in more detail in this chapter, although additional information on impact costs is covered in the next chapter.

Rationale for Developing Costs

Tracking and managing HR costs are important to an organization's success. There are at least nine important reasons for monitoring HR costs. Collectively, they provide a convincing argument for developing a cost tracking system or taking a renewed look at improving the present HR costing system. For some organizations, all of these factors may not be applicable.

■ **To determine the total HR expenditures.** Every organization should know the approximate total HR expenditures. Although this appears to be fundamental, many HR managers still do not know what the organization spends on HR. Total expenditures include costs such as salaries, employee benefits, facilities expense, and other general overhead. A few organizations calculate this expenditure and make comparisons with other organizations, although comparisons are difficult to achieve because of the different bases for cost calculations. Some organizations calculate HR costs in a variety of ways such as unit labor costs, and they set targets for cost performance. An effective cost data collection system enables an organization to calculate the magnitude of total expenditures and helps top management answer two important questions:

- How much *does* the organization spend on its human resources?
- How much *should* it spend on its human resources?

The answers to both questions are important.

- **To determine the relative cost of each individual HR program.** The HR department should know which programs are the most cost effective. Monitoring costs by program allows the HR staff to evaluate the relative cost of a program and determine how costs change. If a program costs more than in previous time periods, it might be appropriate to re-evaluate its impact and overall success. It may be useful to compare specific components of costs to similar internal programs or programs in other organizations. The cost per participant for one program could be compared to the cost per participant for a similar program. Large differences may signal a problem, although there may be legitimate reasons for the differences. For example, it may be helpful to know why recruiting a new programmer costs $2,000 more than recruiting a sales representative. Also, costs associated with items such as program development, program implementation, or other categories could be compared with other programs in the organization and may lead to the development of cost standards.
- **To predict future program costs.** Historical costs provide a foundation for predicting future costs. Cost data from a previous program help develop standardized data to use in estimating the cost of new or proposed programs. Sophisticated cost models provide the capacity to estimate or predict costs with a reasonable accuracy.
- **To calculate benefits versus costs for a specific program.** Probably the most increasingly common and significant reason for collecting costs is to prepare data to use in a benefits-versus-costs comparison for a program. Cost data takes on the same importance as the data that determines the economic benefits of a program. This approach views HR expenditures as investments, with a potential return.

■ **To improve the efficiency of the HR department.** Controlling costs is an important management function, and HR should not be exempted from this responsibility. HR managers must be able to monitor and control the costs of developing and delivering programs. Most HR departments have monthly budgets that project costs by various accounts and, in some cases, by project or program. Cost reports that show how the department is doing are tools to spot problem areas and take corrective action when necessary. From a practical management issue, the accumulation of cost data is a necessity. Some costs serve as efficiency measures for HR departments and ultimately help to evaluate the HR function. The cost per hire, cost per EAP participant, health care cost per employee, and cost per grievance are examples of measures that can serve as indices for tracking efficiency of various HR functions.

■ **To evaluate alternatives to a proposed HR program.** Realistic cost data provides management with data to estimate the cost of a proposed program. The data can be used to evaluate the cost effectiveness of alternatives to a particular program. Consider an example involving the decision of whether to use an external employment agency or the internal recruiting capability. A complete analysis of recruiting costs will reveal precisely the cost per hire for internal efforts. This cost can be compared with cost from agencies or other external sources. Of course, quality and policy decisions may enter the process and may affect the ultimate decision. However, it is important to obtain direct cost comparison and then factor in the qualitative factors.

■ **To plan and budget for next year's operations.** Another reason for tracking HR costs is to prepare for next year's operating budget. The operating budget usually includes all HR costs such as salaries and benefits, although those expenses may be charged to other departments. Collecting current costs is usually the first step in developing a budget. In recent years, the budgeting process in many organizations has been more closely scrutinized and become more sophisticated. The days of adding a percentage increase to last year's budget is, for the most part, gone. HR departments are asked to examine their activities and programs carefully when preparing the budget. A few departments operate on a zero-based budget in which each activity must be justified during the budgeting process. This type of budget assumes no carryover expenses into the next year based on the previous year's activity. This process can be used as the basis for setting priorities for next year's efforts. Proposed projects and their costs are reviewed by top management, and their approval of specific projects lets the HR department focus on the most important efforts for the coming year.

■ **To develop a marginal cost pricing system.** HR expenditures are important when developing marginal cost pricing strategies. In order for management to consider a HR program involving new organizational strategies, they must be apprised of the cost for each strategy. Several organizations developed standard cost data that can easily fit into expansion plans, changes in procedures or policies, and changes in products or services. For example, calculating the costs of employee benefits as a percent of payroll costs is a standard cost item that allows organizations to quickly factor the investment in human resources into business decisions.

■ **To integrate data into the human resource information systems.** An HR department should collect cost data as part of existing databases for the human resources information system. These databases provide information on the contribution of human resource practices to the profitability of the organization.

In conclusion, these nine factors provide convincing rationale for collecting cost data. They clearly show why these data are necessary and why HR departments should collect and monitor HR costs. However, in many organizations this type of data is either inaccurate or not available.[1]

General Considerations

Whether an organization is developing a new cost system or modifying an existing one, several factors about costs are worth considering. This helpful advice to HR professionals includes:

■ **Collect costs even if they are not utilized in HR measurement and evaluation.** Too often, an HR department will neglect to accurately collect and report costs because they will not be used directly in evaluation. Cost data represent useful management tools and are necessary in an effective organization.

■ **Costs may not be precise.** An accurate assessment of all costs associated with a program is almost impossible. With so many hidden costs and cost allocation schemes, it is difficult to develop a completely accurate picture of costs. A lack of precision should not discourage staff members from attempting to monitor and collect costs. A reasonably accurate cost estimate is better than no cost estimate. If used in measuring the contribution, the costs are probably more accurate as the economic value of program benefits.

■ **Use a practical approach in building a system.** The HR department must define the purposes for developing a cost system before it is designed. Tradeoffs in accuracy versus the feasibility of maintaining the system will be necessary. Also, the organization should not be burdened with additional paperwork, calculations, and other analyses that can become unproductive and may not add to the precision of cost data. A system is needed that is simple yet accurate, easy to administer, and easy to understand by those who use it. If possible, it should be a part of current systems in use. Some account categories will be different, but the manner of collecting, compiling, storing, and reporting data should be consistent with established practices within the organization.

■ **Use caution when reporting cost data.** Taken out of context and without proper explanations, cost data might be frightening to top management and disastrous for an HR manager. An example of the misuse of cost data comes from the U.S. General Accounting Office (GAO). The GAO examined the training provided to auditors of the Internal Revenue Service and concluded that training cost the federal government as much as $6.5 billion in lost revenue.[2] The GAO calculated this figure by estimating the revenue that would have been brought in by experienced auditors who were taken off the job to train new employees. The GAO investigated the costs of training 1,103 new employees the IRS hired for five offices in the U.S. It figured that the lost revenue was $840 million from those offices. It arrived at the $6.5 billion figure by multiplying its figures to account for the 7,300 people the IRS hired nationwide during that time.

These costs, which were reported to the press, had one major flaw. The GAO did not bother to calculate the long-term benefits of providing training to new employees who presumably could go back to the job and bring in even more revenue. They examined only the cost side of the ledger and not the benefits. The GAO report concluded that it is essential for the IRS to explore alternatives to its present training programs. The moral of this story: If the costs of a program are reported, the benefits should be reported even if they are estimates; otherwise, a program can appear prohibitively expensive.

■ **The effort to set up a cost system is extensive.** Most organizations use a formal cost accounting system designed to accumulate cost by department, section, product line, and other categories. This type of system is usually adequate for collecting much of the cost data necessary for developing HR program costs. However, if a system is not in place, the effort to develop one is significant, and will usually involve input from the finance and accounting sections. This substantial effort must be fully recognized at the beginning of the project.

EMPLOYEE COSTS

Few organizations would survive without tracking direct employee costs, reported either as payroll, average unit labor costs, or total costs of employees. This critical data must be used regularly to manage the organization efficiently. Fully loaded costs of maintaining employees should be reported in meaningful ways in order to make comparisons with other organizations, particularly those in the same industry. This section briefly outlines these major cost elements.

Direct Compensation

The largest portion of these costs are the wages and salaries paid directly to employees. They are tracked in every organization. Direct compensation also includes various incentives and bonuses, as well as deferred compensation. All of these costs must be included in the total direct payroll cost. Salaries and wages are usually available directly from the payroll system, while some bonuses, incentives, and possibly deferred compensation may be stored on other systems.

Benefits

Few items connected with overall employee costs have increased as dramatically as the cost of employee benefits. Benefit costs as a percent of payroll have risen steadily since their inception in the early 1920s and now hover around 40 percent.[3] Recently efforts have been made to contain health care and rising retirement plan costs. Still, these costs are significant and must be monitored, controlled, and managed. An important challenge to HR professionals is to determine exactly what should go into the cost component. Some benefits such as health plans, retirement plans, life insurance programs, and holidays, are clearly included. Other benefits are more difficult to lump in the total. Free parking, subsidized cafeteria, educational programs, and credit union are sometimes omitted from benefit calculations, but should be included in total benefit costs. Also, to have an accurate estimate of the fully loaded costs, the cost of administering the benefits must be included. These costs include the salaries and direct and indirect expenses of the benefits staff as well as costs for outside services related to benefits administration.

Several measures are available to compare benefit costs. The United States Chamber of Commerce, the International Foundation of Employee Benefits, and the Society of Human Resource Management (all based in the Washington, D.C. area) offer national surveys of employee benefit costs. Also, in many areas, regional surveys are available. One or more of these surveys can be used as a comparison so that the internal cost figure can be adjusted to match the external number.

Direct and Indirect Support

In addition to salaries and benefits, direct expenses related to staffing are significant and should be included in the total employee cost. These include items such as the cost of maintaining an office or workstation for the employee, the cost of equipment such as telephone, calculator, computer, fax machine, and miscellaneous costs such as travel, direct office supplies, and office support. These figures are easily tabulated but, unfortunately, are not monitored in a total amount in many organizations.

Indirect costs related to employment are also significant, and include the costs for support staff, division or corporate overhead, as well as cost of employee facilities such as break rooms and cafeterias. These costs should be calculated or estimated and included as a percent of direct compensation to develop the fully loaded costs.

HR PROGRAM COSTS

There are two basic ways HR department costs can be classified and monitored. One is a cost accounting classification that contains expenditures such as labor, materials, supplies and travel. The other classification is by total program cost broken down into categories of the HR process such as program development, implementation, and monitoring. An effective system will monitor costs by account categories, but it will also include a method for accumulating costs by the HR process category. Many systems stop short of this second step. While the first grouping can sufficiently determine the total cost of an important item such as travel and consulting expenses, it does not provide for program accountability or indicate areas in which costs might be excessive by relative comparisons of programs. For example, the implementation costs of a productivity improvement program in one division should be compared to the same cost category in another division.

Developing a Classification System

When developing an HR classification system, the following steps ensure that the system provides the information needed:

■ **Define which costs will be collected.** A system of cost classification may be subject to several interpretations. All relevant costs must be identified. Cost accounts should be clearly defined to reduce possible errors made in misclassifying costs. There should be little doubt where an item should be charged (i.e., office supplies or duplication). Also, the various process categories should be clearly defined so that items can be properly grouped into those accounts.

■ **Assign the responsibility for developing the system.** Because the implementation of a costing system involves the input of others, responsibilities of each individual or department should be detailed to reduce delays in implementation and errors in the final product.

■ **Review the current expense account classifications.** Each account category should be clearly defined and developed consistent with the organization's current chart of accounts and in a manner that will ease the application and use of the system. The classifications should be practical and should describe the types of costs that make up each account.

■ **Develop the HR program classifications.** Appropriate detail needed for dividing costs into each of these different categories should be developed. Each process category should be clearly defined so that those employees using the system will place the expenditure in the proper category and charge it to the proper account number.

■ **Use standard cost data when appropriate.** There are many situations where standard cost data may be useful. Standard costs can save time and improve the accuracy of total cost calculations. An example of standard cost data is the percent of payroll for employee benefits. Another example is the average per diem for participants when attending an out-of-town HR program.

■ **Carefully select data sources.** A valid data source is critical to the costing system. The source must be readily available, ideally from an existing system. It should be consistent with any other reports of the same data. Typical data sources are payroll records, budget reports, standard cost reports, travel expense records, purchase orders, and petty cash vouchers.

■ **Computerize the system.** The cost accounting system should be computerized to track HR program costs and analyze them efficiently. Using computers will ease the implementation and the acceptance of such a system as well as improve this accuracy.

These steps make the development of a costing system easier. They also help ensure that the system is implemented smoothly and on a timely basis.

Process Classifications

Table 10-1 shows four different methods of developing process categories for HR costs. Method A uses only two categories: support costs and operating costs. Operating costs include all expenses involved in implementing and conducting the HR program; whereas, support costs include all administrative, overhead, development, analysis, or any other expenditures not directly related to program implementation. While this method of categorization is simple, it does not provide enough detail to analyze costs. Method B provides a little more detail because costs are divided into three categories. This is more useful than Method A, but does not provide information on program development/acquisition costs. Method C provides for development costs as a separate item. It still falls short of

TABLE 10-1
HR PROCESS CATEGORIES FOR COSTS

A	B
Support Costs	Participant Costs
Operating Costs	Administrative Costs
	Implementation Costs

C	D
Analysis Costs	Analysis Costs
Development Costs	Development/Acquisition Costs
Administrative Costs	Implementation Costs
Implementation Costs	Operating Costs
	Evaluation Costs

what possibly is a more ideal situation because it does not allow for tracking operating or evaluation costs. Method D represents a more appropriate HR process cost breakdown: analysis, development/acquisition, implementation, operating, and evaluation. Administrative costs are allocated to some or all of these areas. These process breakdowns in Method D are defined below.

Analysis cost. All of the costs associated with initial problem identification, needs analysis, development of objectives, selection of participants, and preparation of an initial program proposal should be included in the analysis costs. Typical costs that are a part of the analysis include consulting fees, special equipment, software packages for analysis, printing materials for surveys and reports, and salaries and benefits of those involved in analysis. These costs are often ignored as a group, but should be tracked and monitored, not because they may be excessive and must be reduced, but because tracking them will show management and the HR staff exactly what was spent on analysis. They are often lower than expected.

Development/acquisition cost. Costs related to the design, purchase, and/or development of the program are included in this cost category. These include the costs for designing specifications, developing program materials, preparing brochures, using external consultants for program development and any other costs associated with developing the final product. If a program is purchased from a vendor, the initial purchase fees and costs are included in this category. (Per participant charges for materials or royalties are included in the implementation category.) Because development costs are usually substantial, the HR staff must decide whether these costs should be spread over the life of the program or considered a one-time charge-off in the first weeks or months of the program. This issue should be discussed with appropriate finance and accounting staff.

Implementation cost. All costs associated with introducing, implementing, and conducting the program should be included in this category. Typical cost items included travel and lodging for participants to attend meetings, salaries and expenses of participants and others involved directly in the program, materials and supplies for the program introduction, and other direct expenses associated with the program's initial implementation. For education and training programs, all delivery costs are included in this category.

Operating cost. Following implementation, routine costs associated with operating and maintaining the program for its duration are collected as operating expense. This category represents all expenses necessary to keep the program operational, including salaries and benefits of individuals who supervise, administer, or coordinate the program, salaries and benefits of participants for the time they are involved in the program, and various support services and materials necessary to keep the program operational. These costs may include administrative expenses or external fees and expenses.

Evaluation cost. The last category includes all costs associated with measurement and evaluation of the program. This category includes instrument design, follow-ups, data analysis and report development for management. If a pilot test is conducted, those costs would also be included. As with analysis, these costs are sometimes lower than expected.

Expense Account Classifications

The most time-consuming step in developing an HR cost system is defining and classifying the various HR expenses. Many of the traditional expense accounts, such as office supplies and travel expenses, are already a part of the existing accounting system. However, expenses unique to the HR department may have to be added to the system. The system design will depend on the organization, the type of programs in place, and the limits imposed on the current cost accounting system, if any. Also, to a certain extent, expense account classifications will depend on how the HR process categories are developed. A description of all the expenses necessary for a system is inappropriate; however, an example may be useful to illustrate how one classification was established. Table 10-2 shows an expense account classification system in one large organization. Each account is defined and assigned an account number. Additional accounts might make the sys-

TABLE 10-2
HUMAN RESOURCE EXPENSE ACCOUNT CLASSIFICATIONS

01—**Salaries and Benefits—HR Personnel**
Includes the salaries and employee benefit costs for HR personnel.

02—**Salaries and Benefits—Other Company Personnel**
Includes the salaries and employee benefit costs for other company personnel.

03—**Salaries and Benefits—Program Participants**
Includes the salaries and employee benefit cost for program participants.

04—**Payments to Employees**
Includes all payments made directly to employees for benefits, bonuses, and awards.

05—**Taxes—Employee**
Includes taxes paid to local, state, and federal authorities for employees.

06—**Meals, Travel, and Incidental Expenses—HR Personnel**
Includes meals, travel, and incidental expenses of HR department employees.

07—**Meals, Travel, and Accommodations—Program Participants**
Includes meals, travel accommodations, and incidental expenses for participants in HR programs.

08—**Office Supplies and Expenses**
Includes expenses incurred for stationery, office supplies and services, subscriptions, postage, telephone, and fax.

09—**Program Materials and Supplies**
Includes the cost of materials and supplies purchased for specific programs and includes such items as videos, binders, hand-out materials, and purchased programs.

10—**Printing and Reproduction**
Includes expenses incurred for printing and reproduction of all material.

11—**Outside Services**
Includes the cost incurred for fees and expenses of outside corporations, agency, institutions, or individuals other than company personnel who perform special services such as management consultants and professional instructors.

12—**Equipment Expense Allocation**
Includes that portion of original equipment cost allocated to specific HR programs, including computers.

13—**System Expenses**
Includes charges for computer and systems services.

14—**Equipment—Rental**
Includes rental expenses for equipment used in administrative work and HR programs.

(continued on next page)

TABLE 10-2 CONTINUED
HUMAN RESOURCE EXPENSE ACCOUNT CLASSIFICATIONS

15—**Equipment—Maintenance**
Includes expenses incurred in repairing and servicing company-owned equipment and furniture.

16—**Registration Fees**
Includes employee registration fees and tuitions for seminars and conferences paid for by the company and membership dues and fees in trade, echnical, and professional associations paid by the company for employees.

17—**Facilities Expense Allocation**
Includes an expense allocation for use of a company-owned facility for conducting an HRD program.

18—**Facilities Rental**
Includes rental payments for facilities used in connection with an HRD program.

19—**General Overhead Allocation**
Includes general overhead expenses prorated to each HRD program.

20—**Other Miscellaneous Expenses**
Includes miscellaneous expenses not provided for elsewhere.

tem more precise and avoid misallocation of expenses. However, from a practical standpoint, this classification seems to be adequate for most analyses of HR costs.

Cost Classification Matrix

A final step in the classification process is to define the types of costs in the account classification system that normally apply to the process categories. Table 10-3 presents a matrix that allows for this comparison. Account classifications represent the categories for accumulating all HR-related costs in the organization. The costs, which normally are a part of a process category, are checked in the matrix. Each member of the HR staff should know how to charge expenses properly. For example, the HR department may rent equipment to use in the development and implementation of a program. Should all or part of the cost be charged to development or to implementation? Costs should be allocated in proportion to the extent the item was used for each category.

Cost Accumulation

With expense account classifications clearly defined and the HR process categories determined, it becomes an easy task to track costs on individual programs. This can be accomplished through the use of account numbers, project numbers, and

TABLE 10-3
COST CLASSIFICATION MATRIX

Expense Account Classification	HR Program Categories				
	Analysis	Development/ Acquisition	Implementation	Operating	Evaluation
01—Salaries and Benefits— HR Personnel	X	X	X	X	X
02—Salaries and Benefits— Other Company Personnel		X	X	X	
03—Salaries and Benefits— Program Participants			X	X	X
04—Payments to Employees			X	X	
05—Taxes—Employee			X	X	
06—Meals, Travel, and Incidental Expenses— HR Personnel	X	X	X	X	X
07—Meals, Travel, and Accommodations— Program Participants			X	X	
08—Office Supplies and Expenses	X	X			X
09—Program Materials and Supplies		X	X		
10—Printing and Reproduction	X	X	X	X	X
11—Outside Services	X	X	X		X
12—Equipment Expense Allocation	X	X	X	X	X
13—System Expenses	X	X	X	X	X
14—Equipment—Rental		X	X	X	
15—Equipment—Maintenance			X		
16—Registration Fees			X		
17—Facilities Expense Allocation			X	X	
18—Facilities Rental			X	X	
19—General Overhead Allocation	X	X	X	X	X
20—Other Miscellaneous Expenses	X	X	X	X	X

a PC-based system. An example will illustrate the use of these numbers. A project number is a three-digit number representing a specific HR program. For example:

Recruiting	110
Employee assessment and testing	115
New employee orientation	112
Minority engineering program	118

Numbers are assigned to the HR process categories. Using the example presented earlier, the following numbers are assigned:

Analysis	1
Development	2
Implementation	3
Operation	4
Evaluation	5

By adding the numbers assigned to the expense account classifications, an accounting system is complete unless other requirements from the existing system must be met. For example, if brochures are printed for the minority engineering program, the appropriate charge for that reproduction is 10-3-118. The first two digits denote the account classification, the next digit the HR process category, and the last three digits is the project number. This system enables easy accumulation and monitoring of HR costs. Total costs can be presented by:

■ HR program (minority engineering program)
■ process (implementation)
■ expense account classification (printing and reproduction)

Cost Estimation

With procedures in place to classify, develop, and monitor HR-related costs, comparing costs with the budget or with projected costs is easy. However, a significant reason for tracking costs is to predict the cost of future programs. This task is usually accomplished through a formal method of cost estimation unique to the organization.

Some organizations use PC-based cost estimating worksheets to arrive at the total cost for a proposed program. Table 10-4 shows an example of a cost estimating worksheet to calculate costs for analysis, development/acquisition, implementation, operating, and evaluation. In addition to these worksheets, current charge rates for services, supplies, and salaries are available. These data become quickly outdated and should be prepared periodically as a supplement.

An effective way to predict costs is to analyze historical costs; that is, to track the actual costs incurred in all phases of a previous program from analysis to evaluation. This approach shows the amount of money spent on a program as well as the amount spent in the various categories. Until adequate cost data are available, it is necessary to use the detailed analysis in the worksheets for cost estimation.

In some organizations, a cost model might be appropriate for analyzing and estimating costs. A model is a simplified representation of a real-world situation that stimulates the behavior of HR costs under various specified conditions. It is a step-by-step procedure that enables the user to predict the cost of a proposed

TABLE 10-4
Cost Estimating Worksheet

Analysis Costs	Total
Salaries and Employee Benefits—HR Staff	___
Meals, Travel, and Incidental Expenses	___
Office Supplies and Expenses	___
Printing and Reproduction	___
Outside Services	___
Equipment Expenses	___
System Expenses	___
General Overhead Allocation	___
Other Miscellaneous Expenses	___
Total Analysis Cost	═══

Development/Acquisition Costs		Total
Salaries and Employee Benefits		___
Meals, Travel, and Incidental Expenses		___
Office Supplies and Expenses		___
Program Materials and Supplies		___
Videotape	___	
35mm Slides/Transparencies	___	
Artwork	___	
Manuals and Materials	___	
Other	___	
Printing and Reproduction		___
Outside Services		___
Equipment Expense		___
System Expenses		___
General Overhead Allocation		___
Other Miscellaneous Expense		___
Total Design and Development Costs		═══

Implementation Costs		Total
Participant Costs		___
Salaries and Employee Benefits	___	
(No. of Participants × Avg. Salary × Employee Benefits Factor)		
Meals, Travel, and Accommodations	___	
(No. of Participants × Avg. Daily Expenses × Days of Program)		
Program Materials and Supplies		___

(continued on next page)

TABLE 10-4 (CONTINUED)
COST ESTIMATING WORKSHEET

Participant Replacement Costs (if applicable)   _____
Lost Production (Explain Basis)   _____
Facilitator Costs   _____
  Salaries and Benefits   _____
  Meals, Travel and Incidental Expense   _____
  Outside Services   _____
Facility Costs   _____
  Facilitites Rental   _____
  Facilities Expense Allocation   _____
Equipment Expense   _____
General Overhead Allocation   _____
Other Miscellaneous Expense   _____
  Total Delivery Costs   =====

Operating Costs   Total
Participant Costs   _____
  Salaries and Employee Benefits   _____
  Taxes—Employee   _____
  Payment to Employee   _____
  Meals, Travel, Accommodations   _____
Office Supplies and Expenses   _____
Program Materials and Supplies   _____
Printing and Reproduction   _____
Outside Services   _____
Program Coordination   _____
  Salaries and Employee Benefits   _____
  Meals, Travel, and Incidental Expenses—HR Personnel   _____
Equipment Expense Allocation   _____
Equipment—Rental   _____
Equipment—Maintenance   _____
Facilities Expense Allocation   _____
Facilities Rental   =====
General Overhead Allocation   _____
Other Miscellaneous   _____
  Total Operating Costs   _____

Evaluation Costs   Total
Salaries and Employee Benefits—HR Staff   _____
Meals, Travel, and Incidental Expense   _____

(continued on next page)

TABLE 10-4 (CONTINUED)
COST ESTIMATING WORKSHEET

Participant Costs	_____
Office Supplies and Expense	_____
Printing and Reproduction	_____
Outside Services	_____
Equipment Expense	_____
Systems Expense	_____
General Overhead Allocation	_____
Other Miscellaneous Expenses	_____
Total Evaluation Costs	═══
TOTAL PROGRAM COSTS	═══

HR program or, in the absence of accurate accounting data, to construct the cost of a program already conducted.[4]

IMPACT COSTS

Cost reduction or containment is often a goal of HR programs. In these cases, an important task is to determine the specific amount of cost savings or containment with each output variable. While the conversion of the outputs of HR programs to monetary units are covered in the next chapter, this final section illustrates the potential of HR impact costs in organizations.

Turnover

Few variables linked with HR programs are as important as turnover. Several types of programs including training, recruiting, employee relations, compensation, and benefits are aimed at reducing turnover. One reason for the significant attention to this variable is the tremendous cost for an excessive turnover rate. In some organizations, turnover has been estimated to cost as much as three times the annual base salary of the employee.[5] This figure becomes staggering when several hundred employees leave unexpectedly during the course of the year. In one financial services company, the cost of annual turnover for branch managers was estimated to be $10,000,000.[6] Many studies and cost estimates of turnover are documented in HR literature.

Absenteeism

As with turnover, absenteeism can be a chronic problem of organizations. It not only results in significant costs, but results in many inconveniences and irritations along the way. When an employee unexpectedly does not show up for work, a variety of events or activities must take place. While each of these items will vary considerably with the setting and organization, an increase in cost from absenteeism usually results. Several HR programs, ranging from supervisory training to motivational efforts, are aimed at reducing absenteeism and its corresponding cost reduction. Often, estimating the cost of absenteeism is difficult. One recent study by the commerce clearing house places the cost of absenteeism at between $247 to $534 per employee per year.[7] A reduction of one percentage point (e.g., 7 percent to 6 percent) can represent a significant cost savings in a large organization.

Grievances

In both unionized and non-union plants, the cost of grievances can be significant and consequently should be monitored regularly. Excessive grievance rates bog down the organization, diverting productive time to unproductive activities to resolve differences. In addition to these costs, external costs are associated with grievances and sometimes include settlements and back pay. Many labor relations programs are aimed at grievance reduction and have shown dramatic results.[8]

Safety and Health

Safety and health problems are usually expensive for the organization in terms of direct costs of accidents and increased insurance premiums. In addition, excessive accidents and health problems can lower productivity and quality and reduce morale. Many HR programs focus on the reduction of accident frequency rates, OSHA incidence rates, and strive for improvement in a healthy work environment. The results represent important cost savings as well as other benefits.[9]

Job Dissatisfaction

Job dissatisfaction is directly related to turnover. As employees become more dissatisfied with their jobs, they are more likely to leave. Excessive job dissatisfaction can also hamper recruiting, further adding to costs. A variety of HR programs are designed to improve employee satisfaction, and they have achieved excellent results.[10] Employee benefits, career development, job redesign, and employee relations programs often include job satisfaction as one of their objectives. While the costs are difficult to pinpoint, there have been some attempts to estimate them.[11]

Customer Dissatisfaction

With the increased focus on customer-driven organizations, HR programs often are implemented to directly link to this important output variable. The cost of a dissatisfied customer has been an important topic in many quality control and total quality management programs.[12] Because of its importance, this issue is covered in more detail in the next chapter.

SUMMARY

This chapter presented information necessary to develop a cost system to accumulate, monitor, and report the costs of HR programs. Cost information is necessary even when it is not used directly in program evaluation. When information is collected for evaluation, it can also be used in analysis.

HR costs can be divided into three categories. The first category represents the total cost of an organization's employees, which is usually large and consequently must be properly managed. The second category is the HR department's actual expenses for staff and programs, which is usually under the direct control of the HR staff and must be properly classified, collected, monitored and reported to ensure an efficient HR delivery system. A final category, HR impact costs, represents the opportunity for HR programs to reduce or contain important costs in the organization.

REFERENCES

1. Greer, C. R. *Strategy and Human Resources: A General Managerial Perspective.* Englewood Cliffs: Prentice Hall, 1995.
2. Geber, B. "GAO Raps IRS Training," *Training,* June 1990, pp. 16, 21.
3. Thompson, R. "Benefit Costs Surge Again," *Nation's Business,* February 1993, pp. 38–39.
4. Cascio, W. F. *Costing Human Resources,* 3rd Edition. Boston: PWS-Kent, 1991.
5. Phillips, J. D. "The Price Tag on Turnover," *Personnel Journal,* December 1990, pp. 58–61.
6. Schoeppel, C. "Turning Down Manager Turnover," In *Measuring Return on Investment.* J. J. Phillips. (Ed.) Alexandria: American Society for Training and Development, 1994, pp. 213–234.
7. "No-Shows Cost in Lost Productivity and Service," *Managing Office Technology,* December 1993, p. 66.

8. Cascio, W. F. *Managing Human Resources: Productivity, Quality of Work Life, Profits,* 4th Edition. New York: McGraw-Hill, Inc., 1995.

9. Karasek, R. and Theorell, T. *Healthy Work.* New York: Basic Books, 1990.

10. Kotter, J. P. and Heskett, J. L. *Corporate Culture and Performance.* New York: The Free Press, 1992.

11. Cranny, C. J. and Smith, P. C. *Job Satisfaction.* New York: Lexington Books, 1992.

12. Rust, R. T., Zohorik, A. J., and Kenningham, T. L. *Return on Quality.* Chicago: Probus Publishing Company, 1994.

CHAPTER ELEVEN

Data Analysis and Interpretation

Most HR professionals will agree that data analysis and interpretation is one of the most confusing tasks of the measurement and evaluation process. This confusion often results from misunderstanding the techniques and procedures involved as well as fear of statistics and data analysis. This chapter explores these issues in four parts, using a simplified, jargon-free approach. Figure 11-1 illustrates these four parts. The first part of the chapter addresses the critical issue of isolating the impact of an HR program. In almost every situation, other important variables will influence the impact of an HR program, and these factors must be taken into account. The second part of the chapter discusses converting data to monetary values. It is one thing to collect the data, but it is a different process to assign a monetary value to it. This process alone keeps many HR professionals from following through with a cost/benefit analysis. Statistical techniques, covered in the third part of the chapter, are extremely important in summarizing data and calculating relationships between groups of data. When presented in a simplified, straightforward manner, statistics can be very understandable and helpful for HR practitioners. In this part, references to other works provide more detail for the serious student of statistical analyses. The final part focuses on calculating the actual return on investment (ROI), and presents common approaches to calculate values that can be used in comparison with other types of investment.

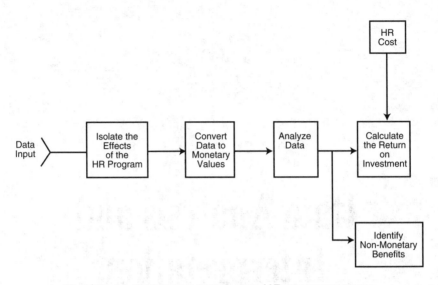

FIGURE 11-1. CALCULATING THE HR CONTRIBUTION.

In many situations, the cost of the program must be compared with the benefits; therefore, monetary benefits should be itemized and reported. The chapter presents general cautions throughout to keep the HR professional from straying into unknown or murky waters.

ISOLATING THE EFFECTS
OF THE HR PROGRAM

The situation is often repeated. A performance improvement is noted after a major HR program has been implemented. The two events appear to be related. A key executive asks "How much of this improvement was due to the HR program?" This potentially embarrassing question is often asked but rarely answered with any degree of certainty by the HR staff. While the change in performance may be related to the program, other factors may also have contributed to the improvement. The program is only one of many variables that can influence performance. This section explores several techniques that can be used to answer the question "What impact did the HR program have on performance?" with a much greater degree of certainty.

Identifying Other Factors: A First Step

As a first step in isolating HR's impact on performance, the HR staff should attempt to identify all the key factors that could have contributed to the improvement. This step communicates to interested parties that other factors may have influenced the results and emphasizes that the HR program is not the sole source of improvement. Consequently, the credit for improvement is shared with several possible variables and sources—an approach that is likely to gain the respect of management.

There are several potential sources for identifying major influencing variables. HR program participants are usually aware of other influences that may have caused performance improvement. After all, it is the output of their collective efforts (output, quality, costs, or time) that is being monitored and measured. In many situations, they may have witnessed previous movements in performance measures and can pinpoint the reasons for improvement. Program designers and developers are another source for identifying variables that have an impact on results. They may have noted these influencing variables during needs analysis and program development. In some situations, supervisors of participants may be able to identify variables that influenced the performance improvement. This is particularly useful when program participants are nonexempt employees (operatives), who may not be fully aware of the variables that can influence performance. Finally, middle and top management may be able to identify other influences. Perhaps they have monitored, examined, and analyzed the variables previously.

Taking the time to carry out this step creates additional credibility for the process by focusing attention on other variables that may have influenced performance. It moves beyond the scenario in which results are presented with no mention of other influences, a situation that often destroys the credibility of the analysis. It also provides a foundation for some of the strategies described next, by identifying the variables that must be isolated to show the effects of the HR program.

Use of Control Groups

The most credible approach for isolating the impact of an HR program is the use of control groups in an experimental design process. This approach involves an experimental group that has the benefit of the program and a control group that does not have the program. The composition of both groups should be nearly identical and, if feasible, the selection of each group should be on a random basis. When this is possible, and both groups are subjected to the same environmental influences, the difference in the performance of the two groups can be attributed to the HR program. Chapter 6 presented more detail on the control group arrangement.

Control group arrangements show up in many settings. One example is a Federal Express analysis that used control groups in measuring ROI.[1] The study focused on 20 employees who went through the company's two-week training

program soon after being hired to drive company vans. The employees' performance was compared with a control group of 20 other new hires whose managers
were told to do no more (or less) on-the-job training than they normally would.
Performance was tracked for the two groups for 90 days in categories such as accidents, injuries, time-card errors and domestic airbill errors. The 10 performance
categories were assigned dollar values by experts from engineering, finance, and
other groups. The results showed a 24 percent return on the investment.

Because this is the most effective approach for isolating the impact of an HR program, it should be used for programs that represent a significant expenditure, have a
wide exposure, and are closely linked to organizational objectives. In these situations, it is important that the analysis of the program impact be highly accurate. Program implementers must clearly understand the research design process and the role
of their efforts in the process. Most participants are willing to participate in an experiment when they understand its purpose and see the value of their participation.

Trend Line Analysis

Another useful technique for approximating the impact of some HR programs
is trend line analysis. In this approach, a trend line is drawn on a graph from a point
that represents the beginning current performance level of participants and extends
to a point that represents the anticipated performance level without the HR program. Upon completion of the HR program the actual performance of employees
is compared to the level the trend line predicted performance would be without the
HR program. Any improvement of performance above what was predicted can
then be reasonably attributed to the HR program. While this is not an exact
process, it provides a reasonable estimation of the impact of an HR program.

Figure 11-2 shows an example of this trend line analysis taken from an electronics manufacturer. The data is slightly exaggerated to illustrate the process.
The reject rate for defective components is presented before and after an HR program that was conducted in July. As shown in the figure, there was already a
downward trend on the reject rate prior to conducting the program. Although the
program apparently had a dramatic effect on the reduction of rejects, the trend
line shows that reject rate reduction would have continued, based on the trend that
had been previously established. It is tempting to measure the improvement by
comparing the average six-month reject rate prior to the program to the average
six months after the program. A more accurate comparison, however, is to use a
six-month average after the program and compare it to the trend line value at the
midpoint of the six-month period after the program (October–November value).
In this example, the difference is .75 percent (1.45–.7).

A primary disadvantage of this approach is that it is not necessarily accurate,
although it may be as accurate as other methods described here. The use of this

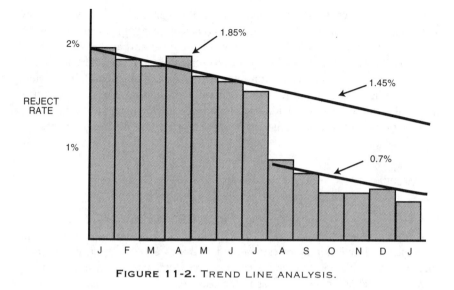

FIGURE 11-2. TREND LINE ANALYSIS.

approach also assumes that the events that influenced the performance variable prior to the program are still in place after the program, except for the implementation of the HR program. Finally, this approach assumes that no new influences entered the situation. The trends that were established prior to the program will continue in the same relative direction. This may not always be the case.

The primary advantage of this approach is that it is simple, inexpensive, and takes very little effort. If historical data are available, a trend line can quickly be drawn and data estimated. While this process is not exact, it does provide a quick analysis of the program's impact.

Forecasting Methods

A more analytical approach to trend line analysis is to use forecasting methods to predict the level of performance that might occur in the future if the HR program had not been undertaken. This approach represents a mathematical analysis of the trend line analysis above. Instead of drawing a straight line, a linear equation is used to calculate a value of the anticipated performance improvement. A linear model is appropriate only when one other variable influenced the output performance, and that relationship can be characterized by a straight line.

The primary advantage of this process is that it can be an accurate predictor of the performance variables that would occur without implementing the program, if appropriate data and models are available. The method is simple for linear relationships. However, a major disadvantage to this approach occurs when many variables enter the process. The process becomes more complex and requires the use of sophisticated statistical packages for multiple variable analysis. Even then, the data may not fit the model. Unfortunately, many organizations have not developed mathematical relationships for output variables as a function of one or more inputs. Without them, the forecasting method is difficult to use. If the numbers are available, they could provide useful evidence of the impact of training. The presentation of specific methods is beyond the scope of this book and is contained in other works.[2]

Participant Estimation

An easy method to isolate the impact of an HR program is to secure information directly from program participants. This approach assumes that participants are capable of determining or estimating how much of a performance improvement is related to the HR program. As the source of the performance, participants may have reliable input on the issue. Because their actions produced the change, they should have some estimation as to how much of the change was caused by the HR program. Although their input is an estimation, it will usually have considerable credibility with management groups because participants are at the center of the change or improvement resulting from the HR program.

As an added enhancement to this method, management may be asked to approve the participants' estimates. For example, in an HR program involving a performance management system (performance appraisal and training) for Yellow Freight Systems, participants estimated the amount of savings attributed to the program.[3] Table 11-1 shows a sample of these estimates. Managers at the next two levels above participants reviewed and approved the estimates. So, in essence, the managers actually confirmed participants' estimates.

The process has some disadvantages. It is an estimate and, consequently, it does not have the accuracy desired by some HR managers. Also, the input data may be unreliable because some participants are uncomfortable with providing these types of estimates. Finally, some participants may be incapable of estimating improvements, even if they sincerely try. They might not be aware which factors exactly contributed to the results.

The approach has several advantages. It is a simple process and easily understood by participants and by others who review evaluation data. It is inexpensive, takes little time and analysis, and results in an efficient addition to the evaluation process. Although it is an estimate, it originates from a credible source: the individuals who actually produced the improvement.

TABLE 11-1
SAMPLE OF PARTICIPANT ESTIMATES

TERMINAL IN DIVISION I	IMPROVEMENT	PERCENTAGE OF IMPROVEMENT ATTRIBUTED TO PERFORMANCE MANAGEMENT SKILLS	DOLLAR VALUE*
A	To reduce high cost per bill due to poor planning on pickup and delivery and low sales, manager installed job models and feedback systems, coached supervisors and drivers, and praised all employees for improved performance. Cost per bill decreased an average of $1.30.	25	6,928 (C)
B	In new terminal with cost per bill running high, manager installed job models and used coaching and rewards for supervisory, clerical, and sales staff. Terminal's profits increased from $43,253 to $49,024.	10	27,680(R)
C	Terminal had low bill count and high cost per bill. Manager installed job models and feedback systems and used interpersonal skills. Cost per bill decreased an average of $1.79 over same period before the program.	5	800 (C)
D	Terminal had low bill count, which contributed to a high cost per bill. Manager installed job models and feedback systems, and used rewards and coaching with office staff, supervisors, and sales representatives. Cost per bill decreased an average of 92¢; number of bills increased from 7,765 to 9,405 per month. To improve sales growth, sales manager created job models, coached sales repre- sentatives, and used interpersonal skills	25	9,856 (C)

(continued on next page)

TABLE 11-1 (CONTINUED)
SAMPLE OF PARTICIPANT ESTIMATES

TERMINAL IN DIVISION I	IMPROVEMENT	PERCENTAGE OF IMPROVEMENT ATTRIBUTED TO PERFORMANCE MANAGEMENT SKILLS	DOLLAR VALUE*
	with representatives and customers. Number of bills increased from 7,290 to 9,765 per month; total bill count increased from 65,614 to 87,892 per month; at an average revenue of $110 per bill, the 22,278 additional bills brought in $2,450,580 in extra revenue.	10	245,058 (R)
E	Terminal had low bill count and high cost per bill. Manager installed job models and had his sales manager and operations manager install job models, also. All managers used rewards, coaching, and interpersonal skills. Cost per bill decreased from $22.49 to $21.00; number of bills increased from 11,716 to 12,974 per month.	50	56,060 (C)
F	Terminal had rising cost per bill with a fluctuating bill count. Manager used job models and feedback reports. Cost per bill decreased from $17.13 to $15.46; number of bills rose from 6,160 to 7,357 per month.	10	5754 (C)

*(R) indicates a revenue gain; (C) indicates decreased costs.

Management's Estimate

In some cases, upper management may estimate the percent of improvement attributed to the HR program. Although the process is subjective, the source of the estimate is a group that usually allocates funds and has a sense of what the value should be. With this approach, the source of these estimates is not usually based on direct knowledge of the process. For example, Litton Guidance and Control Systems implemented a successful self-directed team process.[4] Management identified other factors such as technology, procedures, and process changes that could have contributed to the improvement. Adjustments were made to account for these factors. After the other factors were considered, management then applied a subjective factor, in this case 60 percent, to represent the portion of the results that should be attributed to the HR program. The 60 percent factor was developed at a meeting with top executives and therefore had the benefit of group ownership. Applying this factor, the HRD program took credit for 60 percent of the improvement in quality and productivity. While this process is subjective, the input or action comes from those who often provide the funds for the program. Sometimes their comfort level is what's most important. Because of the subjective nature of the process, this adjusted estimating process allows for a greater comfort level.

Customer Input

A helpful approach in some situations, such as an empowerment program, is to solicit input directly from customers concerning the impact of the program. In these situations, customers are asked to indicate their reasons for choosing a particular product or service or to indicate how their reaction to the product or service organization has been influenced by individuals and their skills and abilities. This type of input focuses directly on what the HR program is often designed to improve. For example, following a merger, one bank conducted a teller training program. Market research data showed that after training the percentage of customers who were dissatisfied with teller knowledge was reduced by 5 percent.[5] (Teller knowledge was increased by training.) Therefore, 5 percent of the reduction of dissatisfied customers was directly attributable to the training program.

Expert Estimation

Another approach to identifying factors that influence the impact of an HR program is to rely on external or internal experts to estimate what portion of results can be attributed to an HR program. With this process, the experts must be carefully selected based on their knowledge of the process, program, and situation. For example, an expert in quality might be able to provide estimates of how much quality improvement can be attributed to an HR program and what percent can be attributed to other factors. In another situation, an external expert can possibly estimate the extent to which improvement is made without the program. This amount is subtracted from the improvement, and it is assumed that the remainder can be attributed to the HR program. This approach appears to be most effective when the expert has been involved in similar programs and has estimated the impact in other settings. In another situation, the expert identifies other factors contributing to the results and estimates the impact of those factors based on previous experience or the use of historical data.

A potential variation on this approach may include using the external expert to produce the estimates from participants and supervisors and to then provide guidance on how to analyze and summarize the data. In some cases, it is helpful to have an expert actually facilitate the process with participants and supervisors. Experts, consultants, or researchers are usually available for almost any field in which there is training. They can bring their experience with similar situations into the analysis. This process has an advantage in that its credibility often reflects the reputation of the expert or independent consultant. Sometimes top management will place more confidence in external experts than in their own internal participants and supervisors.

CONVERTING DATA TO MONETARY UNITS

An earlier chapter presented the types of data collected for program evaluation. Before this data can be used to compare benefits with costs, it must be converted to monetary values. This section provides additional insight into practical ways to convert data to monetary values. Conversions of hard data (output, quality, cost, time) are discussed first, followed by soft data conversion.

Converting Increased Output

Changes in output are the goal of many HR programs and in most situations the value of increased output can be easily calculated. For example, when implementing a sales incentive program, the change in output can easily be measured. The average sales before the program was installed is compared to the average sales after the program. It is calculated by multiplying the increase in sales by the average profit per sale. In another example, consider a packaging machine operator in a pharmaceutical plant. The operator packages drugs in boxes ready for shipment. Machine operators participate in an employee involvement program to learn how to increase production through better use of equipment and work procedures. The value of increased output is more difficult to pinpoint than the sales increase example. One approach is to calculate the unit labor cost of the packaging operation. Additional output of a unit ready for shipment saves the company the unit labor cost. Using this approach, the increase in output multiplied by the unit labor cost of packaging is the added value of the program. While this figure may not be exact because increases in output may affect the unit costs, it is usually accurate enough for measuring the return on an HR program.

Direct Cost Savings

Converting cost savings to monetary values appears to be redundant. An HR program that produces a cost savings usually contributes an added value equal to the amount of the cost savings. However, the time value of money may slightly alter these values. An amount of money at one point in time is worth more than the same amount at a later time. A simple discounted cash flow adjustment will place this comparison on an equal basis. Also, a cost savings generated by an employee or a group of employees over a long period might have a greater value than the actual savings, because costs normally increase during the period. This is best explained with an example. A group of employees operate a distribution center for publications. Supervisors have specific cost control responsibilities for their particular unit. They are held accountable for the direct variable costs and a portion of the fixed costs that are partially under their control. When costs seemed unusually high, the organization implemented cost control techniques as part of a continuous process improvement (CPI) program. Supervisors learned how to analyze costs and use the various reports to control costs. Both fixed and variable costs were monitored for a six-month period before and after the program to measure improvements. Part of these costs included equipment, wages, and supplies, all of which increased during the one-year period. To pinpoint an accurate value of the cost savings, the first six-month period costs were adjusted upward to what represented a cost target for comparison during the post-program period. Actual costs were compared with the target costs to determine the value of the cost savings as a result of the HR program, assuming no other factors influenced the cost savings.

Converting Time Savings

Many programs are aimed at reducing the time to perform a task, deliver a service, or respond to a request. Time savings are important because employee time is money, in the form of wages, salaries, and benefits paid directly to the employee. Several economic benefits are derived from time savings as described below.

Wages/salaries. The most common time savings results in reduced costs of labor involved in the HR program. The monetary savings are the hours saved multiplied by the labor cost per hour, which can be an allusive figure. While the average wage, with a percent added for benefits, will suffice for most calculations, it may be misleading. Some experts suggest that other cost factors be included such as support costs to maintain the employee. Whatever figure is used in the calculations must be clearly explained in the HR evaluation. A conservative figure is probably best because most managers feel more comfortable in dealing with the average wages plus benefits.

Improved service. Another potential benefit of time savings is better service, particularly when production time, implementation time, construction time, or processing time is reduced so that the product or service is delivered to the client or customer in a shorter period of time. As a result, there is improved customer satisfaction, the value of which is difficult to quantify and will be discussed in the soft data section in this chapter. In some situations, reductions in time can avoid penalties. For example, with processing invoices in accounts payable, a reduction in processing time can avoid late payment penalties and possibly earn a discount. A reduction in time to complete a construction project can earn the company a sizable bonus.

Opportunity for profit. A sometimes hidden, but potentially rewarding, benefit of time savings is the opportunity to make additional profit. For example, when a sales representative reduces the average time for a sales call, that representative has more time for sales calls. These additional calls should increase sales, which add to profits with little or no additional sales expense.

Converting Improved Quality

Quality improvement is an important and frequent target of HR programs. Total Quality Management (TQM) programs are developed to improve the quality of products, services, and processes. The cost of poor quality to an organization can be staggering. According to quality expert Phillip Crosby, an organization can probably increase its profits by 5 percent to 10 percent of sales if it concentrates on improving quality.[6] To be effective, the measurable impact of a quality improvement program must be determined. To calculate the return on the program, the value of the quality improvement must be calculated. This value may have several components as described below.

Scrap/waste. The most obvious cost of poor quality is the scrap or waste generated by mistakes. Defective products, spoiled raw materials, and discarded paperwork are the results of poor quality. This scrap and waste translates into a monetary value that can be used to calculate the impact of an improvement in quality. For example, in a production environment, the cost of a defective product can be easily calculated because it is the total cost incurred at the point the mistake is identified minus the salvage value. The costs of paper and computer entry errors can be significant. For example, the cost of an error on a purchase order can be enormous if the wrong items are ordered.

Rework. Many mistakes and errors result in costly rework to correct the mistake. The most costly reworks occur when a product is delivered to a customer but must be returned for correction, or when an expensive program is implemented with serious errors. In determining the cost of rework, labor and direct cost are both significant. Maintaining a staff to perform rework is an additional overhead cost for the organization. In a manufacturing plant, the cost of rework is in the range of 15 percent–70 percent of a plant's productivity. In banks, an estimated 35% of operating costs could be blamed on correcting wrong work.[7]

Customer/client dissatisfaction. Customer and client dissatisfaction represents a tremendous loss for the organization when errors and mistakes are made. In some cases, serious mistakes can result in lost business. Customer dissatisfaction is difficult to quantify, and attempts to arrive at a monetary value may be impossible. Usually, the judgment and expertise of sales and marketing management are the best sources for estimating the cost of a dissatisfied customer. It may be more realistic to list an improvement in customer satisfaction as an advantage of improved quality without trying to quantify it.

However, experts in service quality insist that customer and client dissatisfaction can be measured. Some refer to this as measuring the market damage of poor service quality. One approach is to survey customers who have had good and bad experiences and ask them whether they are likely to do business with that particular company again. Later, the same people can be surveyed to find out whether they did do business with the company. Then researchers use a formula to measure the monetary damage bad service did to repeat business.[8]

Inspection and quality control. In some organizations, a response to the demand for improved quality is to employ additional inspectors or to beef-up the quality control staff. Quality control inspectors often inspect products after they have been produced or inspect supplier products as they are received. Although some inspection may be necessary to determine the level of quality, it is not a solution to a poorly designed or manufactured product or an ineffective service delivery system. An HR program designed to improve quality should reduce the level of inspection and quality control needed and that should ultimately result in specific reductions in the number of inspectors, a measure that can be translated into a monetary value savings.

Cost of Quality. The quality problem is extensive, and various components affect the cost of poor quality. These components are sometimes grouped and often referred to categorically as preventive costs, appraisal costs, and failure costs. Crosby contends that total expenditures for these items should be no more than 2.5 percent of sales.[9] Although it may seem challenging to calculate the numbers, some consultants and practitioners are able to make this calculation using surveys. This process requires employees to estimate how much time they spend doing work that falls into each of the three categories above. The figure is then multiplied by the standard labor wage rate and adjusted with a benefits factor. Paul Revere Insurance Companies uses a survey process to estimate this cost. Each team lists the amount of time each member devotes to each category in an average week as well as the specific costs incurred by variations from quality standards. The numbers were not precise, but were estimates, and resulted in a total figure of 44 percent of overhead. The result was amazingly consistent among the divisions. This measure provided an indication of the magnitude of the problem and served as a source of ideas for the team throughout the year. It also served as a benchmark by which to measure the team in years to come.[10]

Converting Soft Data

While soft data are not as desirable as hard data, they are important in HR measurement and evaluation. The difficulty with soft data often arises in assigning monetary values to the data. Most assignments of value are subjective and must be used with some caution. Several approaches are available to convert the soft data to a monetary value and are presented below.

Historical costs. Occasionally an organization will develop and accumulate cost for specific soft data items. For example, some organizations monitor the cost of grievances. Although an extremely variable item, the average cost per grievance provides a basis for estimating the cost savings for a reduction in grievances. Because of their relative accuracy, historical costs, if available, should always be used to estimate the value of soft data items.

Expert opinion. Expert opinions, either internal or external, are sometimes used to estimate the value of soft data improvements. Internal experts are those employees who are proficient and knowledgeable in their fields. For example, a purchasing expert may estimate the salvage value of defective parts, an industrial engineer might estimate the time that it takes to complete a task or perform a function, and a marketing analyst might estimate the cost of a dissatisfied customer. Using internal experts provides excellent opportunities to recognize individuals in the organization. Chances are, their expert analysis will not be challenged because others in the organization have no better basis to make the estimate. External experts usually possess a string of impressive credentials including education, research, publications, and experience in a particular field. One consultant, for example, estimated the cost of work slowdowns and was able to use the figure with several organizations by providing an expert opinion on the item. An important caution should be exercised, however, when using experts. You should always ascertain that they are indeed recognized as experts and that they are credible.

External studies. Extensive analyses of similar data in other organizations may be extrapolated to fit an internal situation. For example, many experts have attempted to calculate the cost of absenteeism. Studies on absenteeism usually show that the average cost of absenteeism per incident is in the $80–$100 range.[11] Although these estimates can vary considerably, they may serve as a rough estimate for other calculations with some adjustments for the specific organization.

There are literally hundreds of studies conducted in the literature covering the cost of variables such as absenteeism, turnover, tardiness, grievances, complaints, and loss of time due to accidents. Typical publications to pursue would be *Academy of Management Journal, Journal of Applied Psychology, Personnel Psychology, Human Resources Management, HR Magazine, Human Resource Development Quarterly,* and *Personnel Journal.* A variety of databases are available, such as ERIC, which can help a practitioner locate this data.

Practitioners rarely venture into external studies probably because there is not enough dialogue between the HR researchers and the practitioners. Each group seems to have a misunderstanding of the other's role, and they only mesh at times when it is convenient for both. Practitioners should learn more about research studies and publications and possibly influence future research.

Participant estimation. Employees directly involved in an HR program may be capable of estimating the value of an improvement. Either during the program or in a follow-up, participants should be asked to estimate the value of the improvements. To provide further insight, participants should also be asked to furnish the basis for their estimate and their level of confidence in it. Estimations by participants are credible and may be more realistic than other sources because participants are usually directly involved with the improvement and are knowledgeable of the issues. If provided encouragement and examples, participants are often creative at estimating these values. For example, in one organization, in response to a special HR program, staff managers were asked to estimate the value of reducing the time to recruit a new employee. Although their responses were not precise, they provided a credible estimate of this value from the customers of the recruiting section.

Management estimation. A final strategy for converting soft data to monetary values is to ask managers who are concerned about the program's evaluation to estimate the value of an improvement. Several management groups may be targets for this estimation including supervisors of program participants, top management (who approves the expenditures), and the members of a program review committee whose function is to direct the program. With this approach, managers estimate what it is worth to improve on a particular soft data item such as solving problems, resolving conflicts, or increasing customer satisfaction. When management develops an estimate, it becomes their figure. Because it has ownership, this estimate can be useful in the analysis of the HR program.

Soft data value example. In some cases, it might be appropriate to combine strategies to arrive at an estimation of the benefits from an HR program. The following example comes from an actual case and focuses on three strategies: expert opinion, external studies, and management estimation. A large regional federal savings bank was experiencing a higher than desirable turnover rate. It developed an HR program to reduce turnover. To measure the payoff of the program, the HR staff needed to estimate the cost of turnover, an illusionary figure in most organizations. The total cost includes:

- replacement costs (i.e., recruitment, selection, employment testing, and orientation)
- training costs to bring new employees up to the contribution level of the employees who left the organization
- lost production (because new employees are not at full contribution)
- lost time of individuals involved with the turnover problem (i.e., supervisors, managers and specialists involved in the issues of recruiting and training),
- administrative costs tied to all of these processes

Calculating the precise cost of turnover is a difficult task, and the bank did not want to devote resources to develop it. Consequently, a combination of strategies were used to estimate turnover costs.

First, the HR staff searched the literature to see whether turnover had been calculated for financial institutions. In a bank of similar size, the cost of turnover had been developed by the internal audit department and verified by a consultant who was an expert in turnover reduction.[12] The cost of turnover was calculated to be $25,000 per turnover statistic. Thus, this initial figure had the advantage of an external study of costs developed at a similar institution and had the credibility of expert opinion. However, there is always a question of whether data in one organization should apply to another, even though both organizations are in the same type of business.

Next, the HR staff met with top executives to agree on a turnover cost value to use in gauging the success of the program. It presented management with the external study and agreed on an estimate that was half the amount from the study,

$12,500. This was considered conservative because other turnover studies typically yield greater values. However, management felt comfortable with the estimate, and used it for the benefits side of program evaluation. Although not precise, this exercise yielded a figure that was never disputed. For additional information on how to calculate the cost of turnover, see other references.[13]

In summary, these strategies are effective for converting soft data to monetary values when calculating a return on an HR program. One word of caution is in order. Whenever a monetary value is assigned to subjective information, it needs to be fully explained to the audience receiving the information. When there is a range of possible values, the most conservative one should be used to ensure credibility for the process.

DATA ANALYSIS TECHNIQUES

General Guidelines

One of the most critical and confusing tasks in the measurement and evaluation process is data analysis. An appropriate data analysis is essential for credible, valid, and reliable results. Data analysis does not have to be confusing. It is a logical process that can be easily learned by the HR staff. Before approaching the use of statistics, a review of a few very basic guidelines for analyzing evaluation data should be helpful.

Review for consistency and accuracy. While this guideline may be obvious, additional checks may be necessary to ensure the accuracy and consistency of the data. Incorrect or insufficient data items should be eliminated from the analysis. A simple scan of data will usually reveal extreme data points or values that may seem impossible to obtain. Accuracy is of utmost importance because the analysis, interpretation, and conclusion will only be as reliable as the data itself. Proper attention to this step will pay off in other stages of the analysis.

Use all relevant data—negative and positive. Some organizations only report successes from programs. In most program evaluations, the individual conducting the evaluation wants improvement. This, however, creates an opportunity for a built-in bias. Improvement as a result of the program will not always happen. Data may be both positive and negative, and the evaluator may be tempted to eliminate data that does not support the desired outcome. All relevant data should be used for a valid and credible analysis. If not, there should be an explanation of why it was deleted.

Treat individual data confidentially. Frequently, data collected will be the result of individual performances and decisions. When analyzing, interpreting, and reporting results, the confidentiality of the sources should be an important concern unless there are conditions that warrant their exposure. The same atmosphere of confidentiality used in collecting data should be used in the analysis and reporting phases. This should be clearly communicated to the participants before the evaluation begins.

Use the simplest statistics possible. Usually there are several ways to analyze data and a variety of statistical techniques are available to compare changes in performance. Conducting additional analyses, which may serve no further benefit, should be avoided. The analysis should be kept simple and limited to data necessary to draw the proper conclusions. For example, the values of implemented suggestions from a new suggestion program are measured. Three ways to report the average are available: the mean, the median, and the mode. The mean value is usually the appropriate value. It adds very little to the analysis to present the median and the mode. While these two numbers can be easily determined, they may confuse the audience receiving the evaluation results.

Statistics in Perspective

The terms "statistics" and "data analysis" are almost synonymous. According to *The Random House Dictionary,* statistics is the "science that deals with the collection, classification, analysis, and interpretation of numerical facts or data, and that, by use of mathematical theories of probability, imposes order and regularity on aggregates of more or less disparate elements." Unfortunately, the use of statistics frighten many of those involved in HR evaluation. Full coverage of statistics is not presented here. Many other books serve that purpose.[14] The material that follows discusses a few basic concepts and provides enough insight to perform simple analyses on frequently occurring situations.

One useful way to present raw data is by using a frequency distribution. A frequency distribution is a graph that displays the values that a variable can assume along with the frequency of occurrence of these values. Table 11-2 illustrates this concept. The data in the table represent pre-program and post-program measurements of performance for a group of 15 employees. A unit hour is a measure of work pace equal to the allowed minutes of work produced in an hour's time. One way to present the data is to group it into small ranges called class intervals.

These groupings can be plotted on a diagram to yield what is called a frequency histogram as shown in Figure 11-3. This graphical presentation of the data reveals that after the HR program was implemented more employees reported a unit hour rating in the range of 60–64 than any other range. The graphical presen-

TABLE 11-2
PRE-PROGRAM AND POST-PROGRAM MEASUREMENTS

EMPLOYEE NUMBER	PRODUCTION RATES (UNIT HOURS) BEFORE TRAINING	AFTER TRAINING
1	43	47
2	45	59
3	61	79
4	59	69
5	66	63
6	54	55
7	49	51
8	52	58
9	55	72
10	60	63
11	50	61
12	55	60
13	58	65
14	56	63
15	63	67
Total	826	932

tation of data can be useful to show the central tendency (where most of the items are grouped) and also the dispersion (the extent to which the data is scattered).

Measures of Central Tendency

The most common measures of central tendency are the mean, median, and mode. The mean is the arithmetic average for a group of numbers. It is calculated by adding all of the values and dividing by the total numbers and presents in a single number a summary of the characteristics of the entire group such as the average absenteeism rate for a group of employees. The mean is the number that best represents the set of data. It is the most useful statistic to reflect performance after completing an HR program.

The median is the middle value in a stream of numbers arranged in order of magnitude. There are an equal number of values above and below the median. In the case of an even number of data items, the median is the average of the two middle values. The median can serve as a useful shortcut to determine the estimate of the whole group when the mean is not readily available or is not required.

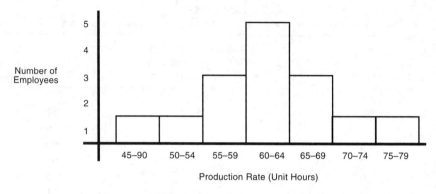

FIGURE 11-3. A FREQUENCY HISTOGRAM.

The mode of a set of numbers is the value that occurs with the greatest frequency; i.e., the most common value. The mode has limited application and may not even exist at all in some data. For instance, if all of the employees had different levels of performance, there would not be a mode for the distribution. When the three measures are almost equal, the distribution is called normal or bell-shaped.

Measures of Dispersion

The degree to which data varies from the average, or mean, is called dispersion. Three common measures of dispersion are the range, variance, and the standard deviation. The range is the simplest measure of dispersion. It is the difference between the largest and smallest of a set of numbers. This value provides a simple picture of how much the data varies from one extreme point to the other. A larger range usually reflects more dispersion.

The variance is the average value of the squares of the deviations from the mean and reflects the degree to which the numbers vary from the mean. By itself the variance is not very useful because it represents squared values. A more useful value is the standard deviation, calculated by taking the square root of the variance. As the name implies, standard deviation represents how much the data deviates from the mean value for the group. For example, a large standard deviation for an average attendance means that there is a wide variation among the absenteeism records for the group of employees. If the standard deviation is low, then the data are grouped very closely to the mean value.

In the frequency histogram, the data graphically simulates a bell-shaped curve if the center points of each of the rectangles are connected. If there were many items with smaller intervals, the histogram would form a bell-shaped curve as shown in Figure 11-4. Much data in its normal state are distributed in a similar manner. For this kind of distribution, which is called a normal distribution, approximately 95 percent of the values are within two standard deviations of the mean as illustrated in the figure. In other words, two standard deviations on both sides of the mean (for a total of four) account for approximately 95 percent of the total of the values. Therefore, the range will equal approximately four standard

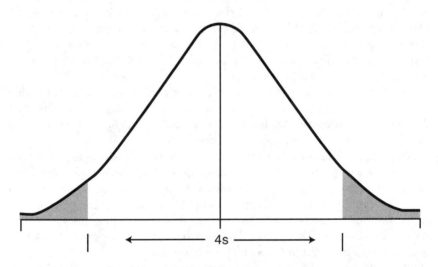

FIGURE 11-4. THE NORMAL DISTRIBUTION OR BELL-SHAPED CURVE.

deviations for normal distributions. This represents a shortcut way to approximate the standard deviation.

Measures of Association

In program evaluation, occasionally there is a need to know if a relationship exists between two or more groups of data. These groups of data are usually referred to as variables. This relationship is useful in predicting performance based on program results or prerequisite criteria. An example will help illustrate this point. A large aerospace firm evaluated its cooperative education program. Among the items of evaluation, the employer wanted to know if the grade point average (GPA) of participants in the program is related to future success measured by their rates of promotion and salary increases after program completion. This information would answer the question: "Are co-op students with higher grades more successful?" The answer to this question could alter the firm's co-op recruiting strategies.

In another example, an electronics manufacturer employs individuals who test completed electronic components. Candidates for this job must complete a training program prior to employment. At the end of the program, a test is administered that covers the procedures and tasks necessary to perform component testing effectively. After candidates are hired, their test scores at the end of the program are compared to the production efficiency and quality of their work after employment. The efficiency relates to the number of component tests completed. Quality represents the percentage of the components tested properly. A direct relationship between the end-of-the-program scores and after-the-program performance helps validate the test and also provides a predictor of performance without the expense of a follow-up.

These two examples illustrate the need to determine whether a relationship exists between two variables and the extent of the relationship. The term that describes the relationship is called correlation, and the extent of the relationship (or quality) is measured by a correlation coefficient.

A basic approach to examining data for a possible relationship is to plot the two variables on a diagram called a scatter diagram and visually determine the likelihood of the correlation. Doing this shows whether a relationship exists between two variables. Figure 11-5 gives an example. The relationship can be expressed in the form of an algebraic equation process known as curve fitting. The line through the data is a trend line that can be extended to show approximately where data will be located past the data points on the graph.

The method of determining the equation of a relationship is called the method of least squares. When the equation of the relationship is known, test scores can be plugged into the equation, and the corresponding values for production efficiency can be calculated. The specific formulas for determining the equations are beyond the scope of this book. Several resources are appropriate for providing information on these calculations.[15]

Several different types of correlation coefficients are available depending on the type of data, how the data are arranged, and the relationship between the two variables. Most of the data used in evaluation will be numerical and come from sources such as performance measurements. For this type of data, the correlation coefficient used is the Pearson's Product-Moment Correlation Coefficient. This coefficient applies only when there is a linear relationship, i.e., a straight-line relationship with no curve in the trend line of the graphical plot of the data. Fortunately, in many cases there is a linear relationship, particularly with performance data. This coefficient will be used in the remainder of this chapter. For additional information on the other correlation coefficients and when they should be used, consult other references.[16]

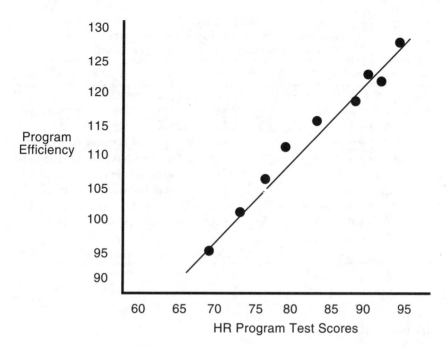

FIGURE 11-5. SCATTER DIAGRAM OF TWO VARIABLES.

The correlation coefficient varies between −1 and +1. The minus denotes negative correlation and the plus denotes positive correlation. When a perfect negative correlation exists, the coefficient is −1; when there is no correlation between the two variables the coefficient is 0; when a perfect positive correlation exists, the coefficient is +1. This measure presents in a single number a summary of the characteristics of the entire group such as the average absenteeism rate for a group of employees.

The range between these two extreme values represents the degree of correlation. As a rough guide, Table 11-3 shows ranges of possible correlations and their rough interpretations. These are only approximate, and the actual interpretations of a specific correlation value depend on the confidence placed on that value. A word of caution is in order about correlation. The determination of a relationship between two variables does not mean that one necessarily caused the other. There could be other outside factors that influenced the changes. Therefore, as with many areas of statistics, this process provides additional useful information but does not always provide the specific answers to the relationship puzzle.

TABLE 11-3
RANGES OF CORRELATION COEFFICIENTS
AND THEIR APPROXIMATE INTERPRETATIONS

CORRELATION VALUE	GENERAL DESCRIPTION
−1.0	Perfect negative correlation
−.8 to −1.0	Very high degree of negative correlation
−.6 to −.8	High degree of negative correlation
−.4 to −.6	Medium degree of negative correlation
−.2 to −.4	Low degree of negative correlation
+.2 to −.2	Probably no correlation
+.2 to +.4	Low degree of positive correlation
+.4 to +.6	Medium degree of positive correlation
+.6 to +.8	High degree of positive correlation
+.8 to +1.0	Very high degree of positive correlation
+1.0	Perfect positive correlation

Statistical Inference

When performance improves after an HR program, a likely question should be asked: "Did the improvement occur because of the program or could it have occurred by chance?" In other words, would the same results have been achieved without the HR program? How accurate are the conclusions? These questions can be answered through hypothesis testing. Statistical analyses are used to establish a confidence level for conclusions made concerning differences in groups of data. Normally conclusions are based on a 95 percent confidence level, which means that 95 percent of the time, on the average, the conclusions will be correct.

A few HR program evaluations are based on an hypothesis. An hypothesis is a proposed explanation of the relationship between two or more variables such as performance and an HR program. For example, "Production employees performance will improve as a result of the HR program" is a statement that is either rejected or not rejected based on the evaluation data, the result of the statistical analysis, and a statistical test. The hypothesis is "tested." (Some researchers prefer to use the terminology "fail to reject" or "not rejected" rather than "accept." The rationale is that in some situations failing to reject the hypothesis on the basis of a single test may not be sufficient to accept the hypothesis.) While the development of hypotheses, statistical analyses, statistical testing, and the types of errors associated with statistical testing are important, they are beyond the scope of this book and are presented in other works.[17]

Statistical Deception

No chapter on data analysis can be complete without some discussion of statistical deception that might result in erroneous conclusions from data. Numerous examples of statistical deception appear regularly.[18] Statistics can prove almost anything. The following are common ways that statistics can deceive the casual observer, often unintentionally.

Unsupported Results. Presenting conclusions from data without proper statistical analysis is a common deceptive practice. Too often conclusions are reached because they are desired, not because of data analysis. The necessity for conducting a thorough analysis cannot be over emphasized. Without support, data are subject to distortion and may be useless.

An improperly selected sample used in an experimental versus control-group comparison may yield results that are inconclusive. If the experimental group contains only high achievers and the control group represents the general population, the improvement in the experimental group from a statistical point of view may be conclusive; however, because of the bias in the sample selection, the results may be completely distorted. Random sampling and proper sample sizes usually can overcome biases in the selection.

Improper Use of Percentages and Averages. Another error involves the use of different bases for comparisons that show an improvement. For example, an HR program in quality improvement resulted in a reduction in the error rate from 20 units per 1,000 to 15 units per 1,000. There are two ways to show that improvement. Normally, it can be expressed as a 25 percent reduction, a change in 5 divided by 20. However, another way to express the result is that the new error rate is 33 percent less than the old rate. In this case 5 is divided by 15 to give 33 percent. There is a big difference in the two numbers.

Another deception comes in the use of averages. It is not unusual for a set of data to have a different value for the three types of averages: mean, median, and mode. An HR staff member can select the one that suits the situation, depending on what message is needed, and disguise it under the term "average."

Graphical Distortions. Visual presentation of data in the form of graphs and charts can distort the true comparisons of data. For example, examine the two charts shown in Figure 11-6. The same data are presented in two different charts; only the scale of the vertical axis is changed. The one on the right shows a very small amount of increase; the one on the left shows a large increase in proportion to the horizontal axis. This difference can easily account for a distorted picture of what happened.

Consider another example. The change in output in a brewery resulting from the implementation of an HR program is presented visually. Because the output is in barrels of production per employee, a drawing of a barrel is used to show the

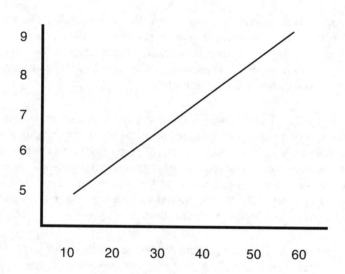

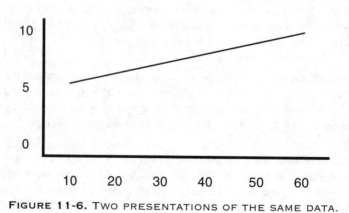

FIGURE 11-6. TWO PRESENTATIONS OF THE SAME DATA.

visual differences in the output. Figure 11-7 shows a 100% improvement. The barrel on the left shows the output before the program; the one on the right shows output after the program. The one on the right is twice as tall as the one on the left. The basis of comparison is a vertical axis only. However, the taller barrel has

Before the
Program
(50 Tons
Per Employee)

After the
Program
(100 Tons
Per Employee)

FIGURE 11-7. DISTORTION IN VISUAL PRESENTATION.

a wider base. Therefore, a 100 percent improvement looks like at least a 200 percent improvement.

Drawing Erroneous Conclusions. Much caution should be exercised when results from a single program, particularly on a pilot or experimental basis, are used to make inferences about the entire target population. If care is taken to select a random sample and the proper statistical analysis is conducted, then the predictions for the remaining population will usually be accurate. However, without this attention, distortions can easily enter the situation. Consider this extreme example. Following a pilot HR program on work simplification, one participant suggested a way to simplify a procedure that saved the company almost $10,000 annually. The report worded one of the conclusions this way:

> If every employee could save $10,000, then, with an employment level of 450, the resulting savings would be $4,500,000. And since the program cost is only $50,000, a 9000 percent return on investment would be realized.

The conclusion is very misleading. Although one employee $10,000, the average savings per participant were closer to $200. Using a single statistic to make inferences about the entire population suggested a vastly distorted improvement.

Another distortion example involves a correlation between two variables. A correlation does not necessarily show a cause-and-effect relationship. Suppose the production output for a group of employees correlates with age. The older the employee, the greater the output. Using this correlation to draw a conclusion, the best recruiting strategy might be to hire older employees, possibly in their sixties. Further analysis of the data reveals that the employees in the sample were in their early twenties to mid-thirties. No employees in their forties or fifties were in the sample. More than likely, performance would begin tapering off as employees approach upper-age ranges.

In summary, the common methods of statistical deception represent traps the HR program evaluator must avoid when analyzing, interpreting, and presenting data. Otherwise, not only will the results be misleading, but valuable credibility can be lost. For additional information on how to avoid statistical deception, see other references.[19]

CALCULATING THE RETURN

The return on investment is an intriguing and important calculation for the HR professional. Yet, it is a figure that must be used with caution and care because it can be interpreted or misinterpreted in many ways. This section presents some general guidelines to help calculate the return and interpret its meaning.

Defining Return on Investment

The term "return on investment" (ROI) may appear to be out of place in HR. The expression originates from finance and accounting and usually refers to the pretax contribution measured against controllable assets. In formula form,

$$ROI = \frac{\text{pretax earnings}}{\text{average investment}}$$

It measures the anticipated profitability of an investment and is used as a standard measure of the performance of divisions and profit centers within a business.

In many situations a group of employees is involved in an HR program at one time, so the investment figure should be the total costs of analysis, development, implementation, operating, and evaluation lumped together for the bottom part of the equation. With these considerations, the return on investment in human resources becomes the following formula:

$$ROI = \frac{\text{pretax earnings}}{\text{average investment}}$$

The formula could be multiplied by 100 to convert it to a percent. To keep calculations simple the return should be based on pretax conditions and avoid issues such as investment tax credits, depreciation, tax shields, and other related items. The total program costs are all related costs including analysis, development, implementation, operating, and evaluation. The net benefits could result from cost savings, additional revenues, or improvements. They are not limited to any particular type of benefit, but are converted to a monetary value. It is recommended that annual benefit be used in the formula.

To illustrate this calculation, consider an HR program designed to reduce error rates. Because of the program, the average daily error rate per employee dropped from 20 to 15. Before the program, employees spent an average of two hours correcting errors. If employees average $20.00 per hour and 20 employees completed the program, the weekly operational savings for this program using base pay savings only is $1,000. The annual savings is $52,000. If the HR program costs $40,000, the return on investment after the first month is

$$ROI = \frac{\$52,000 - \$40,000}{\$40,000} \times 100 = 30\%$$

ROI is usually useful for evaluating expenditures relating to an HR program. Although the term is common and conveys an adequate meaning of financial evaluation, the finance and accounting staff may take issue with calculations involving the return on investment for an HR program. Because of this, some HR professionals suggest that a more appropriate label would be return on human resources. Others avoid the word "return" and just calculate the monetary savings as a result of the program, which is basically the benefits minus costs. These figures may be more meaningful to managers who use ROI calculations for capital expenditures.

ROI may be calculated prior to an HR program to estimate the potential cost effectiveness or after a program to measure the results achieved. The methods of calculation are the same. However, the estimated return before a program is usually calculated for a proposal to implement the program. The data for its calculation are more subjective and usually less reliable than the data from a program completion. Because of this factor, management may require a higher ROI for an HR program in the proposal stage.

When to Use ROI

The calculation of the return for an HR program is not feasible, realistic, or desired in all cases. Even if the perceived benefits have been converted to monetary savings, the mere calculation of the return communicates more preciseness in the evaluation than may exist. An ROI calculation should be used when the program benefits can be clearly documented and substantiated, even if they are subjective. If management understands and buys into the method of calculating the benefits, then they will have confidence in the value for the return. The nature of the program can also have a bearing on whether or not it is realistic to calculate a return. Management may believe, without question, an ROI calculation for a gain sharing program. They can easily see how an improvement can be documented and a value tied to it. On the other hand, an ROI for an employee assistance program may be difficult to accept—even for the most understanding manager. Therefore, the key considerations are how reliable are the data and how believable are the conclusions based on subjective data.

While it is dangerous to suggest precisely where ROI calculations may be appropriate, Table 11-4 provides some rough guidelines on where the potential applications are most likely. The table shows the relative use of ROI in the various functions of human resources, based on the examination of the literature and input from a variety of HR executives. Information on typical programs and appropriate comments are also provided. Some organizations establish criteria to use in selecting calculations. Typical criteria include:

■ The length of time the program is expected to be viable.
■ The importance of the program in meeting the organization's goals.
■ The cost of the program.
■ Visibility of the program.
■ The size of the participant group.

TABLE 11-4
ROI APPLICATIONS IN HUMAN RESOURCES

HR FUNCTION	RELATIVE USE OF ROI	TYPICAL PROGRAMS FOR ROI CALCULATIONS	COMMENTS
Recruitment and Selection	Low	Special recruitment programs; recruiting segments such as college recruiting; new employee orientation	Difficulty in capturing benefits and converting them to quantitative measures.
Education and Training	Moderate	Sales training; technical training; supervisory training	Much progress has been made. More improvement is needed.
Career Development	Low	Career path program	Difficult to convert to monetary values.
Compensation	Moderate	Skill-based pay; incentives; bonuses	Difficult to work with traditional compensation programs in terms of the return on investment. Alternative reward systems show more promise.
Employee Benefits	Low	Wellness/fitness programs; child care program	New benefits should be subjected to ROI calculations.
Fair Employment	Low	Sexual harassment prevention	Very difficult to convert to monetary benefits. Usually justified based on regulatory issues or community needs.
Labor Relations	Low	Labor management cooperation program	Programs justified in non-monetary benefits.
Safety and Health	High	Accident prevention programs; Loss control program	Easy to measure and capture costs.
Employee Relations	Low	Absenteeism control program; Turnover reduction program	As new programs are implemented, they should be subjected to ROI calculations.
Productivity/ Quality Improvement	High	Gain sharing; TQM	Virtually every program should have an ROI calculation.
Employee Involvement	Moderate	Suggestion systems; Empowerment program	New programs should be subjected to ROI.

Still other organizations set targets for the percent of programs that are planned for ROI calculations. These targets become policy that translates into specific goals for the HR staff and focuses attention on this important aspect of HR evaluation.

Targets for Comparison

When a return is calculated, it must be compared with a predetermined standard to be meaningful. A 30 percent ROI is unsatisfactory when a 50 percent ROI is expected. There are two basic approaches to setting targets. First, the normally accepted return on any investment may be appropriate for the HR program. Second, because the ROI calculation is more subjective than the ROI for capital expenditures, management may expect a higher target. This figure should be established in review meetings with top management who should be asked to specify the acceptable ROI for the program. It is not uncommon for an organization to expect an ROI for an HR program twice that of the ROI for capital expenditures.

ADDITIONAL METHODS FOR EVALUATING INVESTMENTS

Because of the limitations with ROI, other approaches for evaluating HR investments should be explored. Several methods are available that reflect efficiency in the use of invested funds. The most common approaches are described next.

Payback Period

A payback period is a common method for evaluating a capital expenditure. With this approach, the annual cash proceeds (savings) produced by investment are equated to the original cash outlay required by the investment to arrive at some multiple of cash proceeds equal to the original investment. Measurement is usually in terms of years and months. If the cost savings generated from an HR program are constant each year, the payback period is determined by dividing the total original cash investment (development costs, outside program purchase, etc.) by the amount of the expected annual savings. The savings represent the net savings after the program expenses are subtracted.

For example, if the initial program costs are $100,000, with a three-year useful life and the annual net savings from the program is expected to be $40,000, then

$$\text{Payback period} = \frac{\text{total investment}}{\text{annual savings}} = \frac{100,000}{40,000} = 2.5 \text{ years}$$

The program will "pay back" the original investment in two and a half years. The payback period is simple to use but has the limitation of ignoring the time value of money.

Discounted Cash Flow

Discounted cash flow assigns certain values to the timing of the proceeds from the investment. The assumption, based on interest rates, is that money earned today is more valuable than money earned a year from now. Several ways of using the discounted cash flow concept are available. The most popular one is probably the net present value of an investment. This approach compares the savings year by year with the outflow of cash required by the investment. The expected savings received each year is discounted by selected interest rates. The outflow of cash is also discounted by the same interest rate. Should the present value of the savings exceed the present value of the outlays after discounting at a common interest rate, the investment is usually acceptable with management. The discounted cash flow method has the advantage of ranking investments, but becomes difficult to calculate and may be too complex for the average user.

Cost-Benefit Ratio

Another method for evaluating the investment in HR is the cost-benefit ratio. Similar to the ROI, this ratio consists of the total of the benefits derived from the program expressed in monetary units, divided by the total cost of the program. A cost-benefit ratio greater than 1 indicates a positive return. A ratio of less than 1 indicates a loss. The benefits portion of the ratio is a tabulation of all the benefits derived from the program converted to monetary values as described earlier in this chapter. The total costs include all the cost categories as described earlier. The ratio has been used to evaluate projects, particularly in the public sector, beginning in the 1900s. Since then, it has been used for project evaluation in a variety of different settings.

Many HR practitioners prefer to use the cost-benefit ratio because it is not usually connected with standard accounting procedures. Although the benefits are converted to monetary values, steering away from the standard accounting measures is a more comfortable approach. Sometimes there is a feeling that the accounting measures communicate a preciseness that is not always available when calculating the benefits or the cost portion of the equation.

Consequences of Not Providing an HR Program

A final method for calculating the return on HR that has received recent attention is the consequences of not implementing an HR program. An organization's inability to perform adequately might mean that it is unable to take on additional business or that it may be losing existing business because of an untrained, unmotivated, underpaid, or disruptive workforce. This approach, at least intuitively, provides the basis for many preventive programs such as safety and health, affirmative action, litigation prevention, and labor management cooperation efforts. This method involves:

- Establishing the existence of an actual or potential loss.
- Obtaining an estimate of the worth of the business in actual or potential value and if possible, the HR program's value to the organization in terms of profit.
- Isolating the factors involved in a lack of performance that may create the loss of business or the inability to take on additional business. This includes lack of staff, lack of training, inability to staff quickly, inadequate facilities in which to expand, inadequate equipment, and excessive turnover. If there is more than one factor involved, determine the impact of each factor on the loss of income.
- Estimating the total cost of HR using the techniques outlined in an earlier chapter and comparing costs with benefits.

This approach has some disadvantages. The potential loss of income can be highly subjective and difficult to measure. Also it may be difficult to isolate the factors involved and to determine their weight relative to lost income.

A FEW WORDS OF CAUTION

The HR professional should use caution when developing, calculating, and communicating the return on investment for HR programs. The ROI is important and should be the goal of many HR programs. While there are many ways to calculate the return on funds invested or assets employed to produce benefits, the calculation for a return on an HR program should be based on as much tangible data as possible. The method of calculation and its meaning should be clearly communicated, and more importantly, it should be accepted by management as an appropriate measure for HR evaluation. Management ultimately decides the acceptability of a return, and they should be involved in defining how a return is calculated and setting targets by which programs are considered acceptable within the organization. After all, an adequate return as viewed by management is what is most important.

Occasionally sensitive and controversial issues will be generated when discussing a return on HR. It is best to avoid debates over what is measurable and what is not measurable unless clear evidence exists to support the arguments. Sometimes a tendency exists to consider some items so fundamental to the survival of the organization that any attempt to measure them is unnecessary. For example, when a program is designed to improve customer service, there may be a tendency to avoid measuring the impact of the program and subsequently not calculate the return because of the assumption that if the program is well designed, it will improve customer service. This argument may not be sufficient for some cost-conscious managers.

Each time a return is calculated for a program, the HR manager should use the opportunity to educate other staff members and colleagues in the organization. Even if the program is not in their area of responsibility, managers will be able to see the value of this approach to HR evaluation. When possible, each project should serve as a case study to educate the HR staff on specific techniques and methods.

SUMMARY

This chapter discussed four key issues in calculating the HR contribution. The first and one of the most critical is the concept of isolating the HR program, which determines the extent to which the improvement was caused by the HR program. The second issue involves converting data to monetary values. Regardless of the type of data, a process or strategy exists that can be extremely helpful in reducing the data to monetary values to use in ROI formulas. The use of statistics, a third issue of data analysis, is sometimes confusing for many HR practitioners. The chapter reported a few simple and common statistics with some caution for their use and abuse. The final issue is what some professionals consider to be the ultimate level of evaluation: calculating the return on investment. While not appropriate for every program, it is desirable in some situations and should be used in the analysis of those situations. The organization should determine which types of programs will ultimately command a return on investment calculation and then set goals to meet their targets.

REFERENCES

1. Hassett, J. "Simplifying ROI," *Training,* September 1992, 54.

2. For additional information, see Makridakis, S. 1989. *Forecasting Methods for Management* (5th Ed.). New York, NY: Wiley.

3. Zigon, J. "Performance Management Training," In *In Action: Measuring Return on Investment,* Vol. 1., J. J. Phillips, Ed. Alexandria: American Society for Training and Development, p. 262.

4. Graham, M., Bishop, K., and Birdsong, R. "Self-Directed Work Teams," In *In Action: Measuring Return on Investment,* Vol. 1., J. J. Phillips, Ed. Alexandria: American Society for Training and Development, p. 105.

5. Rust, R. T., Zahorik, A. J. and Keiningham, T. L. 1994. *Return on Quality: Measuring the Financial Impact of Your Company's Quest for Quality.* Chicago: Probus Publishers.

6. Crosby, P. B. *Quality Is Free.* New York: New American Library, 1979.

7. Zemke, R. "Cost of Quality: You Can Measure It," *Training,* August 1990, pp. 62–63.

8. Zemke, R. "Cost of Quality: You Can Measure It," *Training,* August 1990, p. 62.

9. Rust, R. T., Zahorik, A. J. and Keiningham, T. L. 1994. *Return on Quality: Measuring the Financial Impact of Your Company's Quest for Quality.* Chicago: Probus Publishers.

10. Townsend, P. L. *Commit To Quality.* New York: John Wiley, 1991.

11. Martocchio, J. J. "The Financial Cost of Absence Decisions," *Journal of Management,* March 1992, pp. 133–152.

12. Creery, P. T. and Creery, K. W. *Reducing Labor Turnover in Financial Institutions.* New York: Quorum Books, 1988.

13. Hom, P. W. and Griffeth, R. W. *Employee Turnover,* Cincinnati, Ohio: South-Western College Publishing, 1995.

14. *The Economist Guide to Business Numeracy.* New York: John Wiley & Sons, Inc., 1993.

15. Anderson, D. R., Sweeney, D. J., and Williams, T. A. *Introduction to Statistics Concepts and Applications.* St. Paul: West Publishing Company, 1991.

16. Bobko, P. *Correlation and Regression.* New York: McGraw-Hill, Inc., 1995.

17. Levin, J. and Fox, J. A. *Elementary Statistics in Social Research,* 5th Edition. New York: Harper & Row, Publishers, 1994.

18. Crossen, C. *Tainted Truth: The Manipulation of Fact in America.* New York: Simon & Schuster, 1994.

19. Dewdney, A. K. *200% of Nothing.* New York: John Wiley & Sons, Inc., 1993.

CHAPTER TWELVE

Communication of HR Program Results

With program results in hand, what next? Should they be used to justify new programs, gain additional support, or build good will? How should results be presented? An actual situation illustrates the importance of communicating results. A promising HR executive enjoyed an excellent reputation among his colleagues. His programs were effective and the results were impressive as evidenced by an occasional article in professional HR publications about the organization's HR programs. An external consultant, impressed with one of the feature presentations, clipped an article, attached a congratulatory note, and sent it to the CEO. The article came as a surprise to the top executive. Not only had the CEO missed the article, but he was unaware of the program's success. He inquired and was surprised to learn that many of the HR programs were considered successful, some with bottom line results. The HR executive learned a valuable lesson: successful programs must be communicated internally to the appropriate audiences to gain the support and commitment needed for continued success.

The least desired communication action is to do nothing. Communicating results is almost as important as producing results. The old saying, "results will speak for themselves," is not accurate. If they are not "spoken" in the right places, key individuals may not get the necessary information. Getting results without communicating them is like planting seeds and failing to fertilize and cultivate the seedlings. The yield will just not be as great. This brief and final chapter explores the critical issue of communication of HR program results. An entire chapter is devoted to this step to underscore its importance. It provides useful information to help present evaluation data to various audiences and covers both oral and written reporting methods. The end result of the effort is a repositioning of HR function from an activity-based process to a results-based process.[1]

THE PROCESS OF COMMUNICATING RESULTS

The skills required for communicating results effectively are as important as those involved in producing the results. Yet, the communication process varies little from other types of communications in business and professional settings. Regardless of the message, the audience, or the media, a few general principles are important when communicating HR program results.

- ■ **The communication must be timely.** Usually, program results should be communicated as soon as they are known and are packaged for presentation. From a practical standpoint, it may be best to delay a communication to a convenient time, such as the next edition of the newsletter or the next general management meeting. Several questions about timing must be addressed. Is the audience prepared for the information, when considering the content and other events? Are they expecting it? When is the best time to have the maximum impact on the audience?
- ■ **The communication should be targeted to specific audiences.** The communication will be more efficient when it is designed for a specific group. The message can be specifically tailored to the interests, needs, and expectations of the group. The length, content, detail, and slant will vary with the audience.
- ■ **The media should be carefully selected.** For a specific group, one medium may be more effective than others. Face-to-face meetings may be better with some groups than special bulletins. A memo to top management may be more effective than an evaluation report. The selection of an appropriate medium will help improve the effectiveness of the process.
- ■ **The communication should be unbiased and always modest.** Facts must be separated from fiction, and accurate statements must replace opinions. Some target audiences may view communication from the HR department with skepticism and may look for biased information and opinions. Boastful statements will sometimes turn off individuals, and most of the content of the communication will be lost. Observable, believable facts carry more weight than extreme or sensational claims, although the claims may be needed to get initial attention.

■ **The communication must be consistent.** The timing and the content of the communication should be consistent with past practices. A special communication at an unusual time may create suspicion. When a particular group, such as top management, regularly receives communication, the information should continue even if the results are not good. If selected results are omitted, it might leave the impression that only good results are reported.

■ **Testimonials are more effective if they are from individuals with audience credibility.** Attitudes are strongly influenced by others, particularly by those who are admired or respected. Testimonials about HR program results, when solicited from individuals who are generally respected in the organization, can have a strong impact on the effectiveness of the message. This respect may be earned from leadership ability, position, special skills, or knowledge. The opposite of this principle is true. A testimonial from an individual who commands little respect and is regarded as a poor performer can have a negative impact.

■ **The audience's perception of the HR department will influence communication strategy.** Perceptions are difficult to change. A negative opinion of the HR department may not be changed by the mere presentation of facts. However, the presentation of facts alone may strengthen the opinion of individuals who already have a favorable impression of the department. It provides reassurance that their support is appropriate. The department's credibility should be an important consideration when developing an overall communication strategy. An HR department with high credibility and respect in the organization may have a relatively easy task in communicating results. A department with low credibility may have a problem when trying to be persuasive in a communication. However, communicating significant program results can have a positive effect on increasing the credibility of the department.

These general principles are important to the overall success of the communication effort. They should serve as a checklist for the HR professional when disseminating program results to a variety of individuals. Determining which group needs what information deserves careful thought, because as problems can arise when a particular group receives inappropriate information or another is omitted altogether.

COMMUNICATING WITH TARGET AUDIENCES

The reasons for communicating program results vary with the organization and specific needs. Table 12-1 shows the most common reasons, along with the tar-

TABLE 12-1
COMMON TARGET AUDIENCES

AUDIENCE	REASON FOR COMMUNICATION
Top Management	To secure approval for HR programs; to allocate resources of time and money.
All Management	To gain support and build credibility for the HR department's actions.
Participants' Superiors	To obtain a commitment for a subordinate to be involved in an HR program.
Potential Participants	To create a desire to participate in a program.
Current Participants	To enhance reinforcement of the HR process.
HR Staff	To show the importance of measuring the results of HR programs.
All Employees	To stimulate interest in HR department efforts.
Stockholders	To secure endorsement of the HR department's efforts.

get audiences. An organization should develop its own tailor-made list of reasons. The list should be reviewed prior to developing a communication strategy for reporting significant results.

Selecting the Audience

Probably the most important target audience is top management, who are responsible for the allocation of resources for the HR department. They need information in order to approve expenditures and to gauge the success of the HR function. Without a stream of information about HR effectiveness, top management will form an opinion about HR based on whatever data is available.

The entire management group should be informed about HR program results in a general way. Management's support for, and involvement in, the HR process is important to the success of the effort. The department's credibility is another key issue. Communicating program results to management can help establish this credibility.

The importance of communicating with a participant's supervisor is probably obvious. In many cases supervisors must allow their employees to be involved in HR programs and are required to support HR programs. An adequate return on investment in HR programs improves their commitment to the HR function, as well as enhancing HR's credibility with them.

Occasionally, results are communicated to create a desire for individuals to participate in a program. Potential participants are an important target for communicating results, especially for voluntary programs.

Participants need feedback on the overall success of their efforts. Some participants may not have been as successful as others in meeting program objectives. Communicating results creates peer pressure to make the program work and to improve results for the future. For those achieving excellent results, the communication will serve as reinforcement. This target audience is often overlooked under the assumption that participants do not need to know about the overall success of the program.

HR staff members should receive information about program results. For small staffs, the individual conducting the evaluation may be the same person who coordinated the program. For larger departments, evaluation may be a separate function. In either case, the program designer must have the information on the program's effectiveness so that adjustments can be made when the program is to be repeated.

All employees and shareholders may be less likely targets. General interest news or stories may build respect for the function and positive attitudes about the organization. Shareholders are interested in their investment, and stories about a significant ROI will peak their interest.

While Table 12-1 shows the most common target audiences, others may exist in a particular organization. For instance, all management or all employees could be subdivided into different departments, divisions, or even subsidiaries of the organization. The number of audiences can be quite large in a complex organization.

Selecting the Message

When considering a particular audience, the following questions should be asked about each potential group:

- Is the audience interested in the subject?
- Do they really want to hear the information?
- Is the timing right for this audience?
- Is the audience familiar with the views of the HR department?
- How do they prefer to have results communicated?
- Are they likely to find the results threatening?
- Which medium will be most convincing to this group?

Three general principles should be followed when communicating with a specific audience:

- **Get to know the audience.** The HR department should know each audience to the greatest extent possible. Some audiences, such as program participants, are well known. Others, such as top management or various segments of the management group, may not be known to the HR staff as well as they should be. Special efforts may be needed to understand their concerns and the issues they face.

■ **Find out what information is needed and why.** Each group will have its own needs relative to the information desired. Some will need detailed information, while others want brief summaries. A quick review of this issue will help streamline the process.

■ **Try to understand each audience's viewpoint.** This relates back to the first principle—know the audience. Each will have a particular viewpoint about the results. Some audiences may want to see the results, while others may not. Still others will be neutral. The staff should try to understand the different viewpoints. With this understanding, communications can be tailored to each group. This is especially critical when the HR professional expects an audience to react negatively to communication.

COMMUNICATING WITH TOP MANAGEMENT

No group is more important than the top management group when it comes to communicating program results. Improving communications with this group involves developing an overall strategy that may include all or part of the following actions.[2]

Strengthen the Relationship with the CEO

The individual responsible for HR should establish an informal and productive relationship with the chief executive officer of the organization. If this is a direct reporting relationship, this process is a natural development; otherwise, it will require special attention. Both the CEO and the HR executive should feel comfortable with open communications regarding HR needs as well as program results. One approach to better communications is to establish frequent, informal meetings with the chief executive to discuss problems with current programs, new program needs, and performance deficiencies in the organization. Candid and informal conversations can provide the CEO an insight not possible from any other source. It can also be helpful to the HR manager in determining direction for the HR function.

Show How HR Programs Have Helped Solve Major Problems

While specific results of current programs are comforting for an executive, solutions to immediate problems may be more convincing. Consider this example. One organization experienced a serious problem with turnover. Costs were unusually high and service had begun to deteriorate. This was a complex problem, and the HR director began to look for solutions. Several actions were planned, including the implementation of new HR programs. The collective effort of all actions yielded favorable results, with improvements in costs and quality. The HR department got its share of the credit. The HR function helped turn around an unprofitable situation.

Communicate Program Results Routinely

When an HR program achieves significant results, appropriate top executives should know about the results. A brief memo can accomplish this by indicating when the program was implemented, what its goals were, and what results were achieved. Presented in a for-your-information format, this communication should state only facts and very little opinion. The credit for success should be given to program participants and their supervisors. HR programs, including plans, activities, and results should also be communicated to the top executive group, unless of course the information is insignificant. Frequent information from the HR department can have a positive impact on the top group.[3]

Appoint Top Executives to HR Committees

An effective way to enhance commitment from the top group is to ask them to serve on an HR committee. The HR department should use committees to provide input and advice to the HR staff on a variety of issues, including program needs, problems with the present programs, and program evaluation. Committees come in a wide variety of types, as illustrated in Chapter 4. Regardless of the scope, committees can be helpful in informing executives about programs accomplishments.

For example, one organization appointed several executives to a salary administration committee. The committee's functions included job evaluation, program design, and program changes. The committee met frequently to review the effort, monitor the results, and make changes to correct problems. The executives were made aware of the results of the program on a continuous basis, and top executive involvement became crucial to the success of salary administration in the future.

Conduct an HR Review

An effective way to communicate HR program results to top executives is through the use of an HR review meeting. While this review can be conducted more frequently, an annual basis is common. The primary purpose is to apprise top management about what has been accomplished with HRD and what is planned for the future. The review meeting can last from two hours to two days, depending on the scope of the meeting and the amount of HR program activity. Table 12-2 presents a typical agenda.

This meeting cannot be taken lightly because it may be the most important event on the HR department calendar during the year. It must be planned care-

TABLE 12-2

HR REVIEW AGENDA

■ Review of HR programs for the past year.
■ Methods of evaluation for selected programs and the results achieved.
■ Significant deviations from the expected results (both good and bad).
■ Basis for determining HR needs for next year.
■ Planned programs for the coming year (secure support and approval).
■ Proposed methods of evaluation and potential payoffs.
■ Problem areas (lack of support, systems problems, or other potential problems that can be corrected by top management).
■ Concerns from top management.

fully, executed on a timely basis, and controlled in a manner to accomplish its purpose. This approach has been used in many organizations, and the reaction has been extremely favorable. Top management is interested in what the HR department accomplishes because the process involves all employees. Most of all, they want to have input into decisions for new programs.

DEVELOPING THE EVALUATION REPORT

The type of formal evaluation report used to communicate results depends on the amount of detailed information developed for the various target audiences. Brief summaries of program results with appropriate charts may be sufficient for most communication efforts. For other situations, particularly for the evaluation of significant programs requiring extensive funding, more detail is needed and a full evaluation report may be necessary.[4] This report then can be used as the basis for other reports for specific audiences and various media. At a minimum, the report should contain the sections outlined here.

Management Summary

The management summary, a brief overview of the entire report explaining significant conclusions and recommendations, is designed for those individuals who have only a casual interest or who are too busy to read a detailed report. Although usually written last, it appears first in the report for easy access. One page is usually sufficient.

Background Information

The background information provides a general description of the events that led to the creation of the program. If applicable, the section summarizes the needs analysis. It also presents specific issues and events that were critical to the development and implementation of the program. This section lists the objectives and gives a brief description of the program as well as other detailed information the audience may need.

Evaluation Strategy

The evaluation strategy describes all of the components that make up the total evaluation process. It discusses several components of the results-based HR model, presented in Chapter 3. It begins with the purposes of evaluation for this particular program, then describes, the data collection techniques and presents them as exhibits. Other useful information related to the design, timing, responsibilities, and execution of the evaluation are included.

Data Collection and Analysis

The report usually presents the data collected in both raw and finished formats. In some cases a summary is appropriate. This section presents special data analysis issues including how the effects of the program are isolated from other factors and how the output data are converted to a monetary value. The methods of data analysis are presented with appropriate explanations and interpretations. If appropriate, the report states the hypothesis along with the confidence level and the outcome of hypothesis testing.

Program Costs

This section presents program costs. A summary of the costs, by cost components (process category) or by particular accounts, may be appropriate. Recommended categories for cost presentation are analysis, development, implementation operating, maintenance, and evaluation costs. While the assumptions made in estimating costs are discussed in this section, there is no need to explain the complete system for assigning and allocating cost. A footnote to explain that a description of the system is available is sufficient.

Program Results

The program results section, probably the most important part, presents a summary of the results with charts, diagrams, tables, and other visual aids. If applicable, this section presents a cost/benefit analysis along with the ROI. It also outlines various program benefits and presents a complete picture of both hard and soft results.

Conclusions and Recommendations

A final section presents the overall conclusions based on an analysis of all the information. If appropriate, this section gives brief explanations on how each conclusion was derived. If not obvious, the impact of these conclusions is explained. This section presents a list of recommendations including changes in the HR program, if necessary, as well as brief explanations for each recommendation. The conclusions and recommendations must be fully consistent with the findings described in the previous section. While this appears obvious, it is not unusual to find reports with conclusions that are in conflict with the results.

While these components are the key parts of a complete evaluation report, the report can be scaled down as necessary to provide needed documentation. This process may appear complicated; however, it is necessary to communicate results when a comprehensive evaluation has been conducted.[5] This report is an important "last step" in the evaluation process.

MANAGEMENT MEETINGS

If used properly, management meetings represent a fertile opportunity for communicating program results. In the proper context, HR results can be an important part of any organizational meeting.[6] A few examples will illustrate the range of possibilities.

Staff Meetings

Staff meetings are held to review progress, discuss current problems, and disseminate information. These meetings can be an excellent forum to discuss the results achieved with an HR program, when the program is related to the activities of the particular group. Information on program results can be sent directly to executives to use in staff meetings, or a member of the HR staff can attend the meeting to present the information. For example, a large waste management company discussed a progress report on an organizational change program at its staff meetings.

Supervisor/Leader Meetings

Regular meetings with first-level supervisors are quite common. Topics that will help supervisors be more effective in their work are usually discussed. A discussion of an HR program, with corresponding results, can be integrated into the regular meeting format. In one example, a new safety awareness program was announced in a routine supervisors' meeting. After the program was implemented, the results were discussed at subsequent supervisors' meetings throughout the year.

Panel Discussions

Although not common in all organizations, panel discussions can be used to discuss important issues and solutions to problems. A typical panel might include two or more supervisors or managers who discuss how they used an HR program to solve a problem common to other supervisors. A successful discussion that includes the results of an HR program can provide other supervisors and top management with convincing data on the success of the program. In one organization, a selected group of supervisors discussed ways in which they have lowered turnover by using an HR program. Each panel member achieved significant progress with turnover reduction and discussed his specific techniques.

Management Clubs and Associations

Management clubs, leadership associations, and local company chapters of management associations are becoming increasingly popular. These organizations usually open their membership to all professional, technical, and managerial employees. Regular meetings are a major part of their activities, with the majority of the meetings focusing on management-related topics. HR program results can be an appropriate topic in these meetings. In one company, a monthly meeting featured a member of the HR staff who discussed the results of an assessment center for selecting supervisors. In a featured presentation, the staff member outlined the program statistics since its inception and the specific results achieved. By showing management that the program worked, the presentation gained additional support for HR.

Annual "State of the Company" Meetings

A few organizations initiated an annual meeting for all the members of management in which the CEO reviews progress and discusses plans for the coming year. A few highlights of major HR program results integrated into the CEO's speech can have a positive effect on the HR department. They can show top executive interest, commitment, and support. These highlights of program results can be presented along with operating profit, new facilities and equipment, acquisitions, new products, and next year's sales forecast.

In summary, whenever a management group is convened in significant numbers, the possibility of communicating HR program results should be considered.

HR NEWSLETTERS

Although usually limited to large HR departments, a highly visible way to communicate program results is through the use of an HR newsletter. Published on a periodic basis, usually monthly or quarterly, a newsletter usually has four basic purposes:

■ To inform management about HR activities, programs, and plans.
■ To build commitment and support for the HR function.
■ To explain to the managers their role in the HR process.
■ To communicate HR program results.

Possibly a more subtle reason for a newsletter is to show the importance of the HR function. Published by the HR staff, the newsletter is usually distributed to management, or at least to key managers, in the organization. Some publications target the first level supervisors, while others target department heads. The format and scope of the newsletter can vary considerably. A simple two-page newsletter, front and back, may work well for a small organization, while a comprehensive, four-color, 12-page newsletter may be appropriate for a large organization with an adequate budget. Still other organizations put the information online for access on desktop PCs. Regardless of format, several topics are appropriate for this newsletter and are shown in Table 12-3.

While this list may not be suited for every newsletter, it represents the variety of topics that should be presented to the management group. The newsletter should not be too boastful; otherwise, it might turn off even the most supportive managers. It should present facts and leave out most of the opinions of the HR staff. Facts are hard to dispute, and opinions and comments from executives outside the HR department will be respected. When presented in a professional manner, the newsletter can meet the four objectives listed above.

THE GENERAL INTEREST PUBLICATION

To reach a wide audience, HR professionals sometime use general interest, in-house publications. Whether a newsletter, magazine, or newspaper, this publica-

Table 12-3
Topics for HR Newsletter

- Significant HR program results documented in an easily understood format, including the method(s) of evaluation and the measurement of the impact.
- Announcements of major HR change programs with the expected results.
- Progress reports on major programs in the development stage, with a request for comments.
- Cost/benefit analysis or ROI calculations for a specific program.
- A brief summary of the feedback from participants in an HR program reporting initial success and including brief interviews with participants.
- Comments from a top executive about the organization's HR policies.
- A feature story of a key supportive manager, emphasizing the manager's efforts and involvement in HR programs.
- A section spotlighting a member of the HR staff who is achieving results with programs in a partnership with supervisors.
- A schedule of planned programs with a brief description including objectives and target audience.
- Changes in benefits, employee services, compensation plans, and recognition systems along with the rationale for the changes.

tion usually reaches all employees, and the material is limited to general interest articles, announcements, interviews, and helpful data. HR program results may be an appropriate topic when the program has wide participation and the results have general interest appeal. The information must be carefully selected. A few of the types of articles that may be included are described below.

Program results. Results communicated through this media must be significant to arouse general interest. For example, a story with a headline, *New Safety Program Results in One Million Hours Without a Lost Time Accident,* will catch the attention of many people because they are involved in the effort and understand the significance of results. A report on the accomplishments of a single group of participants may not create interest unless the audience can relate to those accomplishments. The results of many HR programs occur weeks or even months after the program is completed. Participants need reinforcement from many sources in order for them to meet program objectives. Communicating program results, to a general audience that includes the participant's peers, offers encouragement (or sometimes additional pressure) to participants to reach desired accomplishments.

Building interest. Stories about participants involved in an HR program and the success they achieve create a favorable image that may be appropriate for a publication. This type of article can show employees that the company invests time and resources in its employees. These articles provide information about programs that employees may not otherwise receive, and sometimes create a desire for involvement in these programs. This desire to participate may be necessary to obtain a future desired level of participation. For example, one organization conducted a program for potential new supervisors. Although the program was not described as a pre-supervisory program, employees understood that those who were selected for participation were being groomed for supervision. The program was highly visible and involved department visitations as well as classroom assessment. The company's monthly newspaper published information about the program including interviews with participants. The article resulted in a long list of employees expressing a desire to be included in future programs.

Participant recognition. General audience communication can bring recognition to participants in an HR program, particularly those who excel in some aspect of the program. For example, one organization, a large pipe manufacturer, features an article in its in-house publication on all top award winners for the suggestion system program and includes the details and results of their suggestions.

When participants are selected for a prestigious and well-respected program, the recognition can enhance self-esteem. One aerospace company sends promising executives to a prestigious university executive development program. Each year, the company's newsletter lists the participants and describes the program and its goals.

Human Interest Stories. HR activities are a wonderful source of human interest stories. A rigorous program with difficult requirements for selection can provide the basis for an interesting story on participants who have been involved in it. For example, in one steel plant, the editor of the company newspaper participated in a rigorous training program for sales representatives and wrote a stimulating article about what it is like to be a participant. The article described the entire course, its agenda, how it was presented, and its effectiveness in terms of the results achieved. The feature made an interesting story about a difficult development activity. Reprints of the article were used in recruiting sales representatives.

Annual Reports. Some organizations publish annual reports on the condition, success, or results of a specific HR program. One construction firm publishes an annual report of its employee assistance program, detailing program costs, program utilization rates (compared to other plans), and the successes (without names). Another firm, a large Japanese-owned automobile manufacturing plant, publishes an annual report of its suggestion plan, including costs and results.

The benefits and opportunities for the HR departments to use the in-house publication to let employees know about current events in the HR department are endless.

BROCHURES/BOOKLETS/PAMPHLETS

In addition to memos, reports, and newsletters, other forms of written communications can be effective in getting the message out about HR programs results. Brochures, booklets, and pamphlets have proven to be effective in a variety of applications. Four examples are presented here.

Program brochures. A brochure might be appropriate for programs conducted on a continuing basis in which participants are selected from many potential applicants. The brochure should be attractive and should present a complete description of the program, with a major section devoted to results obtained with previous participants, if available. Measurable results and reactions from participants, or even direct quotes from individuals, can add spice to an otherwise dull brochure. For example, a large electric utility established a comprehensive leadership development program, called leadership challenge, aimed at developing future executives. The brochure for the program contained descriptions of projects and the results achieved by former participants.

Program Summaries. A detailed description of programs can be distributed to the management group, particularly in large organizations. Some necessary items to include in these summaries are general description, program specifics, and the target audience. The brochure should be attractively packaged. If the program has been in existence for some time, evaluation data can be presented. For example, in a basic resources firm, a gain sharing program was implemented in most plants. A brochure for the program listed the results in productivity gains and cost reduction, in addition to describing how the program works.

Recruiting brochures. For some jobs and trainee programs, candidates are recruited from outside the organization. Brochures can help bring individuals into programs for target positions such as management trainees, nurses, account executives, salespersons, and other entry-level professionals. These brochures usually devote little attention to the results obtained from the formal entry-level selection and training program. Most brochures aim to describe the program and the entrance requirements. They should include information on the success of those completing the program, and possibly a few quotes from past participants about the importance of the program. For example, one large engineering firm produced a results-based recruiting brochure for its cooperative education program. The brochure contained feedback data from participants, quotes from interviews with former participants, and actual statistics on co-op retention and advancement when compared to non co-op graduates.

Special achievement. Occasionally, the HR department may have an opportunity to publicize a success story—an achievement linked to an HR program. A pamphlet on this story, developed and distributed to the management group in general management meetings or staff meetings, can be beneficial. The brochure should focus on tangible results such as reducing costs, increasing productivity, improving quality, and improving service times. It should detail what was done, how it was done, and what was achieved with subtle tie-ins to HR programs. A large package delivery firm did just that when it implemented an employee empowerment program. Periodically, it published pamphlets to feature individuals who had taken the spirit and concepts of the program to ultimate extremes. These pamphlets clearly showed what individuals could, and should, do to make the program work.

If developed and presented in a professional manner, these brochures, booklets, and pamphlets are effective and inexpensive ways to let others know about HR programs and the results they have achieved. Reporting on the results can add accountability and build credibility.

SUCCESS STORIES

A final approach to communicating program results involves the use of the subtle success story (SSS), which is an extension of the special achievement above. In this approach, success stories are publicized when a success can be linked to an HR program. Publicity is usually low key, and initially it may not be obvious who initiated the communication or even why it was communicated. The subtle idea is to let the management group see a successful performance story that was a result of an HR program. Publicizing success stories can have several advantages. It shows the entire group a success related to HR. Top managers, who expect results from HR programs, will certainly connect the two events. This approach can encourage participants in the program who did not get similar results, and for the employees who are featured, the story reinforces the importance and significance of their accomplishments. It provides a positive recognition for their efforts, and it reinforces the objectives of the HR program to the entire target group. It shows them that if they meet program objectives, the organization will give them recognition.

The subtle approach is used so that unnecessary attention is not directed to the HR department. The stars of the show are the participants who have made the program work. No one wants to listen to the HR department tooting its own horn about its programs. With this approach, critics will not treat valuable information as propaganda.

The various methods for communicating HR program results can be creatively combined to fit any situation. Here is a successful example using three approaches: a success story, management meetings, and a pamphlet.

A production unit achieved outstanding results through the efforts of a team of two supervisors. These results were important key bottom-line measures of absenteeism, turnover, lost-time accidents, grievances, scrap rate, and unit hour. The unit hour was a basic measure of individual productivity.

These results were achieved through the efforts of the supervisors who applied the basic skills they learned in a supervisor development program. During a panel discussion presented in a question-and-answer session at a monthly meeting for all supervisors, the two supervisors outlined what they do to get their results. They mentioned that they learned many of the techniques in the supervisory training program.

The comments were published in a pamphlet for distribution to all supervisors through department heads. The title of the publication was *Getting Results: A Success Story,* and the cover of the 8½ × 11, four-page pamphlet was attractive, but the contents were more important. The inside cover detailed the specific results, along with additional information about the supervisors. A close-up photograph of each supervisor taken during the panel discussion was included. The next two pages presented a summary of the techniques used to secure the results. The pamphlet was used in staff meetings as a guide to discuss the points covered in the panel discussion. Top executives were also sent copies. In addition, the discussion was videotaped and used in a subsequent training program as a model for applying information learned in the program. The pamphlet served as a handout.

From all indications, the communications effort worked. All levels of management responded favorably. Top executives asked the HR department to prepare and conduct additional similar meetings. Other supervisors began to use more of the approaches presented by the two supervisors.

SUMMARY

This chapter presented the final step in the results-based HR model introduced earlier. Communicating program results is a crucial step and if this step is not taken seriously, the full impact of the program results will not be realized. The chapter began with the general principles of communicating program results. It presented a communications model that serves as a guide for any significant communications effort. The various target audiences were discussed and, because of its importance, emphasis was placed on the top management group. The chapter presented a suggested format for a detailed evaluation report. Much of the remainder of the chapter included a detailed presentation of the most commonly used media for communicating program results, including meetings, periodic publications, and other written materials.

REFERENCES

1. Schuler, R. S. "Repositioning the Human Resource Function: Transformation or Demise?" *Academy of Management Executive,* 1990, Vol. 4, No. 3, pp. 49–60.
2. Anthony, P. and Norton, L. A. "Link HR to Corporate Strategy," *Personnel Journal,* April 1991, pp. 75–86.
3. Majors, G. and Sinclair, M. J. "Measure Results for Program Success," *HRMagazine,* November 1994, pp. 57–61.
4. Hinrichs, J. R. "Commitment Ties to the Bottom Line," *HRMagazine,* April 1991, pp. 77–80.
5. Witzling, L. P. and Greenstreet, R. C. *Presenting Statistics.* New York: John Wiley & Sons, 1989.
6. Gross, W. D. "Pump Up HR Productivity!" *Personnel,* August 1989, pp. 51–53.

Appendix One

(See Table 1-5 for Checklist)

Scoring: Assign a numeric value to each of your responses to the questions in Table 1-4 based on the following schedule: 5 points for the most correct response, 3 points for the next most correct response and 1 point for the least correct response. Total your score and compare it with the analysis that follows.

The following schedule shows the points for each response:

POINTS	POINTS	POINTS	POINTS
1. A – 5	6. A – 3	11. A – 1	16. A – 3
B – 3	B – 1	B – 3	B – 5
C – 1	C – 5	C – 5	C – 1
2. A – 3	7. A – 5	12. A – 5	17. A – 1
B – 1	B – 3	B – 1	B – 3
C – 5	C – 1	C – 3	C – 5

(continued on next page)

POINTS	POINTS	POINTS	POINTS
3. A – 1	8. A – 1	13. A – 3	18. A – 1
B – 3	B – 3	B – 1	B – 3
C – 5	C – 5	C – 5	C – 5
4. A – 5	9. A – 3	14. A – 1	19. A – 3
B – 1	B – 1	B – 3	B – 5
C – 3	C – 5	C – 5	C – 1
5. A – 5	10. A – 5	15. A – 3	20. A – 3
B – 1	B – 3	B – 1	B – 5
C – 3	C – 1	C – 5	C – 1

Rationale: Explanations for responses is given below.

1. Performance measurements should be developed for all HR function. When that is not feasible, at least a few key measures should be in place in each function; otherwise, a function may be perceived to be unimportant or not a contributor.
2. *Major* organizational decisions should always involve input from the HR function. HR policy makers should have input into key decisions in which human resources are at issue.
3. Whenever possible, the investment in human resources should be measured by improvements in productivity, cost savings, and quality. Although other types of evaluation are important and acceptable, these measures are the ultimate proof of results.
4. The concern for the method of evaluation should occur before the program is developed. In the early stage, some consideration should be given to how the data will be collected and how the program will be evaluated. This ensures that the proper emphasis is placed on evaluation.
5. HR programs should never be implemented without a provision for at least some type of formal method of measurement and evaluation. Otherwise, the contribution of the program may never be known.
6. The costs of all individual HR programs should be continuously monitored. This provides management with an assessment of the financial impact of these programs at all times—not just when the program is implemented.
7. Because these important variables represent a tremendous cost for the organization, the cost of absenteeism, turnover, and sick leave should be routinely calculated and monitored.
8. Cost/benefit comparisons of HR programs should be conducted frequently, particularly when a significant investment is involved. Even rough esti-

mates of payoffs versus estimated costs can be helpful in the evaluation of a program.

9. In an economic downturn, the HR function should go untouched in staff reductions or possibly beefed up. Ideally, the function should enhance the bottom line by improving productivity or by reducing costs that can keep the organization competitive in the downturn.

10. Because employee benefits represent a signficiant portion of operating expenses, they should be routinely monitored and compared to national data, industry norms, and localized data. Projected future costs of benefits should also be periodically reviewed.

11. The CEO should frequently interface with the executive responsible for human resources. It is important for the CEO to know the status of the HR function and receive input on employee morale. This provides an opportunity for the CEO to communicate concerns, desires, and expectations to the HR executive. Frequent meetings are important.

12. The top HR executive should report directly to the CEO. A direct link to the top will help ensure that the HR function receives proper attention and commands the influence necessary to achieve results.

13. Line management involvement in the implementation of HR programs should be significant. Line management's participation in the design, development, and implementation of HR programs will help ensure their success. Line management should be considered in a partnership with the HR staff.

14. The entire HR staff should have some responsibility for measurement and evaluation. Even when some individuals are devoted full time to the effort, all staff members should have a partial responsibility for measurement and evaluation. Staff members should also have training in measurement and evaluation methods. This comprehensive focus on evaluation is necessary for successful implementation.

15. Human Resources Development (HRD) efforts should consist of a variety of education and training programs implemented to increase the effectiveness of the organization. HRD involves more than just courses or short seminars. It should include a variety of instructional methods aimed at improving organizational effectiveness.

16. When an employee completes an HR program, his or her supervisor should require use of the program material and reward the employee for meeting or exceeding program objectives. This positive reinforcement will help ensure that the appropriate results are achieved.

17. Pay-for-performance programs should be considered for most employees, both line and staff. Although usually limited to a few key line employees, these programs can work for all employees. Through gain sharing plans,

bonuses, and incentives, employees can see the results of their efforts and are rewarded for their achievement. This is fundamental to a results-oriented philosophy for the HR function.

18. Productivity improvement, cost reduction, or quality work life programs should be implemented in many locations and should achieve positive results. These programs are at the very heart of bottom-line HR contributions and have been proven successful in all types of settings. The HR function should take the lead to ensure that these programs are administered efficiently and are successful.

19. The results of HR programs should be routinely communicated to a variety of selected target audiences. Different audiences have different interests and needs, but several important audiences should receive information on the success of HR programs. While some may need only limited general information, other audiences need detailed, bottom-line results.

20. The impact of the HR function on the bottom-line contribution can be estimated with little additional cost. If measurement and evaluation is an integral part of the organization's philosophy, data collection can be built into the human resources information system. It adds a little cost but should generate data necessary to calculate program results.

ANALYSIS OF SCORES

Total score should range from 20 to 100. The higher the score, the greater your organization's emphasis on achieving results with the HR function.

Score Range	Analysis of Range
80–100	This organization is truly committed to achieving results with the HR function. Additional concentrated efforts to improve measurement and evaluation for the HR function is not needed. There is little room for improvement. All HR subfunctions and programs appear to be contributing to organizational effectiveness. Management support appears to be excellent. Top management commitment is strong. This HR department is taking the lead in measurement and evaluation by showing the contribution it can make to the organization's success. Chances are, it is a vital part of an effective and successful organization.
61–80	This HR department is strong and is contributing to organizational success. The organization is usually better than average in regard to measurement and evaluation. Although the attitude

toward achieving results is good, and some of the approaches to evaluation appear to be working, there is still room for improvement. Additional emphasis is needed to make this department continue to be effective.

41–60   Improvement is needed in this organization. It ranks below average with other HR departments in measurement and evaluation. The attitude toward results and the approach used in implementing HR programs are less than desirable. Evaluation methods appear to be ineffective and action is needed to improve management support and alter the philosophy of the organization. Over the long term, this department falls far short of making a significant contribution to the organization.

20–40   This organization shows little or no concern for achieving results from the HR function. The HR department appears to be ineffective and improvement is needed if the department is to survive in its current form and with its current management. Urgent attention is needed to make this department more effective in contributing to the success of the organization.

This instrument has been administered to HR managers and specialists attending local, regional, or national HR conferences. The typical respondent has been the individual responsible for the HR function. The instrument was administered anonymously and the respondents were provided ample time at the beginning of the meeting to complete it. Questions and answers were allowed during the administration of the instrument. To date, there have been over 700 usable responses representing an average score of 61.4 with a standard deviation of 7.7.

The score can reveal much about the status of human resources in an organization and the attitude toward measurement and evaluation. A perfect score of 100 is probably unachievable and represents utopia; however, it is the ultimate goal of many HR executives and a few other key executives. On the other extreme, a score of less than 20 reveals an ineffective organization, at least in terms of the contribution of the HR function. The organization will probably not exist for long in its current form or with the current staff.

Although the analysis of these scores is simplistic, the message from the exercise should be obvious. Achieving results from HR function is more than just evaluating a single program or service. It represents a comprehensive philosophy that must be integrated into the routine activities of the HR staff and supported and encouraged by top executives.

Appendix Two

CEO: Check Your Commitment to the Human Resources Function

(See Table 4-1 for Checklist)

NUMBER OF YES RESPONSES	EXPLANATION
25–30	Excellent top management commitment, usually reflective of a successful organization. This organization is maximizing the efforts of the HR function.
20–24	Top management commitment is adequate, but there is a need for additional emphasis. While top executive support exists, it needs some improvement.
15–19	Inadequate top management commitment. Improvement is necessary for the HR department to become an effective and viable part of the organization.
10–14	Very little top management commitment exists. The HR function cannot be effective in this organization.

Appendix Three

FEEDBACK QUESTIONNAIRE FOR HR PROGRAM

Note to Developer: Use only appropriate questions and statements.

Program Title and Number: _____ Date: _____

Name: _____ Location: _____

Coordinator/Facilitator: _____

	Not Successful At All			Completely Successful	
Objectives	1	2	3	4	5

Please indicate the degree of success in meeting each objective.

1. _____ ☐ ☐ ☐ ☐ ☐
2. _____ ☐ ☐ ☐ ☐ ☐
3. _____ ☐ ☐ ☐ ☐ ☐
4. _____ ☐ ☐ ☐ ☐ ☐
5. _____ ☐ ☐ ☐ ☐ ☐

Instructions: For each statement, select the best response that reflects your level of agreement, using the following ratings.

Rating   Description
1   Strongly Disagree
2   Disagree
3   Neither Agree or Disagree
4   Agree
5   Strongly Agree

	Strongly Disagree			Strongly Agree	
Program Content	1	2	3	4	5
1. The program content was relevant to my job.	☐	☐	☐	☐	☐
2. The program content was timely and up-to-date.	☐	☐	☐	☐	☐
3. The program can be transferred to my job.	☐	☐	☐	☐	☐

Comments on Program Content _____

_____

_____

Program Materials

4. The program materials were of good quality.	☐	☐	☐	☐	☐
5. The level of difficulty of this program was appropriate.	☐	☐	☐	☐	☐
6. The workbooks/manuals were helpful in this program.	☐	☐	☐	☐	☐

Comments on Program Materials _____

_____

_____

Program Facilitation/Coordination

7. The method of facilitation was appropriate for this audience.	☐	☐	☐	☐	☐
8. The interaction/involvement was appropriate.	☐	☐	☐	☐	☐

Comments on Program

_____

_____

	Strongly Disagree				Strongly Agree
	1	2	3	4	5

Facilitator/Coordinator

9. The facilitator/coordinator was knowledgeable of the program material. ☐ ☐ ☐ ☐ ☐
10. The facilitator/coordinator was prepared. ☐ ☐ ☐ ☐ ☐
11. The facilitator/coordinator's skills were effective. ☐ ☐ ☐ ☐ ☐
12. The facilitator/coordinator was responsive to particpants. ☐ ☐ ☐ ☐ ☐

Comments on Facilitator/Coordinator _____

_____

_____

Exercises

13. The exercises were of good quality. ☐ ☐ ☐ ☐ ☐
14. The exercises were relevant to the program. ☐ ☐ ☐ ☐ ☐
15. The exercises helped to meet program objectives. ☐ ☐ ☐ ☐ ☐

Comments on Exercises _____

_____

_____

Overall Evaluation

16. The learning environment was adequate. ☐ ☐ ☐ ☐ ☐
17. The pacing of the program was appropriate. ☐ ☐ ☐ ☐ ☐
18. The program length was just right. ☐ ☐ ☐ ☐ ☐
19. The sequencing of the program was appropriate. ☐ ☐ ☐ ☐ ☐
20. This program met my needs. ☐ ☐ ☐ ☐ ☐
21. I would recommend this program to others. ☐ ☐ ☐ ☐ ☐
22. On a scale of 1 to 10, how do you rate this program (1 = Not effective; 10 = Extremely effective)? _____
23. What was the most effective part of this program?

_____

_____

24. What was the least effective part of this program?

_____

_____

_____

25. Do you have any suggestions for improvement of this program?

_____

_____

_____

Comments on overall evaluation _____

_____

_____

Changes in Knowledge/Skills

26. As a result of this program, what additional knowledge have you gained? What new skills have you acquired or improved?

_____

_____

_____

27. As a result of this program, what do you estimate to be the increase in your personal effectiveness, in areas related to this program, expressed as a percent?
                                        _____%

Planned Improvements

28. Please indicate specific actions you will undertake as a result of this program (please be specific):
    1. _____
    2. _____
    3. _____
    4. _____

29. What benefits should your company realize from the program?

_____

_____

_____

30. What personal benefits did you have receive from this program?

_____

_____

_____

31. As a result of applying what you have learned, please estimate value to your organization over a period of one year.

_____

32. What is the basis of this estimate?

_____

_____

_____

33. What confidence, expressed as a percentage, do you place in your estimate? (0% = No confidence; 100% = Certainty)

_____%

34. Other comments.

_____

_____

_____

Appendix Four

PERFORMANCE IMPROVEMENT PLAN

_____   _____
            Name   Title

_____   _____   _____
   Department   Location   Telephone #

_____   _____   _____   _____
Today's Date Start Date   Completion Date   Major Event Dates

This plan is for _____

Total Annual Value of Improvement	**Significant Non-monetary Improvements**
$_____	1. _____ 2. _____ 3. _____ 4. _____ 5. _____

I. Improvement Area _____

Target Performance _____ Current Performance _____

Net Improvement _____ Annual Value of Improvement _____

Action Items	Target Date	Completion Date
1. _____		
2. _____		
3. _____		
4. _____		
5. _____		
6. _____		
7. _____		
8. _____		
9. _____		
10. _____		

Calculations: Non-monetary Improvements

                                 1. _____

                                 2. _____

Index